MAO ZEDONG

Man, Not God

By **Quan Yanchi**

FOREIGN LANGUAGES PRESS   BEIJING

First Edition 1992
Second Printing 1996

Translated by Wang Wenjiong
English text edited by Gale Hadfield

Paperback: ISBN 7-119-01445-5

© Foreign Languages Press, Beijing, China, 1992

Published by Foreign Languages Press
24 Baiwanzhuang Road, Beijing 100037, China

Distributed by China International Book Trading Corporation
35 Chegongzhuang Xilu, Beijing 100044, China
P.O. Box 399, Beijing, China

Printed in the People's Republic of China

Contents

Publisher's Note

MAO ZEDONG: Man, Not God by Quan Yanchi, is based on the recollections of Li Yinqiao. Li, Mao's bodyguard for many years, once received this request from Mao: "If what happens in my family is a secret to others, it is not a secret to you. But don't write about me while I'm still alive; wait until I die, and write truthfully when you do."

This is a candid book about a statesman of world fame, recording truthfully the life and thoughts of Mao as a husband, father, comrade-in-arms, the peasant's son. In entertaining anecdotes it captures moments of joy and sorrow in the life of this outstanding national leader. Since most of the contents of this book have never before been made public, it will provide the reader with a refreshingly different perspective from any other works about Mao. It is a book which will not disappoint anyone who desires to know more about this great man.

Highlighting the book are photographs, published here for the first time.

Mao Zedong with Li Yinqiao and his family

Mao with his daughter Li Ne

Mao with his relatives

Mao in his study

Preface

Li Yinqiao worked for Mao Zedong for fifteen years, first as a plain bodyguard and later as a section leader, then deputy-commander and finally, commander of Mao's bodyguard. Mao once said to him, "If what happens in my family is a secret to others, it is not a secret to you," adding, "but don't write about me while I'm still alive; wait until I die, and write truthfully when you do." When Li was leaving Mao in 1962, Mao told him, "I'm not going to have any new bodyguard commander after you. I've been able to keep you for so long because we got along well with each other. I'm not going to find a replacement after you leave." So Li was the last to command Mao's bodyguard.

As a friend of Li's, enjoying his trust, I sent him a list of questions about Mao Zedong, but I was not sure he would answer them. Some of them asked about Mao's likes, dislikes, fears, and if Li had seen Mao throw a tantrum or quarrel with anyone—questions he might find too embarrassing to answer, but questions, nevertheless, whose answers, I believed, people were as eager to know as I was.

However I was wrong. In response to my questions, the former commander of Mao's bodyguard recalled to the best of his ability his days with Mao, answering without reservation. As I listened to his answers, my image of Mao grew fuller, sharper and more life-like, an image that strengthened my belief that Mao is the greatest man China has produced in this century.

Li was not the only one to whom I addressed my questions. My interviewees included more than a dozen others who had at some time worked for Mao and were now working in various places all over the country. They responded to my questions with no less enthusiasm than did Li, but Li remained the most important of them all in answering my inquiries.

When recalling in old age, his numerous experiences, Li, like any other veteran revolutionary, may have erred with respect of details as to people, events, times and places. But what readers will find in this book is nevertheless a truthful record of the enormous contributions made by a great man to history.

How I Became Mao's Bodyguard

It would be impossible to explain in just a few words why Mao Zedong made me his bodyguard. But amongst all the factors leading up to his choice, the fact that I had never wanted the job was perhaps the most significant of them all. The more unattainable a thing is, the more tantalizing it seems. Mao, a great man but also a human being, was no exception to this rule. Perhaps it is improper to speak thus of him; but anyway, this is what happened.

Soon after Spring Festival in 1947, during the 1946–49 War of Liberation in China, I joined Zhou Enlai's bodyguard. This was at the time when the war between the Kuomintang and the Communists was approaching its final outcome. An élite army of 230,000 men under the command of General Hu Zongnan, Chiang Kai-shek's favourite disciple, had mounted an offensive on the liberated areas in northern Shaanxi Province. In the face of the enemy's onslaught, the Central Committee of the Communist Party left Yan'an and began to engage in guerilla warfare in that part of the province.

It was around August eighteenth when the several hundred of us in the office of the Central Committee reached the Yellow River. It was the toughest period during the entire war in northern Shaanxi. General Liu Kan had sent as many as seven brigades in hot pursuit of us, following us from Suide to Mizhi, and from there on to Jiaxian County and then the Yellow River.

For several days there had been torrential rains without any letup, drenching us to the bones. The river was swollen, its roar could be heard from miles away. Mao was in a bad mood, not so much because of the grim situation which we were facing, as because of the rumours circulating amongst us that we were going to cross the Yellow River. Mao always meant what he said; he was a man not to be expected to give in easily to opposition, or change his mind. He had said, "We will not cross the Yellow River until we defeat Hu Zongnan." Now, with Hu's army which was under Chiang Kai-shek's direct control, yet to be put out of action, and with seven brigades of troops hot on our heels, crossing to the other side of the river was out of the question as far as Mao was concerned. Besides, northern Shaanxi was then looked upon as a symbol of strength by the army and the people in their life-and-death struggle with the Kuomintang; they would fight on, come hell or high water, so long as "Chairman Mao remained in northern Shaanxi."

Zhou Enlai diplomatically pointed out to Mao that the section of river in front of us was not the Yellow River, but was called the Jialu, and thus we would be crossing the latter, and not the former. But that did not make Mao feel any better, for where we were the Jialu empties into the Yellow River, and that section is called "The Yellow River Fork" by the local people.

Finally a decision was made to cross the Jialu, the only alternative left to us under the circumstances. The enemy had occupied the hills behind us, and their bullets were cutting through the air above our heads and driving into the mud at our feet. We had only three companies to block the enemy's advance and they were quite a distance from us. There was only one guard company protecting those of us in the Central Committee office, and Mao had only one platoon of bodyguards, with Yan Changlin as the platoon leader. In the event of a charge by the enemy, there would only be a little over a hundred of us against several tens of thousands of them.

Ren Bishi, then secretary of the Secretariat of the Central Committee, was in charge of taking us across the river. But negotiating that river was no easy thing. The swollen river surged along with deafening roar, its towering waves threatening to submerge the whole world. The goat-skin rafts were capsized the moment they were lowered into the river and, tossed like leaves, disappeared in the angry rapids.

Caught between a formidable river and several tens of thousands of pursuing troops, I, for all my experience as a seasoned soldier, could not help feeling a little scared.

Mao looked grim, but retained his composure. He lifted two fingers, and pressing them lightly against each other, said, "Give me a cigarette!"

It wasn't said loudly, but it reverberated like thunder over those of us accompanying him on the march.

"Get him a cigarette, quick! Comrade Desheng wants a smoke!"

"Comrade Desheng wants a smoke!"

"A smoke!" "A smoke!" "A smoke!"

Li Desheng was Mao's assumed name when he fought in northern Shaanxi. He had stopped smoking for some time on account of poor health, so his bodyguards were not carrying any cigarettes. And with all of us drenched to the skin by the successive downpours, who would have dreamt of being asked for cigarettes?

Mao sat down on a rock, still holding his fingers up. Finding that he had been kept waiting for too long, he flared up, roaring, "Where's my cigarette?"

Comrade Desheng was angry. Immediately everyone of us began to search our pockets for cigarettes. Then those down the column were heard talking excitedly, as Mao's horse-keeper walked up followed by a noisy crowd, beaming happily. What a welcome sight! The horse-keeper was carrying matches and cigarettes wrapped in a piece of yellow oilcloth.

Immediately the guards, as instructed by Zhou Enlai, spread a light cotton-padded quilt over Mao.

Still deep in thought, Mao lit his cigarette. He took long puffs at it, watching it burn. Then he held his breath, and we all followed suit, gazing at the blue smoke rising from the cigarette. Loud gun reports could be heard, but Mao seemed totally oblivious of them. A deep furrow formed between his eyebrows. Then puffs of smoke began to escape from his nostrils and between his teeth, but before they were completely exhaled, they were drawn back forcibly with a loud hiss.

In what seemed like a fraction of a second, or an eternity, the cigarette burned down to a mere stub. All of a sudden Mao rose from the rock, and throwing away what remained of the cigarette with a vengeance, declared in an earth-shaking voice, "We are not going to cross the Yellow River!"

Mao resumed his walk along the river fork, his steps steady, unhurried. His bodyguard ran up to him, but Mao dismissed him in irritation. Alone, he walked in the front, facing a thicket of enemy guns, followed by several hundred of us. In a confrontation like this, a single shot from the enemy troops, to say nothing of a hail of bullets, would have been enough to change the course of history. But miraculously, all the enemy guns fell silent as Mao walked past them for a few hundred metres, until he disappeared beyond a mound....

"Bang!"

It sounded like a gun going off accidently or a salute to Mao Zedong. And then, as if startled from sleep, the enemy troops opened fire, filling the air with their din.

This dramatic confrontation with the enemy troops was to be repeated three or four times during the war in northern Shaanxi.

Ignoring the guns' reports, Mao sat down to take a break and sang a few lines from a Beijing opera aria.

After the break Mao walked up a hill. Half way up he stopped in a village that had seventy or eighty households in it. It was a small hill with scarely any trees or water. There was a temple there called the White Dragon Temple, apparently for the convenience of praying for rain. As Mao's visit to the village was accompanied by a downpour, the villagers took him as the incarnation of the dragon. Down the hill Liu Kan's troops bivouacked, the bonfires they built streching as far as the eye could see. That night Mao slept on the hill; he snored loudly whilst the rain poured down.

The next day, August 19, Ye Zilong and Wang Dongxing summoned me. Ye was then chief staff officer of the Central Committee detachment and Wang, his assistant. We met in front of a cave-house* in the village.

"A transfer of work for you," Ye was always to the point when he talked. "We want you to be Chairman Mao's bodyguard. You've been a bodyguard all these years and are experienced."

"The transfer means we trust you. We thought it over for a long time before we reached the decision, " said Wang, and stressing the political importance of their decision, he added, "It's an honourable job and important. You mustn't disappoint us."

I bent my head, reluctant to tell them what I thought of their decision. Only the day before, Mao, in a fit of anger, had dismissed Yan Yongsheng, his former bodyguard. Since I first joined the army at the age of eleven, about ten years ago, I had been first an orderly, then a guard and now a bodyguard, so their decision did not surprise me. But those who had been in the army as long as I had were now officers, with

---

*Such houses, carved out of the hill-sides (or cliffs) are a common sight in northern Shaanxi Province.

the rank of lieutenant or colonel.

"Well, what do you say?" asked Ye. It was just a routine question, but I found myself blurting out, "No, I don't want to be his bodyguard. I've been a bodyguard for too long."

Since they had not anticipated such a response, they looked a bit surprised and ill at ease. Realizing that I had gone too far in my refusal, I backed down. "Of course," I said, "I'll go along if this is a decision by the Party...."

"Glad to hear you say that," said Ye, looking relieved. "I believe you'll prove your worth with the new assignment."

"You may begin today," said Wang, knitting his brows. "It's only a temporary arrangement until we make a final decision on this matter."

That's how I was brought to the side of Mao Zedong.

One day on the march Mao didn't say a word to me throughout the whole day; he didn't even look at me, although I was walking between him and Zhou Enlai. I became suspicious. "Ye and Wang must have reported that conversation to the chairman," I said to myself, "and the chairman must have got angry with me when he heard it. They might have saved their breath since they didn't know what was on my mind."

We were driven almost stumbling down the hill by the rain. The river had risen at the foot of the hill, and the soldiers who could swim were throwing a bridge over it under the direction of Wang Dongxing. The pursuing troops had by now reached the top of the hill and the loud reports of their guns were causing us to begin to panic.

"It looks like it'll be some time before they can finish," Mao said to Staff Officer Liu, after looking at where the men were putting up the bridge. "Set up the radio transmitter."

The moment the transmitter was ready for work, calm was miraculously restored amongst us, and the anxiety that had gripped us earlier vanished. Sitting underneath an army cotton-padded quilt which we held over him, Mao read the telegrams from the war zones and wrote his instructions in pencil, which he handed to Liu to be transmitted to the headquarters of the various field armies.

Droning, a few enemy airplanes appeared and began to circle above us. We asked Mao to take cover at the foot of the hill, but Mao, without taking his eyes off the telegrams he was reading, and pointing with his pencil towards the hilltop concealed behind the clouds, said, "Do they

5

want to be killed? I think they know better than you do what to do."

Sure enough, the planes never moved to dive, nor dropped their bombs. After droning for some time they flew away, crestfallen.

Now the bridge was ready. Spanning the river were thick ropes, their ends fastened to huge rocks on the banks and buried under dirt. In the river below, there were piles of boulders. Doors from the houses on the other side of the river were laid across the ropes and boulders. Standing in the swift currents were groups of soldiers, stripped to the waist, serving as the "piers" of the bridge. Mao Zedong halted when he reached the river. Looking at the "piers," he was apparently touched, for his eyes misted over. He took a quick look over his shoulders, saying to those behind him, "You go across first, comrades!"

"We want you to go first, Comrade Li Desheng!" the comrades shouted in one voice.

"We want you to go first, Comrade Li Desheng!" the "piers" joined in.

But Mao insisted. Standing their ground, those on the bank and in the river repeated their requests: "We want you to go first, Comrade Li Desheng!" There were only a few hundred of them, but their shouts, amplified by the echoes in the valley, were loud enough to make one's blood boil. Then Zhou Enlai stepped onto the bridge, and after walking quickly down the length of it and back again, to ensure that it was secure, he went up to Mao and said in a low voice, "The comrades will never go before you, Comrade Chairman. Let's get on the bridge before the men in the river catch cold."

The shouts continued. Mao took a glance at those in the river and on the land. It was then, and only then, that he looked me full in the face. Immediately I blushed. In the face of the comrades shouting their requests, I was seized by an inexplicable sense of shame and yet secretly I felt that I was being misunderstood.

Mao stepped onto the bridge with me following immediately behind. We walked across the churning river.

One day we were billeted at Yangjia Yuanzi. Yan Changlin, the guard platoon leader, and some bodyguards were trying to build a fire to dry our wet clothes. Mao was sitting cross-legged on a kang*, studying a military map by the light of an oil lamp. The firewood was too wet to catch fire and was filling the room with smoke so thick that you couldn't see the man opposite you. Mao coughed loudly, and Yan, wiping away tears caused by the smoke, shouted to me, "Take Comrade Desheng out for fresh air! Quick!" I was coughing, too. With one leg on the kang and the other on the floor, I offered to help Mao off the bed, saying, "Come and get some fresh air, Comrade Desheng.... You can return to the map when the smoke is gone."

Mao pushed away my hands. Making a few more marks on the map, he rose from the kang without help. Supporting himself by laying his hands on the wall, he made his way out of the cave-house, coughing all the way.

The rain had stopped; the receding clouds were revealing a sky studded with bright stars. Mao stopped, took a deep breath in the wind and coughed out phlegm from his throat. Wiping away tears that had been caused by the smoke, he began to pace the courtyard, picking his way slowly amongst pools of water on the ground. He must have heard me following closely behind him, but he didn't turn around. The misunderstanding between us must be very great indeed ... I was overwhelmed by pangs of sadness.

Suddenly Mao stopped. Looking at the sky, he asked me slowly, "What's your name?"

I was surprised. Here was Mao Zedong talking to me at last! Bracing myself up, I answered at attention, "My name is Li Yinqiao, Comrade Chairman."

"Li—Yin (silver)—Qiao (bridge), I see," Mao was still looking at the sky. "But why not Jin (gold) Qiao? Where do you come from?"

"Anping County in Hebei Province."

"What do your parents do?"

"My father's a farmer. He does a bit of trading in grain when there isn't much work to do in the fields. My mother's a housewife, but she pitches in when work gets heavy in the fields."

"Your family is very much like mine. Which of your parents do you

---

*A raised platform-style bed, traditionally built of baked mud, which was heated from underneath by a chimney from the stove, the smoke from which would keep the occupants warm during the harsh northern winters.

like better, your mother or father?"

"I like my mother better. My father has a quick mind, is good at accounting, but he has a bad temper and drinks heavily. We don't eat the same food; it's pan cakes for him but coarse corn buns for the rest of us. He beats people for no great offence. My mother's a kindhearted woman, she treats people nicely. I like her better."

"The more you tell me about your family the closer I feel to you. Your mother must be a Buddhist."

"How do you know she's a Buddhist?"

"You said she's kindhearted. All Buddhists are like that. They're compassionate people."

I was amazed. After all those political lectures, what Mao said came as a surprise to me. Instantly the distance I had felt between us disappeared and along with it much of my inhibition and uneasiness. I asked in a low voice, "Is your mother also a Buddhist?"

"I like my mother better, too. Yes, she was a Buddhist, a woman with a golden heart. When I was a boy she used to take me to the temples to pray. But when I grew up I quit praying. No matter how hard you pray, it doesn't relieve the people of their agony."

"Better to rebel than to pray."

"Well said," Mao nodded in agreement and resumed his stroll. When he stopped again, he looked at me and asked, "Well, do you want to be my bodyguard?"

At that moment my heart must have stopped beating: I grew completely mute. I lowered my head. What should I say? All indications revealed that Mao had learned about my unwillingness. I decided to tell him the truth and suffer for it, rather than try to hide it and finish up a hypocrite.

"I wouldn't," I murmured my answer.

Silence, an unbearable silence. I had never felt so helpless in all my life. It seemed as if someone had put the answer into my mouth and I had repeated it mechanically.

Breaking the silence, Mao said in a slightly strained voice, "I see. Anyway, it's good of you to tell me the truth; I like that. But will you tell me why you don't want to work for me?"

"I've been doing this job for too long. I've been nothing but an orderly ever since I joined the army in 1938. I'd like to be with the combat troops."

"I see, a thirty-eighter and still a guard; not much progress, I should say. Is that the reason? No other reasons? For instance, you'd rather stay with Comrade Zhou Enlai than join me...." A "thirty-eighter" was one who joined the revolution in 1938 when China rose in a full-scale war against the Japanese aggressors.

"Oh no! I don't mean that," I protested loudly and was beginning to sweat for fear of being misunderstood. "Seeing some action has always been my wish. I've worked for Comrade Zhou Enlai for some time and he knows what I want; it'll be easier to talk him into letting me go when the situation improves. How could I ask you to let me go soon after I join you?"

"How do you know I wouldn't let you go?"

"You ... you don't like changes."

"What? I don't like changes? Who said so?"

"Never mind who. That old horse you have, you don't want to change it for a better one. Whatever you're accustomed to—those clothes of yours, those writing brushes, ink slabs, tea mugs—you become emotionally attached to them and refuse to replace them with new ones, even though the new ones are much better. Take that willow-wood walking stick you are using now. It's just a common wooden stick, isn't it? Sun Zhen'guo used it to carry his luggage. He gave it to you when he left Yan'an and now you refuse to use any other stick. When it fell down the mountainside the other day, you had it recovered rather than get a new one. If you hate to part with a wooden stick, would you be willing to let a human being, who breathes, go, once you have grown accustomed to his service?"

"Ha, ha, ha!" Mao laughed. "You must have watched me closely, haven't you? Anyway, I like you and want you to work for me. What shall we do? Someone's got to compromise."

"Then it'll have to be me."

"No, that wouldn't be fair to you. Let us both make a compromise," said Mao, and looking seriously at me, he continued, "The truth of the revolution must be understood: If you work for me, the difference between us will only lie in the division of labour, since we are all servants of the people. When you serve me, you will be serving the people through me. But just trying to make you understand that truth is not

9

enough. You're a thirty-eighter and still a bodyguard, much advanced in seniority but too low in rank. Let me make you a leader: You'll be a group-leader of my bodyguards." After a short pause, he said, sticking up his fingers, "For six months. You'll assist me for six months on loan. What do you say?"

"Fine," I nodded vigorously in agreement.

"Good. Go and talk to Ye Zilong; he'll tell you more about me." Mao dismissed me with a wave of his hand and returned to the cave-house without me.

Later I learned that before our conversation, he had been told of my reluctance to work for him, and was momentarily astonished, before shouting his order to those waiting for his instructions: "Don't you go on looking for other candidates. He's the one I want."

For all my unwillingness, I threw myself heart and soul into my work. The revolution had instilled in me a keen sense of duty where work was concerned. Laziness was unknown to me and I was not capable of idling. Having been an orderly and bodyguard for more than ten years, I never missed a hint and was good at understanding the intentions of those I worked for. So it wasn't long before I became familiar with Mao's ways. Whatever he wanted me to do—whether it was bringing him a cup of tea, food, books, pens, or even refusing a visitor—I could tell just by the expression of his eyes. There were times when I did what he wanted without even this much of a hint from him. This pleased Mao so immensely that on several occasions he patted me on the back of the hands saying, "We're getting along quite well. You're very good at discovering the ways things go."

And so, what I had predicted became a reality: Mao, having developed a liking for me, would not let me go.

One day in February 1948, at Yangjiagou, where the Central Committee Frontline Office was quartered, I was bringing tea to Mao. He was pacing in the cave-house and looked like he was thinking over something important. I placed the tea on the table quietly so as not to disturb him, and quietly turned to leave.

"Yinqiao," I heard him calling behind me, "don't go yet. I want to talk to you."

I turned around. "Yes, Comrade Chairman?"

"Today's the nineteenth," said Mao, bending his fingers. "August,

September, October.... It's February nineteenth, and six months to a day since you came...." Looking at me, he lowered his voice and asked hesitantly, "Do you still want to leave me?"

Torn between two loyalties, I lowered my head, but I decided to tell him the truth. "Yes, I do," I said.

The disappointment in his eyes upset me. I said, "But if you...."

Mao made a vigorous movement with his hands, probably an expression of his painful decision to part with someone he liked. "No. There's our agreement to go by," he said. "I never go back on my word. You may leave me now."

I did not leave him. "Now that you've decided to let me go," I said, "your obligation has come to an end. We can reach another agreement if that is necessary."

Mao smiled. "Fine," he said. "Let's reach another agreement. Make it six months again. You will assist me for another six months and see me defeat Hu Zongnan."

Soon after that, Mao received a message from General Peng Dehuai informing him that he had annihilated five brigades of Hu's army at Yichuan and that Liu Kan, commander of the Kuomintang's twenty-ninth army, had been killed in action.

In August 1948, when we were at Xibaipo, Mao said to me, "We've come to the end of the term of our second agreement, Yinqiao. But I'd like to keep you on loan for still another six months, so that you'll see me defeat Chiang Kai-shek."

"Comrade Chairman," I said, "forget about the loan. I'm not leaving you. I want to stay with you for the rest of my life."

I wasn't lying. During the time I was on loan to him as his bodyguard, I had the opportunity to watch a man of enormous wisdom and superhuman will-power and strength make history. Those were the days and nights that stirred men's souls. Mao so drew me to him with his personal charm and character that I would most willingly have spent the rest of my life waiting on him.

I became deputy commander of Mao's bodyguard in 1953. One day he said to me, half-jokingly and half-seriously, "You're now an officer, Yinqiao, and you don't have to come on guard-duty any more, so we get to see each other only rarely. But I don't like it. Let's agree on still another thing: you put yourself on duty twice a week, so I can see you more often."

"Agreed," said I.

After I was promoted to the position of commander of Mao's bodyguard in 1956, I continued to stand on guard-duty twice a week, so that I could take better care of him.

One day in 1962, before I left Mao to work in Tianjin, I went to see him. He was, as usual, reclining in his bed reading documents, his head resting on a pillow propped against the railing behind a blanket. I had walked to the door quietly and stopped there, thinking I would wait until he finished. Instantly, I heard him calling, "Come in, Yinqiao!"

How did he know I was there? He must have felt my presence, I guess, or, as one would say, his sixth sense told him so.

I stood beside the bed. He held my hand in his, patting it gently on the back with his other hand. We looked at each other in silence.

I was the first one to cry, and immediately tears began to roll down Mao's cheeks. Sobbing, I said, "You had me loaned to you when I didn't want to come. Now you're driving me away when I don't want to leave you. You're making things difficult for me, aren't you?"

"I feel just as sad to see you go," Mao sighed, in tears. "I see my children only a few times a year. You're the only one I saw every day, so you're closer to me than my children are. But I had to think of your future. I shouldn't keep you here at the expense of your career. As a commander of the bodyguard you're very high in position, but you're a mere regimental commander in rank; you deserve something higher than that...."

"But I don't mind. I don't want to leave you," I broke into a loud sob.

Mao pulled me into his arms, and holding me tightly he cried loudly. "After I die, Yinqiao, don't forget to come to my grave ... once a year." Afraid it might be bad for his health if he went on crying like that, I held back my tears, trying to calm him down, but hardly had I uttered the first few words, before I broke into loud sobs once again.

A few days later, with tears in my eyes, I bid Mao Zedong good-bye.

Mao Enjoys a Challenge

The most outstanding trait in Mao's character, as his writings attest, was his readiness to take on a challenge. He responded to the challenges from the Kuomintang with counter-challenges, never conceding an inch. A winner all his life, Mao, as far as I know, never admitted to feeling overwhelmed by his adversaries, nor retreated in the face of heavy odds against him. Whatever he did, he never quit, short of total victory.

Throughout the war with the Kuomintang, he displayed enormous courage in the face of danger, when confronting the enemy. His contempt for them originated in his confidence in his own strength and his conviction that they were doomed. Such confidence and conviction often prompted him to do extraordinary things.

Soon after the Lantern Festival in 1947, 230,000 of Hu Zongnan's troops began to advance on the border areas, by five different routes. In Xi'an paratroopers prepared for a surprise attack on Yan'an.

Upon receiving intelligence reports about the massing of enemy paratroopers, General Peng Dehuai posted a defence regiment at Yan'an airfield, and requested that Mao leave Yan'an as soon as possible.

Mao refused. He said to Peng, "I'll be the last one to leave" and "I'd like to see what Hu's troops look like."

When we in the bodyguard heard of these remarks, we did not take them literally. But General Peng thought otherwise. Looking at us sternly, he said, "The chairman always means what he says. He thinks nothing of his personal safety, but let me tell you that the Party thinks otherwise, and so should you. He mustn't be allowed to have it all his own way on this matter. Carry him away if you have to."

General Peng was proved right shortly afterwards, and we thereby came to know how insistent Mao could be with his demands.

On March 13, fourteen brigades of Hu Zongnan's troops mounted a fierce attack on Yan'an from two directions. Waves of air-raids by more

13

than fifty enemy aircraft continued all day. We asked Mao to leave, but each time we did so he would repeat what he had said before: "I'd like to see what Hu's troops look like."

The earth trembled when a bomb exploded in the courtyard of Mao's cave-house. Mao was holding a cup of tea in one hand, whilst with the other he was making pencil marks on a map, when the bomb went off. Once the smoke which had darkened the cave-house dispersed, Mao could still be seen standing in front of the map, cup in hand, putting dots and dashes on the map to demonstrate the movements of his troops. Not even a drop of his tea had spilled on the floor. Mao's total composure stunned all of us, barely recovered as we were, from the shock of the explosion.

Showing Mao a jagged fragment from a bomb which he had picked up from the courtyard, the staff officer of the bodyguard said to him, "What a close shave, Comrade Chairman! You must leave immediately."

Mao took the piece of metal, and weighing it in his hand, said smiling, "You can make two kitchen knives out of it."

On the afternoon of the 16th, Mao was discussing the war with Zhou Enlai and Peng Dehuai. Commenting on a mobilization rally held a week earlier, at which the participants had brandished a thicket of rifles and red-tasseled spears, shouting slogans at the top of their voices to express their determination to defend the border areas, Mao said, "Now that the masses have been aroused, they will fight with the strength of a hurricane...."

Hardly had Mao finished than two heavy bombs from enemy aircraft exploded near the front door, their shock-waves shattering all the windowpanes and sending the cave-house rocking. The attack caught us unprepared. When we went into the house after the explosion, we saw Mao dusting the dirt off his clothes, saying with a smile, "The blast from them is nothing; it couldn't even throw me off balance. But the storm we raise will be terrible; it will uproot them." At this Zhou and Peng laughed heartily.

In the early evening of that day, the officers who had come to report on the progress of the battle joined in urging Mao to leave Yan'an. Mao made a motion with his hand and, tapping the table lightly, said, "I won't hear any more of it. I'll be the last one to leave here; I've told you that before."

It was only then that we realized the full implication of Mao's, "I've told you that before," and understood why General Peng had been so agitated.

At dusk on the 18th, when Wang Zhen was visiting Mao, loud gun reports could be heard coming from the southeast: the enemy troops' advance party had reached Wujia Zaoyuan.

Heavy, rapid footsteps could be heard and instantly General Peng appeared. The general was an impatient man and a fast talker, but he had seldom been seen running excitedly like this. Panting, he roared, "What's keeping the chairman here? Leave now! Not a minute's delay!"

All the comrades now sensed the danger. A guard broke into Mao's room without asking permission. "General Peng's angry, Comrade Chairman," he said. "Please start immediately."

Wang Zhen rose to leave, saying, "That's all I want to tell you, Comrade Chairman. You must leave as soon as possible."

"It's time to go now, Comrade Chairman," Zhou Enlai joined in the urging.

Mao remained in his chair, unruffled. He asked, "Have all the comrades left?"

"Yes, a long time ago," answered several anxious voices.

"The civilians?"

"They've left, too. All of them."

"Well, then," Mao said satisfied, "bring me my meal."

Asking for a meal when he should be leaving! We were horror-struck until suddenly we remembered that Mao had said he would be the last to leave, and that he wanted to see what Hu's troops looked like.

Now enemy gunfire could be heard distinctly and, reinforced by the explosions of hand-grenades, was growing increasingly louder. It made us terribly nervous. We had put the food in the canteen for use on the road; now we had to take it out again and place it hastily in front of Mao. Mao was known as a fast eater, but that day he took his time, adding to our nervousness. It seemed that he had made up his mind to see "what Hu's troops looked like."

General Peng arrived, as requested by Zhou Enlai. With one foot in the room and the other outside, he asked, "What are you waiting for, Comrade Chairman? What's so special about those damned soldiers that you must see them for yourself? Our men can do that for you. You must get going. Now!"

Mao looked at the agitated general and stubbornly continued with his meal. For a moment the general seemed about to yank the chopsticks from Mao's hand, but he checked himself. Turning around abruptly, he stared hard at the guards and secretaries and boomed: "What are you waiting for? Get the things out!"

Hurriedly the secretaries cleared the things from the desks. Outside, the car engines were roaring.

"Clean up the rooms," said Mao, frowning. "Be sure no documents are left behind. Leave the books we can't carry with us in good order. These books on Marxism-Leninism will do Hu's troops good."

Mao put down his chopsticks, looked around the empty room, and walked out in silence. Outside, he glanced at each one of us, and placing his hands behind his back, gazed at the pagoda for a long time. Then drawing in his lips and forcing saliva down his throat, he turned his eyes to the southeast in the direction of the booming and flashing of the guns. He looked that way for a long time. Two creases, displaying his disdain appeared at the corners of his mouth. "I wanted to see what Hu's troops looked like," he told Zhou Enlai and others around him, "but General Peng wouldn't let me. He told me that his men will do that for me. I couldn't afford to offend him so I had to go along."

Mao walked to his jeep. Before mounting, he looked back at us, declaring in a loud voice, "Get aboard, comrades! We will return!"

A year later, Mao's remark, "I've told you that before," created a problem for Zhou Enlai.

With five brigades of the enemy wiped out and the commander of the enemy's twenty-ninth army killed in action during the battle at Yichuan (a battle which Mao had planned himself), our troops in the Northwest, like those in the rest of the country, were beginning to mount a counter-offensive. The recovery of Yan'an was only a matter of time, but the war situation as a whole called for Mao to move to a place east of the Yellow River, where he could best control the operations.

If Mao had had his way, he would have returned to Yan'an as he had said earlier. Zhou Enlai and Ren Bishi made careful plans to ensure that Mao would agree to cross the river. They remembered Mao's saying,

"I've told you that before," in other contexts, and at one such time he had claimed: "I will not cross the river until I defeat Hu Zongnan." Thoroughly acquainted with Mao's ways, and himself a highly persuasive talker, Zhou opened a conversation with Mao by asking him if he thought the victory at Yichuan could be regarded as the defeat of Hu.

"That's a historical fact which nobody can alter," Mao replied. Thus seizing his opportunity Zhou said, "You said you would not cross the Yellow River until you defeated Hu. Now that's history. The Frontline and Rear Committees should join the Working Committee in order to seize the final victory."

"You mean we should leave northern Shaanxi?" Mao asked before Zhou could say it.

"Exactly," Zhou responded immediately, nodding in agreement. "The Central Committee has achieved its purpose of staying in northern Shaanxi. Now we need to move to a position from where operations can be controlled most conveniently and effectively."

That is why Mao Zedong moved east of the river to Xibaipo, instead of returning to Yan'an.

I remember the two reasons which Mao gave for refusing to leave northern Shaanxi at a time when things were extremely difficult for us. He said, "I've received many telegrams asking me to cross the river. True, a place free from disturbances will make it easier to plan the operations, but I have my reservations. I've lived in a peaceful environment in Yan'an for ten years. If I leave the minute the enemy begins its advance, I would be turning my back on the people of northern Shaanxi and would thus be too ashamed to face them again. I've chosen to stay with them and will not cross the Yellow River until I defeat Hu Zongnan. And there's another reason why I refuse to pull out of here. Hu's army is more than 200,000 strong, whilst we have only 20,000 men — this represents a ratio of ten-to-one. But compared with the situation in the other war zones, the difference is not very great, so the situation here is much better. Since the Party has placed me in charge of military affairs, who else but myself should be here? Our forces have only recently gained the war-initiative in a number of liberated areas. With me in northern Shaanxi, Chiang Kai-shek will have to think twice before he moves Hu's troops elsewhere. Now that the 'Master of the Northwest' is pinned down here, it takes some of the pressure off our troops in the other war zones."

After leaving Yan'an, the Central Committee called a meeting at Zaolin'gou. At the meeting the responsibilities of the five standing members of the Politburo — Mao, Zhou, Zhu De, Liu Shaoqi and Ren Bishi — were clearly defined. Mao told the meeting, "The Party has many things to do, the most important of which is to defeat Chiang Kai-shek's Kuomintang militarily. Until that is achieved nothing else can be done." By a decision of the Standing Committee, Mao was put in charge of military operations throughout China, making him virtual supreme commander of the armed forces, to be assisted by Zhou Enlai in the control of operations.

Throughout the War of Liberation, I stayed close to Mao and Zhou. As I recall, Mao, with Zhou's assistance, was responsible not only for strategic decisions of overall importance; but in addition, almost all the military campaigns of any significance in the various war zones were without exception planned down to the last detail by Mao, and his assistant, Zhou.

Mao once said to Wang Zhen, "I maintain radio connection with the rest of China wherever I am. That's how I kept myself informed of what was going on in the outside world when I was in Yan'an." Indeed, any military campaigns anywhere in China would mean increased work for the radio operators. During the Liaoxi-Shenyang Campaign in the Northeast, Mao sent, as far as I know, a total of seventy-seven telegrams to our forces there. He wrote each one of these messages himself, working on them as if he were writing a novel: setting out outlines and supplying details, which included, in one case, his suggestion to slaughter horses for meat if the men ran out of meat supplies on the eve of the major offensive.

Things were very tough for Mao during the first six months of the war in northern Shaanxi. During that period he was constantly on the move, staying in twelve different counties and thirty-seven different townships and villages. He seldom spent a day without being pursued by four, seven, or over a dozen brigades of Hu's troops. He not only had a local war to fight, but at the same time a national War of Liberation to take care of. I don't think anyone else in China could have coped with that. Richard Nixon is right when he observes in his book *Leaders*, that a wartime leader usually receives more credit than does a peace-time leader, partly because of the dramatic events inherent in a war, and partly because wartime challenges make it easier to evaluate the qualities of a leader.

We once stopped at a small mountain village. As soon as we arrived, we laid out military maps of the war zones. Soon the maps were everywhere: on the walls, *kang* tables, even on the pickle-jars in the house. A steady stream of telegrams from the war zones were brought in by the secretaries and staff officers, and each time they left, they would go away with Mao's instructions to be transmitted.

The enemy, with their radio-wave detectors located us. Soon Liu Kan's troops, four and half brigades strong, began advancing on us with a vengeance. Reports from our mounted scouts kept coming in at frantic speed: "The enemy is thirty *li** away"; "The enemy has advanced to a position twenty *li* from here"; "The enemy is now less than ten *li* away...."

Mao hated to be interrupted when he had important things on his mind. But the enemy was approaching fast, so one of the guards had to "interrupt" him several times to keep him informed of the enemy's advance. The third time he did it, Mao lost his patience. Slamming his large hand down on the table covered with military maps, Mao shouted at him, "What's this eight or ten *li* business? For me there are 9,600,000 square kilometres. You're dismissed. You're no longer needed here."

During the battle at Shajiadian, we were quartered less than twenty *li* away, at Liangjiacha. The action had been planned by Mao with the assistance of Zhou. After the orders had been issued to General Peng, and before the onset of battle, Mao advanced to Liangjiacha from Yangjia Yuanzi. As the outcome of the battle was of great significance to the war in northern Shaanxi, Mao treated it in all seriousness. As soon as he arrived at Liangjiacha, he was on the phone to General Peng, giving him detailed instructions, even as to where trenches should be dug, if they were needed.

Putting down the receiver, Mao asked me, "Anything to drink,

---

*One *li* equals half a kilometre.

Yinqiao?"

Mao wasn't much of a drinker; it took only one glass of wine to turn his face red, so he seldom drank. Except when he ran out of sleeping pills. One glass would make him giddy, and three would surely put him to sleep. It didn't have to be spirits; red wine or brandy would do the job. Or when he was writing or fighting a battle; on these occasions he needed wine to keep him awake several nights on end. Wine could refresh Mao or put him to sleep, depending on the quantity. Now, since he had been running out of sleeping pills for some time, I had stored up quite a lot of drinks for him.

"Yes," I said. "Spirits?"

"No spirits," Mao shook his head. "That fellow, Zhong Song, doesn't measure up to the sharp taste."

"Red wine then?"

Mao thought a while and then shook his head. "This is going to be a battle between the main forces," he said. "It's going to be fought in a narrow strip of land with the enemy on one side and a river on the other, so things will be tough for us." Then, after a brief silence, he asked, "Have you got brandy?"

"Yes, and it's imported."

"Give me brandy, then," he said, tapping his fingers on the blue circles on the map, enclosed by red arrows, as if he were knocking Zhong Song on the head, asking him whether he measured up to brandy in strength.

I placed the brandy next to the map, and a pack of cigarettes and a box of matches next to the bottle. On the other side of the bottle, two oil lamps and three candles stood in a row. A canvas deck chair was placed in front of the table. Every time, prior to the onset of battle, I would get these things ready for Mao. This time, as on any other occasion, Mao stayed close to the telephone. When the frontline was not calling, he would read telegrams from the war zones, study the war maps of Eastern, Central and Northeastern China, which covered the walls and pickle-jars, or compose telegrams. When he talked on the phone, he would look at the map of northern Shaanxi at the same time. When he was too tired to think, he would take several sips of brandy to stimulate his mind. All the while, he chain-smoked, and drank cup after cup of tea, chewing the tea leaves and swallowing them.

The battle at Shajiadian went on for three days and two nights, and Mao confined himself to his room for just as long. He didn't sleep a wink. He consumed five and a half packs of cigarettes and scores of cups of tea. He passed water so many times that we lost count, but he never defecated. By the time the battle ended, Zhong Song's 36th Division had been put out of action and more than six thousand enemy troops had been taken prisoner. Mao wrote a twelve-character line dedicated to Peng, which said: "Who could have defied the enemy but our great General Peng Dehuai?" When he had finished writing, he lifted the still more than half full bottle of brandy from the table and said, "Why, it's the wrong drink!"

That is how Mao Zedong met challenges; that is how he fought a war. The way he took on a challenge often brings to mind the saying of a Hunanese when confronted by challenging adversaries: "I refuse to be bullied!"

I described earlier how Mao threw away the cigarette butt with a vengeance and declared in a loud voice, "We are not going to cross the Yellow River," and how he walked in steady steps along the river bank, past Liu Kan's men with their guns aimed at him. Well, I did not quite finish, and this is what happened next.

As Mao was approaching the hill with the White Dragon Temple upon it, Ren Bishi told Liu, a staff officer who was with him, "Tell the men back there to remove all traces of our stay." Mao, who was about to make his way up the hill, turned around when he heard what Ren said. Planting the willow-wood walking stick in the grassy slope at the foot of the hill, he said, "What nonsense! Put up a sign right here saying 'Mao Zedong climbed the hill from here.'" The comrades disagreed, saying, "Better erase our traces. The enemy's right behind us." Mao said angrily, "So what? Put up that sign! I'd like to know if Liu measures up to anything."

When Mao was half way up the hill, a few shots rang out down the hill. He halted, and fanning himself with his straw hat, asked, "Has the enemy arrived?" As he said so, he sat down on a rock, refusing to go any farther. It was not until our scouts brought back reports that "the shots came from the militia on the other side of the river" and "now they know they're mistaken" that Mao rose from the rock, saying, "No danger, eh? Let's move on."

That was Mao, a man who always defied his adversaries, refusing to yield a single inch of ground. Liu Kan, who, with a superior force, pressed hard at Mao's heels for a year, proved extremely annoying to Mao. A year later, when General Peng was taking orders from Mao for the battle at Yichuan, he asked, "This s.o.b. Liu Kan, do you want him dead or alive?" Mao replied, "The *Romance of Three Kingdoms* tells us that General Zhang Yide could take the head of an enemy commander in an engagement, as effortlessly as taking something out from his pocket, no matter how well his opponent was protected." General Peng responded, "You will have his head, Comrade Chairman." Sure enough, General Peng had Liu killed in action in Yichuan. Incidentally, the general *was* likened, in the army, to Zhang Yide, a legendary general who lived towards the end of the Eastern Han Dynasty (AD 25-220).

Some foreigners describe Mao Zedong as aggressive. They may be right, but the implication of the word differs, depending upon who says it. Perhaps Mao's defiance came from an eagerness to see, in the words of M. Gorky, the renowned Soviet writer, "the storm rage even more violently."

I have good reasons for the attribution.

Mao emerged victorious from the formidable trials of war, including the Korean war. How did he cope with such tests during peace-time? Some of the tests which confronted him were highly dramatic and the manner in which he dealt with them reflect his character and his heroic qualities even better.

In 1955 I went home on furlough as Mao asked. Members of his bodyguard came from every part of China, with one from each administrative region; they were sent on home furlough in turn, not just for family reunion, but in order to find out about the situation in the countryside and report back truthfully to Mao.

I told Mao all that I had seen and heard upon my return. He offered a few words of appreciation and said, "I don't want to be disturbed in the next two months. I want to concentrate on the cooperative movement in the countryside. I'll see no visitors."

During those months his desk was loaded with stacks of paper; not documents but final proof copies. He shut himself up in his room, writing from night until the following morning. In the afternoons he would sleep for a few hours and go back to work as soon as he got up. For about two weeks, he didn't say a word to me, nor even look at me when I brought him his tea. He was visibly tired and excited, as was his wont when he was set to reach a goal.

One summer, the leaders of the Party were going to Beidaihe, a summer resort by the sea, as scheduled by the Central Committee. When I told Mao of the arrangement, he said, "That's fine. Socialist construction in China will soon reach the level of the sea at high tide, so let's go and take a look at it." As he spoke, his eyes shone with the joy of a child looking in amazement at a magic world which had suddenly unfolded itself in front of him; a world vast, magnificent and full of wonders; a world of the future—to which he was confiding his secret longings in a whisper. It was this world to which Mao devoted his whole life.

It was a long time before Mao, his thrill at a beautiful vision appearing to have dissipated, pointed to the mountains of papers on his desk, saying, "Bring them along. Keep them in good order."

Mao kept two boxes for books, each one square metre in size; boxes which young people nowadays would call packing cases. Mao never travelled without these boxes. This time, instead of books, they were to hold his papers and manuscripts. I sorted them out, putting index slips in-between them, and placed them carefully in the boxes. When we arrived at Beidaihe, I put them on his desk in the same order, same position and same category as they had been on the desk back in Beijing. The papers were reports on the cooperative movement from the various provinces and regions. Today one would find amongst them "master-pieces" of exaggeration written by those intoxicated with success. But at that time, I did not realize this and Mao most probably did not notice it either.

Our house, in No. 1 Swimming Area, was a small one-story building in a poplar grove. Mao lived in the east room as he did in Zhongnanhai; he liked his room to be on this side wherever he was living. During our stay there, except for swimming breaks, Mao spent most of his time writing; he received no visitors except for Liu Shaoqi, Zhou Enlai and Zhu De.

It was then that I discovered one more thing about Mao. When he was gripped by a strong emotion, he would write non-stop, his pen moving rapidly over the paper; when the emotion became too intense to be vented in words, he would rise suddenly, and take to the sea to battle with the waves.

One day a windstorm was raging. The heat had evaporated and the sky darkened with thick, inky clouds, churning their way across its expanse. The wind was howling, the sea roaring, thunder crashing and rain lashing, filling the entire world with a cacophony at once passionate, soul-stirring, mad and terrifying. Apparently the sound produced its effect on Mao. He went on writing, not bothering to look out of the windows, and as he wrote on, he gained in speed, his chest heaving slightly. Then, all of a sudden, a bizarre idea struck him.

He slammed his pen down on the desk, rising from his seat abruptly. "Yinqiao," he said, "let's go swimming."

"What?!" I might just as well have been struck by lightning. "Go —go swimming? In this wea—weather?" I must have sounded like someone sleep-talking.

"Isn't this nice weather for a swim?" Mao said, with an unexpected, faint smile, which showed the familiar creases of defiance at the corners of his mouth. "I'm not a woman with bound feet. What can the wind do to me?" Chinese women bound their feet in past ages; the phrase "a woman with bound feet" is a metaphor for a hesitant and over-cautious person.

"You can't do that! Absolutely not!" I cried in horror as if awaking from a bad dream. Taking a few quick steps I planted myself in front of him, blocking his way. "A woman with bound feet!" What made him think of that phrase? "No, you're not going!" I protested.

We were empowerd by the Party to prevent Mao from doing what we believed to be dangerous. Since 1949, when New China was founded, Mao had lost all "freedom of movement." Without the consent of the security departments Mao could not leave Zhongnanhai or his residence. Thus I mustered the guards who formed a "great wall" in front of him; the gates in the wall remained shut no matter how violently he protested. On such matters I listened to nobody, not even Mao himself, excepting Luo Ruiqing, whose orders to us were: "Stay close to the chairman twenty-four hours a day, don't leave him alone even for one second. Keep a close watch on him. Stop him at whatever cost if he wants to swim in the sea, and protect him. Under no circumstances must he be allowed to do such a thing."

Mao was a man of superhuman energy. He thought nothing of staying up three or five nights at a stretch. Usually, we in the guard rotated four shifts a day. Now it was one straight 24-hour shift for each of us to ensure we had enough men to stop him; and what with us trying to remain alert for that long, so that he wouldn't "catch us nodding and slip away," and arguing with him when the urge got the better of him, the job was extremely exhausting.

It was a long time before the storm blew over and the sun shone again, and we grew even more nervous. The sun would give Mao more of an excuse to insist upon his wish and we would have an even harder job preventing him. But the wind on the sea was still blowing at force 7 at least, and the swells were just as heavy.

It happened just as we expected: at ten o'clock in the morning, Mao announced he was going swimming. Immediately the "great wall" rose. This time we had enlisted the help of Mao's physician, Dr. Xu Tao, who listed three reasons why swimming was dangerous after a storm. Being an intellectual, Dr. Xu was more skillful than we were in the art of persuasion. But he shouldn't have come up with Reason No. 3. "Thirdly," the doctor said, "after a storm the beach is littered with shells. They make the beach unsafe. Your feet may get hurt or you may trip over them. This is what happened to Li Weihan; he ended up with a broken leg, and it was a fine day and the sea was calm."

"Who tripped?" asked Mao, staring menacingly at Xu. "If that's what happened to Li, does it mean that it will automatically happen to me? What you say makes me even more determined to go for a swim."

Mao rose angrily and immediately we formed a line to block his way. Saying: "To the sea!" he made for the door as if what lay in front of him was not a human barrier but a vast expanse of land, with nothing standing in his way, or alternatively, a straight thoroughfare. With a determined look, he bore down upon us like a train thundering its way towards us, filling us with terror. We kept backing down, and when we reached the front door, we couldn't hold ranks any longer, but parted so that we wouldn't be "crushed to smithereens."

There was nothing left for it but for me to go along. I immediately

25

alerted the bodyguards and accompanied Mao, carrying swimming trunks, towels, life-buoys and spirits. Dr. Xu also arrived with his first-aid kit, so did the guard-company in response to an emergency call. In the company of this small army Mao headed towards the sea.

The moment I saw the sea I felt frightened. The black expanse of water heaved violently, its huge waves, each several hundred metres across, lashed their way from the horizon to the beach at frightening speed, raising an ear-splitting din like the pounding of guns, or a windstorm raging through a forest, or hundreds and thousands of wild beasts stampeding. The foam, riding the wind for several dozen metres, fell on us like rain. We found ourselves closing up on Mao.

Mao stared at the sea, breathing audibly, his chest heaving, his eyes gleaming defiantly like a soldier about to go into action. After sizing up the sea briefly, he gently pushed aside the surrounding bodyguards, and silently took off his clothes. This silence was more compelling and carried more weight than any spoken words, urging us to follow him come hell or high water, as a bugle call would have done. We stripped as fast as we could, all trembling with anxiety, excitement and the chill of the icy cold foam bearing down upon us.

Now we were all ready. Mao glanced at each of us, enquiring, with a faint smile playing at the corners of his mouth, "Are you scared?"

"No!" But our reply didn't come in unison and wasn't loud enough.

"You don't have to come with me if you don't want to. You can watch from the shore or go back," Mao said nonchalently as he turned around and walked towards the sea. Mao was a big tall man; with a slightly bulging stomach tilting his body backwards a little, so that he walked a bit awkwardly. But nothing, not even a force 7 gale, could budge him if he stood still, holding his body like that. So he walked on, towards the sea, leaving a trail of deep footprints behind.

The guards and bodyguards rushed up to Mao as if responding to a command, surrounding him. Seven or eight young guards, spread out in a line in front of him, were racing towards the sea; following behind him, and on both sides, were four or five of us, walking in big, resolute strides.

A huge wave, rising like a cliff, rushed towards Mao as if greeting an opponent, its white-caps resembling thousands of sparkling goblins hovering above a cliff. Rising and falling with terrific force, it roared its way to the beach like an angry wounded beast.

"Beat it, beat it!" Mao yelled like a child. We plunged clumsily into the receding wave. Halfway, it was caught by an onrushing swell, which, with a deafening noise, rose in a high dark green arch, and before we knew it, the arch had collapsed on us with mighty force, swallowing us up. In the ensuing blackout we experienced the sensation of being air-borne, when in fact, we were enveloped in a huge volume of water; even when we fell on the sand with a heavy thud, we still didn't know what had happened.

"Comrade Chairman! Comrade Chairman!" I heard someone shouting, the voice at once both far off and intimately close. "Are you all right? Are you all right?"

Instantly I came to my senses to find that all of us, including Mao, had been knocked down by the waves. I immediately picked myself up and ran up to Mao. "What happened, Comrade Chairman?" I asked. "Are you all right?"

Pushing away my hands, Mao rose from the beach. Spitting out sand and looking sideways at the wide rolling waves surging up to the beach, he pointed to the sea and unexpectedly declared, "That's what I call a worthy opponent."

My heart sank. When Mao saw an opponent in someone, he would never let him go unvanquished.

Sure enough, barely before we had recovered from the shock, he was returning to the churning sea. Then it happened all over again: we joined him protectively, we were buried in the waves, we were lifted up by them, we were thrown far back to the beach. After this had been repeated several times, we grew frightened; the roar of the sea had brought us to the verge of collapse. We lay on the beach, so exhausted that we were unable to get up again, even with Mao standing right beside us.

Mao looked glum. Frowning, he asked me, "Knocked down for good, Yinqiao? It's just a little water; it can't be as bad as the seven brigades which Liu Kan unleashed on us, can it?" Startled, I got up. Now he was speaking to all of us present. "Are you beaten?" he looked and sounded extremely grave. "If you don't want to stay with me, you can leave me; I will then raise a new team to continue the battle."

That was too much for us. I leaped up with a loud cry, so did all

27

the other guards and bodyguards. Shoulder to shoulder, with linked hands, the burly young guards formed a wedge-shaped human shield, with Mao, assisted by his strong bodyguards following immediately behind. In this formation we rushed into the sea. The waves lunged at us, enveloping us, but we remained on our feet; when they rolled back we advanced. Accompanied by the howling wind, the thundering waves and our loud shouts, the scene was as exciting as two armies locked in life-and-death combat. We kept on advancing like this until we reached the bosom of the sea. Now we tried desperately to stay close to Mao, but each time we were thrown back by the waves. As if in revenge, the sea heaved violently, rising one moment like a cliff and the next, plunging like a bottomless chasm, filling us with mortal fear. Someone was shouting out his last request: "A life-buoy, quick! A life-buoy for the chairman!"

Mao shouted back from the crest of a wave, "No need for alarm! It's only the tide...." Then from the bottom: "Hold on! You can only be washed ashore, not dragged to the bottom...." And then from the crest again: "Show your guts!"

When Mao returned from the swim he looked more satisfied than when he had won the battle at Shajiadian.

When offered or offering a challenge, Mao never showed any hesitation but rather, the confidence to win. He was astonishingly tough and was just as astonishingly willful. When his willfulness turned out to be a source of misjudgement, he could still rally a large force around him and sustain its morale with his self-confidence and his unbending will. All his life Mao was a winner, not in terms of specific political issues but rather, as a man who revealed his heroic nature whenever he was confronted with a challenge.

When the Bombers Came

In the face of death, Mao Zedong never lost his composure. That's how he held himself as he walked past the seven brigades' pursuing troops, with their guns aimed directly at him. If you attribute Mao's composure on that occasion to the fact that he was still quite a distance away from the troops on the hilltop, let me recount what happened on yet another occasion.

After we reached the revolutionary base in the Shanxi–Chahar–Hebei border area, east of the Yellow River, Mao lived in Chengnanzhuang, where the Shanxi–Chahar–Hebei Regional Military Command had its headquarters. Mao called a ten-day meeting of the Party secretaries there in May. When the meeting was concluded, Mao was in high spirits. Without taking a rest, he drafted a long telegram to Deng Xiaoping, who had established revolutionary bases in the Dabie Mountains, and a circular on the convocation of the National Political Consultative Conference.

By the time he had finished with the circular, day was breaking. He took a walk in the courtyard to stretch himself. When he returned to his room, he gathered up the stationery and manuscripts, and said, "I'm going to bed, Yinqiao."

I brought him two sleeping pills and a cup of water. Mao, who had retained the habits of a peasant, slept naked, and would read a bit to put himself to sleep. That morning, after reading the newspapers for half an hour, he put them down next to the pillows and closed his eyes. That was a sign that no second dose of sleeping pills was needed. So I left the room quietly.

Jiang Qing, who lived in a small room adjacent to Mao's, had gotten up; she was a woman with regular habits. General Nie Rongzhen, who had also risen, was returning from his morning stroll. When he saw Jiang, he stopped to shake her hand, as he would each time he met her. After they chatted for a little while, Nie returned to his room. The general had given his room to Mao and had moved to a house in the row behind.

They had just parted when the air-raid siren atop a hill to the north of Chengnanzhuang sounded. My heart sank immediately and I grew so frightened that I held my breath. Chengnanzhuang wasn't Yan'an. In Yan'an, the moment enemy planes entered the air space of the Shaanxi-Gansu-Ningxia border region, we would be informed of their approach by telephone, and would have enough time to take cover after the sounding of the siren. Chengnanzhuang was quite close to Beiping*; what was worse, the aircraft could not be sighted until they were right over the surrounding hills, leaving us very little time to take cover. With Mao's room more than a hundred metres from the air-raid shelter, any delay in getting him there could mean disaster.

Fear left me paralyzed—I kept on circling in front of Mao's room. One may not understand why I did not simply wake Mao up and take him to the air-raid shelter. But it wasn't as simple as that. To Mao, sleep didn't come easily; nine times out of ten, when he lost his temper it was because he couldn't go to sleep. Now he would certainly make a scene if he was awakened and there was no air raid. When anger got the better of him, he was frightening to behold, and would swear loudly: "Get the hell out of here!", "You're to remain on your damned feet as punishment!".... These fits were a hazard to his health and would leave him in low spirits for several days.

Yan Changlin, the guards' platoon leader, came running on tiptoe towards me, as excited as if the house were on fire, but careful enough to ask me in a subdued voice, "What shall we do? Wake the old man up?"

Those of us who had been with Mao for a long time called him "old man" sometimes.

"But he's just taken the sleeping pills and gone to sleep...." I kept on wringing my hands.

"What nonsense! The enemy planes may drop bombs at any moment."

"What if they don't? It'll be too late then."

Before we could decide what to do, three enemy aircraft arrived and began to circle over our heads. We stood frozen, too dumbfounded

---

*The pre-liberation name for Beijing.

to take cover. The only thing we could do now was pray to Marx for protection. If the planes didn't drop bombs, everything would be fine; if they did, then let the bombs kill us first, in order that we wouldn't be stigmatized for life....

After circling twice, the planes flew away, heading towards Beiping. I felt greatly relieved, as if a heavy load had been lifted from me. I almost leaped for joy, feeling grateful to Marx for answering my prayer.

But our sense of relief was shortlived, for we were soon gripped by fresh anxiety. Apparently they had been reconnaissance planes. After them.... Bombers! Unlike the civilian buildings, which were laid out haphazardly, those in the compound of the regional command head-quarters stood in neat rows; they were sitting ducks for the bombers.

As our dilemma remained insoluble, we decided to pass the buck to our superior, Jiang Qing. A meeting was called, attended by Fan, General Nie's secretary, at which it was decided that Mao should sleep on, but an emergency team with a stretcher at the ready, would stand by in front of Mao's room, so that Mao could be carried to the air-raid shelter the moment the bombers came.

It was breakfast time. We were told to take our breakfast in turn, but none of us left for the meal: how could we leave Mao at a time like that?

The air-raid siren on the hill sounded again some time after eight o'clock. There was no time to lose. Before Yan Changlin had finished saying, "Do what General Peng said!", I had rushed into Mao's room.

Before leaving Yan'an, General Peng had told Yan, "In case of an emergency, carry the chairman away; don't pay any attention to his protests. Explain to him when he is out of danger. He'll understand."

Now I was standing beside Mao's bed. "Comrade Chairman, an emergency...."

"What?" Roused from sleep, Mao looked at me with sleepy eyes, anger seeming to well up within him. But before he could say anything else, Yan was lifting him from the bed, saying, "The enemy planes are going to bomb this place, Comrade Chairman. Three reconnaissance planes were here a few moments ago. Just now the air-raid alarm sounded again. It must be bombers this time. Please come to the air-raid shelter immediately."

Now Mao knew what was happening. As we frantically helped him on with his clothes, he put out his hand, saying, "Light a cigarette for me!" Good heavens! What a habit to keep at a time like this! "No time for a smoke, Comrade Chairman!" I shouted.

Frowning he enquired, "Are they dropping bombs now?"

"Aiya, Comrade Chairman," said Yan, stamping his feet in agitation. "They will the moment they come; it'll be too late then. Listen—"

"Nonsense! Light a cigarette!" Mao sounded a bit annoyed.

"Hurry! Hurry!" Now Jiang Qing was shouting at the door. "The planes are diving, they're diving!" Before she could finish, she was gone, except for her short rapid shouts which carried over the distance: "Quick! Quick! Quick!"

It was now or never. I thrust my hands under Mao's arms, whilst Yan threw a cotton-padded jacket on him, and with Shi Guorui and Sun Zhen'guo holding him by the arm, we made for the door, half carrying and half dragging Mao along.

We had just got out of the door, when I heard a shrill noise. I ducked and backed up instinctively, and before I knew it, the yellow earth trembled violently under my feet, and at the same time I heard a loud thud, like rotten eggs exploding. Instantly we froze.

"Oh!" Jiang Qing was heard screaming in the distance. Her scream brought me to my senses, and when I saw what had happened, cold perspiration broke out all over me. Right in front of Mao's room, and within our reach, were three bombs in a cluster. I wanted to cry, or run away, but I was too stupefied to do either. And the next moment something incredible happened. "What happened to them?" Mao gazed at the bombs as if they were objects worthy of philosophical contemplation. Fascinated and bewildered by the whirling gyroscopes of the bombs, Mao was about to bend over them and touch them with his finger....

"Bombs, they're bombs!" Jiang Qing shrilled, stamping her feet, but when the planes dived again, she bounced back towards the air-raid shelter like an over inflated ball. Meanwhile the four of us cried out, as if prodded by a hot poker: "On the double! On the double!", and holding Mao by the arms we flew like mad towards the air-raid shelter.

Waving at us frantically at the entrance to the shelter, General Nie shouted: "Hurry! Hurry! They're going to drop bombs! They're going to drop bombs!"

We were running as fast as our legs would carry us, allowing neither Mao nor ourselves to stop. In the flurry, the cotton-padded jacket almost slipped off Mao's back. I held it in place with one hand and with the other hand held Mao by the arm. We rushed on. Apparently displeased at the figure he was being made to cut, mao protested repeatedly, "Let go of me, let go of me! I don't want to run!"

We had just cleared the back door of the compound when we heard loud explosions behind us; the compound had been hit. When I instinctively looked back, I saw black smoke billowing skyward.

"How foolish you are!" Mao gasped, freeing himself from my grip. "It's the buildings they're after. Once we're out of the compound we're safe. So why the hurry?"

But the planes were about to make another dive. Ignoring his protests, we seized his arms and ran even faster. We had just reached the entrance to the air-raid shelter when we heard another loud explosion quite close behind us. We tried to take Mao into the shelter, but he shook himself free. As we were now much safer by the entrance, we stopped "coercing" him, but tried to persuade him to listen to us: "Shall we go inside the shelter, Comrade Chairman?"

Regaining his breath, Mao complained, "But I haven't had a smoke yet."

As Yan helped him on with the cotton-padded jacket, I gave him a lighted cigarette.

"Let's get in there, comrade Chairman," General Nie Joined in.

"No hurry," said Mao. "It's quite safe here. I want to watch them drop bombs...."

He had hardly finished speaking, when the planes dived again. Fire burst out in the compound, the thick smoke spreading everywhere. Nodding, Mao said, "Now I've seen it." He turned around and walked into the air-raid shelter unhurriedly.

When we ran back to the compound after the planes had departed, the first place we visited was Mao's room. The gyroscopes of the bombs that had not exploded were still spinning in the wind. The bombs that had exploded had left a lot of fragments and debris in the room. Two thermos flasks were smashed, leaving pools of water on the floor. These bombs looked like anti-personnel bombs. We shuddered at the thought of what would have happened if we hadn't taken Mao out of his room in time.

I learned later that ordnance workers, who were opposed to the civil war, often filled shells with sand, making them duds.

Apparently the air strike was premeditated. General Nie ordered an investigation: "It's obviously plotted by criminals. Get them, put them on public trial and shoot them!"

The criminals remained at large until investigations into enemy files, after the liberation of Baoding, resulted in their exposure.

Meng Xiande, deputy manager of the Dafeng Tobacco Factory, which was a producer for the logistics service of the military command, was a Kuomintang spy. He and Liu Congwen, a manager of the officers' mess at the command headquarters, whom Meng had recruited, had planned to kill the leaders of the Central Committee in Chengnan-zhuang, by poisoning their food, but they never got the chance. By virtue of tight security, food for Mao was examined by us bodyguards before being brought to him. So they hatched another plot. They smuggled reports to the enemy's intelligence service in Baoding, and briefed the Kuomintang's Security Bureau in detail on Mao and other leaders of the Party in Chengnanzhuang. These reports were relayed to the enemy's intelligence service in Beiping, by the Baoding agents. The result was the air strike. When they were caught, Meng and Liu were shot after public trial.

Mao once said angrily to Luo Ruiqing when the latter, out of his concern for Mao's safety, tried to prevent him from swimming in the Changjiang (Yangtse) River: "All that worries you is that I may drown in that river." "But what's this safety business all about? You may get killed by bombs right in your own room." One would agree if one knew what Mao meant.

In the Jinggang Mountains, on the Long March, and later on in Yan'an, Mao survived many bombing raids by enemy aircraft. His wife, He Zizhen, was severely wounded in one such raid. Before he left Yan'an, bomb explosions during the course of an air-raid shattered the window panes of his cave-room and nearly brought down the house, but this raid on Chengnanzhuang was even worse. After the founding of New China, he was still exposed to many such raids, two of which had outstanding consequences.

In 1952, Kuomintang aircraft attacked Shanghai when Mao was there on an inspection tour. The security people suspected that the raid was the work of enemy intelligence agents, like the one on Chengnan-zhuang. Long-drawn-out investigations into the so-called "Pan and Yang case" led to the wrong imprisonment of Pan Hannian, a leading official of the Shanghai municipal government. It is most unlikely that Mao had anything to do with these investigations, for as leader of the nation, he was far too busy handling much more important affairs of the Party, the army and the whole nation to have issued any instructions for these investigations. One day in 1956, as I recall, when Mao was swimming in Shanghai, he met Li Liancheng, who was then working in Shanghai after quitting his job as Liu Shaoqi's bodyguard. Mao asked him what he was doing; when Li told him that he was investigating the "Pan and Yang case," Mao had no idea what the case was all about.

In January 1958 Mao was in Nanning. A little after one o'clock in the morning of the 18th, the radars spotted Kuomintang planes heading for Nanning. At the time, Mao was working in his room after swimming during the day in the Yong River. Could the Kuomintang have learned that Mao was in the city attending a working conference of the Central Committee? He Tingyi, deputy commander-in-chief of the air force, who was then with Mao, was alarmed: Nanning had no air defences of its own. He made an emergency call to the military airfield at Liuzhou, ordering the fighters there to intercept the enemy planes in three successive missions, emphasizing that the missions must be effective whatever the cost.

There was a blackout in the city that day. All of us went to Mao's bedroom and asked him to leave for the air-raid shelter. "I'm not going," Mao said, waving his hand. "You can go if you want."

"We're responsible for your safety, Comrade Chairman."

"Chiang Kai-shek once asked me to go to Nanjing. I went as requested. What happened? Nothing! What could he have done to me? Don't think I'm much safer now than I was then?" And pointing at me, he ordered, "Go and light the candles for me."

"No, Comrade Chairman," I said. "Just in case...."

"Go," Mao was growing impatient, "and light the candles. Those bombs of theirs don't have the gut to explode at my feet! Have I ever been afraid of them?!"

The candles were lighted, and Mao continued with his reading. The book was *Chu Ci* (*Songs of the Chu Dukedom*), which he was reading with the greatest concentration and interest.

Things That Upset Mao

If there was anything Mao wouldn't want to see, it was tears. Mao said on one occasion, "I can't bear to see poor people cry. When I see their tears, I can't hold back my own."

One day, after we went east of the Yellow River, Mao was travelling from Chengnanzhuang to Xibaipo in a jeep. The going was rough over the mountain roads. When we were passing through a deep gully, we noticed something unusual in the tall weeds by the roadside. We were immediately alerted, our hands on our guns.

On approaching, we saw a girl about eight or nine years old lying in the weeds, with a peasant woman in her thirties sitting next to her. As our car drove past, I noticed that the girl's eyes were closed, her face sallow; the woman next to her was crying. We relaxed: the girl and the woman didn't present any threat to us. As Mao's safety was our sole concern, we heaved a sigh of relief.

But Mao was shaken by the sight. "Stop the car!" he ordered in a loud voice.

Mao had climbed out of the car before we could go over to assist him as we usually did. With large strides he walked over to the girl and the woman. Touching the girl's hands and forehead, he asked, "What happened to her?"

"She's ill," said the woman, her face streaked with tears.

"What's wrong with her?"

"The doctor said she has a bad cold and is running a fever. But the medicine hasn't worked. She's delirious with the fever. Now she can barely breathe...." She broke into a loud sob.

I saw tears well in Mao's eyes. He turned his head suddenly in the direction of the jeep.

"I'm ready," said Dr. Zhu, who was with him on the trip.

"Come and see what's wrong with the child."

Dr. Zhu examined her with his stethoscope, took her temperature and asked the woman about her illness.

"Is she going to live?" Mao asked, his voice trembling, his anxiety visible.

"Yes."

"Good! Do everything you can to save her," Mao sounded relieved.

"But the medicine...."

"No more medicine?" Again Mao was worried.

"Not really ... but there's only one bottle left."

"What is it?"

"Penicillin."

"Use it then."

"It's imported and we can't get a new supply. It's so precious I didn't even use it on you. Unless it's absolutely necessary...."

"It's absolutely necessary now. Give her the shot, please."

That's how Dr. Zhu parted with the bottle of penicillin that he had kept for a long time and had been extremely reluctant to use. As a result of their limited use, antibiotic drugs were much more effective then, than they are now. After the injection the doctor gave the child some water from his water-bottle. The girl soon opened her eyes and said weakly, "Mom...."

That immediately brought streams of tears down her mother's cheeks from her wide-open eyes. Suddenly she dropped to her knees, saying sobbingly to Mao, "You're a Buddha, a life-saving Buddha!"

Mao's eyes misted over with tears. He turned to the doctor, saying, "Take them home in the other car, doctor." "Keep the child under observation. Join us when she's Okay"

This encounter would always turn Mao's eyes misty when he recalled it. "I wonder what's become of the girl now," he would say. "I wish she had been brought here for treatment...." And many times he would add thoughtfully, "There's hardly any medical service in the countryside. The farmers have to travel dozens of li when they're sick and still there's no guarantee that they will be able to find a doctor. We must do something so that there are doctors in the countryside. Doctors are duty-bound to treat farmers, because they live on the farmers' produce."

Another thing which upset Mao was bloodshed.

"Nonsense!" One may dismiss that in disbelief: if there is such a man it certainly wasn't Mao, a man hardened by the sight of blood, shed in hundreds of battles which he had fought as commander-in-chief; a man who never flinched in the face of the enemy's brutalities; brutalities —which had taken a heavy toll of his loved ones and friends.

But it is in a different sense that I say Mao hated to see bloodshed.

After his move to Beiping, following its liberation, Mao lived in a country house in Fragrant Hills. Quite a few generals were also living there. They had grown so accustomed to the pounding of guns that they were unused to the quiet surroundings of the hills. And we in the guard were so familiar with shooting that we iched for the trigger.

But very soon, once the first shot had sounded in the hills, we discovered a way to stop our itch: there were so many birds there. So we began to shoot freely in the otherwise quiet hills. In those days there weren't any laws for the preservation of wildlife, nor was there anything like Greenpeace. The Second World War had just ended, and the War of Liberation was still going on in the southern part of China; with millions of human lives sacrificed, what did the lives of a few birds matter?

One day Mao was returning from a meeting together with me. When he got out of his car in front of the country house, some of the guards, all sharp shooters, were coming back from sparrow hunting, with quite a lot of game, talking merrily.

Mao looked in the direction of the guards; it was only a casual glance, but then he stood still. Out of respect the guards lowered their voices and slowed down when they saw him.

Mao's eyebrows twitched, slowly drawing together in a frown. He bit his lower lip as was his habit and asked, "What's that in your hands?"

"Some sparrows," one of the guards said, holding up the birds tied to a string. I could clearly see blood all over their bodies, and as he held them up, a drop splashed off and landed at Mao's feet.

Mao's face twitched in pain at the sight of the dead sparrows. He backed up half a step, covering his eyes with his hand, and cried, "Take them away, take them away! I don't want to see them!"

Scared, the guard hurriedly swung the birds, dripping with blood, behind him.

"Who gave you permission to kill them?" Mao said reproachfully, with a deep frown. "They're living things, just like us. How do you have the heart to kill them in their prime? They haven't offended you, have they?"

The hunters were left speechless.

"No more hunting from now on. No one will be allowed to do that again."

"It was started by some of the leading comrades," I told Mao quietly. "They just followed suit...."

"No one will be allowed to shoot birds from now on, leading comrades or not. Tell them that I don't want to see any more birds killed by anyone."

So the hills once again became a haven for the otherwise frightened birds, a haven where they could sing, fly, and raise their young.

In 1958, when Mao was touring the countryside, farmers complained to him that sparrows were costing them tons of crops: thousands of kilogrammes of crops were lost the moment the birds landed on them. Some scientists also claimed that sparrows destroyed more crops than they ate. These complaints upset Mao who exclaimed: "Pests, they're pests!", and, as he had sworn to "do away with all pests" in one of his poems, sparrows were labelled a pest, along with rats, flies and mosquitoes and were condemned to public extermination.

Later, other scientists said that sparrows did as much good as they did harm, because they also fed on caterpillars. The new conclusion put an end to the nationwide effort to exterminate these poor birds.

An incident which occurred during a conversation which most probably took place in 1964, is also unforgettable.

Mao was at a dancing party in Zhongnanhai. During a break he was sitting on a sofa chair when a girl from the air force song and dance ensemble came over and joined him for a chat. When they talked about the life of the members of the ensemble, Mao asked with interest, "Do you find the training exercises strenuous?"

"Oh, yes," said the girl. Then blinking her eyes she added, "You can get hurt in these training sessions."

"Can it be that bad?" Mao couldn't understand.

"It can. I have heard that an actor in a theatrical company from

Tianjin had an accident whilst he was doing sommersault exercises. His neck was hurt so badly that it affected the entire length of his spine...."

"Aiya," Mao grimaced. He looked away from her, and waving his hands, said, "Cut it, cut it!" He heaved a deep breath to recover from the shock, as if he had just witnessed a tragic event and wanted to forget it. Then he rose and hurriedly walked away.

When the music started up again, he did not join the dancers, but sat in a chair with a pained look.

The sight of someone pleading for life would also upset Mao.

Mao came from a peasant's family, but he knew better than the peasant in the Chinese fable who was killed by the very serpent he had saved, by warming it back to life on his chest, when it was nearly frozen to death. When his foes, either military or political, Chiang Kai-shek included, were on the verge of total defeat at his hands, he would never spare the final blow, remembering how the Duke of Chu lost the war he should have won by sparing his opponent instead of delivering him the last fatal blow.

But when circumstances were different, the appeal, "don't kill me," would touch the soft spot in Mao.

Life was extremely difficult when we were in northern Shaanxi. One of the guards deserted when he could no longer endure such hardship. A deserter from amongst the guards was much more dangerous than a deserter from amongst the combat troops, because he was party to a lot of secrets.

A manhunt was immediately organized by the guards, which resulted in the capture of the deserter. Since our hatred for deserters was fuelled by our anxiety and the hardships we had endured during the hunt, we all desired to revenge ourselves on him when he was brought in with his hands tied behind his back.

"Beat the bastard to pulp!"

"Shoot the s.o.b.!"

Mao heard the angry shouts. When he came out from his cave-room, he saw the deserter being escorted towards him. The culprit was a young man. He looked awful, trembling with fear, his baby-face ghastly pale, tear-stained, his clothes torn and dusty. When he heard the shouts, demanding his death, he broke into a loud cry: "Don't kill me!

Please don't! I'm not a turncoat. I just wanted to go home. I beg you for mercy!"

For all his hatred of traitors and deserters, at the pathetic sight of the young deserter, Mao knitted his brows together in pain, his eyes filled with tears. Raising his hand, he ordered in a loud voice, "Turn him loose! Now!"

"But he's a deserter!"

"And a skunk!"

"He's a skunk?" Mao said, his brows still knitted. "He's just a boy. Turn him loose! Don't frighten him like that!"

One of the officers didn't like the idea. "Let such a serious offender go unpunished?" he protested. "Discipline is essential to an army."

"Do you mean you're the only one who knows anything about the army?" Now Mao was talking in a conciliatory tone: "He's just a boy and is new to the revolutionary ranks. He's never lived such a hard life before. He found it too much for him and he got homesick. Don't you think he'd be even more homesick if you lock him up? He's not a traitor; he's just ignorant. Let him go. The better he's fed the less he'll think about home. Do you agree?"

So not only was the deserter spared the punishment, but he was put on the officers' mess for a couple of days. He never tried to run away again.

Mao, as I observed, was a sympathetic man, capable of tender feelings as well as being a staunch revolutionary; he was as strikingly kindhearted as he was steel-willed.

Mao in Tears

"I don't cry easily," Mao once told He Zizhen. "But I can't bear to see poor people cry. When I see their tears I can't hold back my own. When my orderlies leave me I feel sad; I just can't bear to see them go. When some of them were killed, I cried over their death. When one of my old horses dies, or when one of my pens gets worn out, I'm reluctant to replace it. And when in Guizhou, I heard that you were dying from a wound, I cried."

Mao was being candid when he said that, as my experience as his bodyguard for fifteen years will testify.

Mao was a tough man. He never shed tears over his personal misfortunes no matter how tragic they were. The death of his son, Mao Anying, in Korea, during the Korean war upset him so much that he lost his appetite and was unable to sleep; he just sat in the sofa chair, all alone, chain-smoking. But he never cried. There was sadness, longing and anger in his eyes, but no tears, not a single drop.

But that doesn't mean that he never cried; he did, even loudly. I was witness to at least three such occasions, which I shall never forget.

The Beijing opera, "The Duke Bids Farewell to His Wife," was one of Mao's favourites. The Duke of Chu finds himself surrounded by enemy troops at Gaixia. His wife takes her own life in order to make it easier for her husband to break through the enemy encirclement. When the duke reaches the Wujiang River, after making the breakthrough, he, too, takes his life, having disgracefully lost the war which he should have won. Mao saw the opera many times, both shortly before and for some time after the defeat of Chiang Kai-shek; on some occasions he took all the leading Party comrades to the performance. As I have said, Mao was capable of great tenderness. When the duke and his wife became overwhelmed by sadness, knowing that they would never see one another again, Mao would blink back his tears. On one occasion, he warned me in a hoarse voice, pressing one of my coat buttons with his finger: "Never do as the duke did; let that be a lesson for all of us."

Mao was a fan of period plays and Beijing opera. His favourites changed along with his circumstances. When he was fighting in northern Shaanxi, his favourites were "Defenceless City" and "Borrowing Arrows"; he liked them so much that he was often heard singing arias from them. These two operas are based on the tales of three rivalling kingdoms in the years AD 220-280. In "Defenceless City," Sima Yi, of the Kingdom of Wei, advances on Xicheng immediately after capturing Jieting from Ma Su, of the Kingdom of Shu. By the time Zhuge Liang, of Shu Kingdom, has been informed of the approach of Sima Yi, it is too late for him to bring in any troops to defend himself. In order to keep the city from falling, he feigns composure by playing the lute atop the city wall, when Sima Yi arrives. Suspecting an ambush inside the city, Sima Yi orders a retreat. This gives Zhuge Liang time to strengthen the city's defences. "Borrowing Arrows" is yet another tale about Zhuge Liang. One foggy night, during the battle of Chibi, on the Yangtse River, between Cao Cao and the allied forces of Liu Bei and Sun Quan, Zhuge Liang feigns a boat attack on Cao's fleet, accompanied by the rolling of drums. The boats are set up with straw dummies. Mistaking it for a real attack, Cao orders a counter-attack with arrows. Soon the dummies are heavy with arrows badly needed by the allied forces.

When Mao was in Xibaipo directing the three major campaigns —those fought in the Liaoxi-Shenyang, Beiping-Tianjin and Huaihai areas—the phonograph records he listened to for relaxation were those of these two operas. The other Beijing opera from which Mao liked to sing arias was "The Meeting of Heroes," a play about the wisdom and resourcefulness of two strategists, Zhuge Liang and Zhou Yu, commander-in-chief of the allied forces, as displayed in the battle of wits between them during the planning of operations on the eve of the battle at Chibi. "The Duke Bids Farewell to His Wife" came to be Mao's favourite after he moved to Beijing, and during the first few years after the founding of New China. Between 1953 and 1954 he saw "The Story of the White Snake" many times. This is an adaptation from Chinese mythology, about a snake who, after meditation for a thousand years takes on human form, yearns to live in the mundane world, falls in love with Xu Xian, whom she marries, but is condemned to eternal imprisonment in a sealed pagoda as a punishment, by Buddhist Monk Fahai, who is the symbol of feudalism. The tragic story which the opera unfolds never failed to move Mao to tears and send him snuffling.

When Mao was touring Shanghai, in 1958, he was once asked by the leading comrades of the Shanghai Communist Party Committee what operatic pieces he would like to see for an evening's entertainment. He thought for a while and replied, "'The Story of the White Snake,' I think."

When Mao arrived in the auditorium of the club for Shanghai government staff on the night scheduled for the entertainment, the audience rose to their feet and applauded in welcome. Mao waved to them in acknowledgement as he was ushered to his seat in the front row. As he never stood on ceremony in the presence of ranking Party officials, Mao walked to his seat without the usual exchange of formalities with the leading comrades of the Shanghai Party Committee and government seated in the same row as himself; he waved again to the audience before sitting down.

The row was made up of single soft chairs in cloth covers. I sat next to Mao so as to be close to him, as was required of a guard on 24-hour duty. Mao was big-bellied; when he sat down I loosened his waist-belt as usual so that it wouldn't become to tight for comfort.

The performance began as soon as Mao took his seat. Now he was comfortably seated in the soft chair, smoking a cigarette which I lighted for him. Mao was a responsive listener. He had soon extinguished his cigarette without finishing it, giving his full concentration to the performance. He did not ask for any more cigarettes, which was unusual for a heavy smoker like him. When he listened to phonograph records, he would beat time with his fingers, and sometimes sing along. But when watching an opera he was quiet, sitting motionless, all attention, his expression changing with the progress of the story. One moment his eyes would shine with joy, or radiate passion, and the next he would look pensive. It was the same that night. Apparently he empathized with Xu Xian and Lady White Snake, and also with Xiao Qing, Lady White Snake's maidservant, also a snake fairy in human form, who commanded Mao's enormous respect for her sympathy, courage and intelligence. Throughout the performance he was frequently the first to punctuate the singing with applause, when a piece was well done.

When Monk Fahai, the villiain, appeared, Mao's face fell; he even looked a little nervous, his jaw dropped slightly, and his lower lip began to twitch intermittently. He ground his teeth noisily in intense hatred for the monk.

Finally came the climax: Lady White Snake was being torn away from her husband never to see him again. I knew from experience what would happen next. Twice I coughed slightly so as to bring Mao back to reality, but I was too late; by now the boundary between reality and imagination had dissolved for him. His nostrils began to twitch, and tears moistened his eyes. Soon, the tears began to cascade down his cheeks in large drops and splash onto his chest.

I grew uneasy: there were so many people around. I stole a glance at the audience, without making any perceptible movement in my seat, so as not to draw their attention. Fortunately, they were too deeply enthralled by the activity on the stage to notice this mini-"drama" off it.

But soon Mao's reaction began to attract attention. His tears were now streaming down his face and because his nose was blocked he was breathing noisily. I noticed the leading comrades of the Shanghai Party Committee, who were sitting close to us, beginning to look in the direction of the strange noise. They were very brief glances, but enough to upset me: I was failing in my duty to preserve "the image of the leader." I coughed again only to make matters even worse. Rather than stopping Mao, this only drew more glances. So I stopped making any further effort.

Now Mao had broken into loud sobs, totally unaware of his surroundings, and was wiping his eyes and nose. Under the circumstances there was nothing I could do but let things run their course. All I wanted now was for the performance to come to an end, and in fact it was reaching the end, for the monk was condemning Lady White Snake to the pagoda....

And then something quite unexpected happened.

In a sudden outburst of anger, Mao, slamming his big hand down on the armrest of the chair, shot up from his seat, proclaiming, "Revolution! Rebellion! That's the only answer!"

I was totally unprepared for anything like that. With his waist-belt loosened, his pants dropped the moment he stood up. As if propelled by a ramrod, I dashed to him, got hold of his pants and pulled them up. Overwhelmed by shame and fright, I was clumsy and my hands trembled as I tightened his belt. The incident left me with a feeling of guilt, which remained with me for a long time.

But Mao didn't blame me for it; he wasn't even aware of what had happened. And when he walked up to the stage, he was still immersed in the story. Only when the audience burst into applause did he come to and join in the clapping. I felt relieved: Mao had been brought back to reality.

As I remember, when he shook hands with the actress who had played Xiao Qing, he held her hand in both of his, but when he shook hands with Lady White Snake and her husband, he used only one hand.

He did not even look at the monk.

Mao always wore his heart on his sleeve.

Next I am going to relate not one, but a number of occasions on which I saw Mao cry. These incidents are inter-related since they reflect deep-seated and complex social changes that spanned a number of years, changes which began in much the same way that the story of the White Snake begins; namely, the institution of the general line for socialist construction, the great leap forward and the people's communes, popularly known as "the three red banners," which together comprised a national drive to change the face of China.

As I am unfamiliar with the complete history of this drive, my recollections of it are only fragmentary: events which I saw happen or heard about.

On May 14, 1955, when Mao met with the guards in Zhongnanhai after a swim, he told them that he wanted them to be good guards, good pupils and good social investigators. He talked at length on the approach to social investigation, its significance and the attitude of the investigators. He said he wanted them to find out about conditions in their home districts when they went home on furlough and to report their findings when they returned.

Members of Mao's guard-company came from all over the country, at Mao's request, with one, and only one, from each administrative region, so that he could be kept informed of the actual conditions in these places, especially those in the rural areas. Every time a guard returned from home furlough, Mao would ask to be briefed on his findings, and make revisions and comments on the reports which were sent in.

Between late 1957 and early 1958, Mao heard a series of verbal reports concerning the "polarization" and the widening gap between poor and rich that was taking place in some of the rural areas. Each of these reports would leave him visibly disturbed and in search of an answer to the problem.

Around December 1957, Ma Wei, one of the bodyguards, returned from his home with a bun. Made largely from chaff, it looked black and was hard to bite. "This is what the peasants eat back home," Ma said. "Believe me!"

Mao was visibly shaken at the sight of the bun. He immediately knitted and then arched his eyebrows. When he took the bun, I noticed that his hands were trembling. He broke off a piece with some effort and put it in his mouth. He had just begun to chew it when his eyes welled with tears, and as he swallowed the first bite, tears literally streamed down his face.

"Eat it, all of you! Take a bite each!" In tears, Mao passed the pieces around. The one I got was soaked with his tears. He was terribly upset. Gasping, he said loudly, "Eat it! It's the peasants' food, peasants who, who ... grow what we eat...."

We did, with difficulty and reluctance. Mao, his eyes brimming with tears, stared at us and took a significant glance at the nutrition expert who planned Mao's meals. Mao never ate the highly nutritious food the expert recommended; he preferred coarse grain for a staple and home-fare. Once Mao said, tapping a bowl of cooked coarse rice and millet, "When this is the food for every peasant in China, we'll be happy...."

That day Mao ate neither lunch nor dinner. His breakfast-time was at midnight, with lunch the next morning. Now it was time for him to go to bed. When I was massaging him, he said to me blankly, still haunted by the problem, "Ours is a socialist society; coarse buns shouldn't still be the food of Chinese peasants. They shouldn't...." Then he added after a long pause, "We have to do something about it, we must. What's the answer to faster development of socialism?"

For several days after that, I heard him repeat that phrase "We have to do something about it." He discussed the matter with some of the leading comrades of the Central Committee.

On January 28, 1958, Mao raised the call, "Go all out, aim high and catch up with Great Britain in fifteen years," at an extra session of the Supreme Conference of National Affairs.

In March of that year, at a conference in Chengdu he summed up the basic idea of the general line in the slogan: "Go all out, aim high and achieve greater, faster, better and more economical results in building socialism." Two months later, in May, the general line was adopted at the Second Session of the Eighth National Congress of the Communist Party.

The Party conference left Mao in high spirits. He said to me, "China's a poor country, but we have socialist system. The Chinese people will live better than the people of other countries."

One day he was returning with a leading comrade of the Central Committee after seeing off a visitor in Zhongnanhai. I was walking behind him as usual. They were conversing light-heartedly with occasional outbursts of enthusiasm. "They're now calling for a great leap forward. That's a nice way to put it, I think," the leading comrade told Mao.

Mao looked at him, asking, "Great—leap—forward?"

"Yes," the leading comrade said. "It's a movement they're starting. It's in today's *People's Daily*."

"I didn't see that," Mao said. Turning to me he said, "Get me the paper, Yinqiao," and then continued to listen to the leading comrade as he elaborated on the topic of the big leap forward.

The newspaper was brought to him by that leading comrade. After reading the article, he made the following comment on the paper, which I remember was: "Well said."

In 1958, another leading comrade of the Central Committee briefed Mao on a people's commune in Qiliying in Henan Province, which he described as a success well worth a visit by the chairman. Mao went as suggested. Throughout the visit, the leading comrade and the secretary of the provincial Party committee fed Mao with talk about the superiority of the new institution called "people's commune." Mao listened with great interest, looking satisfied, and nodding approvingly, saying, "Good,

good ..." when their description appealed to him. At one point, he interrupted one of them, saying, "The people's commune is good." I must admit that I, too, was excited by their talk.

Mao was staying on his special train at the time. He was a man requiring very little sleep. The first thing he did when he woke up was to read the day's newspapers in bed, whilst smoking and drinking strong tea. He would spend about an hour reading thus before he rose. Except on special occasions he wouldn't break this habit. That day, when he was glancing over the headlines, he was taken aback by something he saw. Releasing a cry and slapping the bed, he said, "Oh, no! How could they print it!"

Startled, I turned around to see Mao jump out of bed in his pyjamas and slap the newspaper he was holding, saying, "Scandalous, it's scandalous!"

The newspaper headlines proclaimed: "The People's Communes Are Good." It was the work of a reporter from Xinhua New Agency who had been with us throughout the visit. He had heard Mao say this and had filed a story on the same day, which was carried in the next day's papers.

"This hasn't been discussed by the Politburo." Mao was visibly upset, and, walking round in circles, kept on saying: "Scandalous!"

Sure enough, objections were raised to the news story. In order to pacify them, Mao explained to a selected audience: "I should be blamed for this." "It was said in a slip of the tongue during the visit. We shouldn't lay all the blame on this reporter." But something had to be done, now that Mao's words had been made public. Soon the issue was brought to the attention of an enlarged meeting of the Politburo at Beidaihe. The meeting decided unanimously in favour of the institution of people's communes, and the decision was announced to the public.

It should be pointed out that at that time, leading comrades at all levels were sincere in their eagerness to see socialism flourish in China. They were perhaps a little impatient, but they all possessed great vision and worked against time in the hope that China would soon emerge strong and prosperous. They believed they would acquire the experience needed for such an endeavour as they went along.

On an inspection tour in Wuhan, another leading comrade tried to sell Mao the idea of public canteens for all. Mao responded by saying,

"Write a report on that and give it to me." Soon the report was worked out by a deputy secretary-general of the Party committee of Hubei Province, at the request of the leading comrade. Mao read the report and authorized its circulation. Meanwhile, the secretary of the Party committee of Henan Province called for an all-out effort to develop the steel industry, agriculture, the highway-system and public canteens for all.

Once, commenting on the reports which he received concerning these new efforts, Mao said, as I remember it, "What these comrades say in their reports is encouraging. Peng Dehuai is the only exception: I have found nothing positive in any of his reports which have reached me."

Mao liked and supported these comrades for their zeal, initiative and boldness, both in thought and action. His support, in its turn, caused them to grow even more zealous and bold. By the end of 1958, the Party policy, summed up figuratively by a ranking Party official as, "the three red banners" and "three long-lives," had taken shape. The first time these policies were publicized was at the time of the Central Committee meeting, in Reception Room 18 of the Great Hall of the People. A ranking official of the Party had brought three final proof copies of articles dealing with "the three red banners" and "three long-lives" to the meeting, and displayed them near the rostrum. There he glowingly expounded upon these policies to the Politburo members, who had gathered to look at the articles, emphasizing that these policies were a refutation of the revisionist clique of the Soviet Union, headed by N. Khrushchov.

In 1959, Mao began to suspect deviations within the Party, and his anxiety mounted. He wanted to know just what was going on, but this wasn't easy for him. I will explain why not later. What I can say now is this: After we moved to the city, restrictions upon Mao's movements grew increasingly tight for security reasons. He had to follow carefully-made plans for all his trips. Such restrictions never eased in spite of his angry protests. A decision of the Central Committee prohibited him from travelling by air.

In 1959, he revisited Henan during an inspection tour of the nation. At a fact-finding meeting, he repeatedly asked the participants, "What about the public canteens? Are they good or not? Tell me the truth. I want you to tell me the truth." All those present at the meeting told Mao that the canteens were well liked. They cited examples of their merits and showed him loaves of bread which they said were baked at the canteens, and were the staple food these canteens provided. Mao broke one of the loaves and offered everyone a piece. The piece I got tasted good. Mao, finding the food satisfactory, said, "If public canteens can feed all the peasants in China with food like this, they really are good."

But still his suspicion persisted. He wanted to see what the conditions in the countryside were like with his own eyes, by way of "raids" or unannounced visits. One day he surprised me by pointing at a village seen at a distance from his speeding train and saying, "Tell them to stop the train. I want to take a look at that village. I'm going to ask for a bowl of stewed pork there and see if they have it." Immediately I made phone calls asking the local officials to be prepared for our visit. When Mao arrived, stewed pork was ready; he wouldn't have been disappointed if he had asked for a roast pig.

By the summer of 1959, the economy had deteriorated to such an extent that it was no longer possible to lie about it. The Central Committee was divided over the great leap forward and the people's communes. In late June, Mao came to Lushan Mountain from Shaoshan. There he called a meeting to evaluate the situation. After bitter argument, the meeting closed with the conclusion that the situation was excellent, prospects bright, but that problems were numerous.

Mao addressed the last session of the meeting in late July. Sitting on the stage were the standing members of the Politburo; its other members were seated in the front row, with the members of the Central Committee behind them. Before the meeting began, Mao scanned the audience; he seemed to want to know if everyone was there, but I knew that he was really looking for Peng Dehuai. Peng had aired his objections to the new policies in a report to Mao. Initially, Mao merely took them as Peng's private opinion, calling them an expression of "bourgeois vacillation," in the course of the argument, and stopped at that. Now, when he could not find Peng, he said in disappointment, "Marshal Peng not here?" I pointed out to him where the general was sitting. Peng was not in the front row as expected, but was sitting in the back one, his newly shaven head gleaming.* Mao bit his lower lip but didn't say anything; apparently he was displeased.

Mao's main target for attack in his speech was "Leftism." He severely criticized some of the leading officials for their impetuosity and gross exaggeration, sometimes using very strong language. But still Mao remained well disposed towards these comrades and sought to protect them; at one point he turned around and said to Zhu De, "The public canteens must disband, but not all of them. You don't like these canteens, but I'm afraid we have slightly different opinions on this matter."

After criticizing "Leftism" Mao made a few unfavourable remarks regarding what he called Rightist views, notably those of Comrade Peng Dehuai. It seemed to me that he was walking a tight rope, blaming right and wrong alike. What he said at one point struck me as quite unusual. "If the army doesn't want me any more," he said, "I will return to the countryside and establish guerillas there; I will raise a new army."

When the meeting was over, some of the participants stayed behind. Peng Dehuai was the first to leave, apparently in pent-up anger. Mao called after him, but either he didn't hear Mao, or he just ignored him.

Leaving the conference hall, Mao was coming down the slope on which the hall was situated. He was accompanied by four leading comrades of the Central Committee. On the way down, one of them stepped aside to relieve himself just as Peng Dehuai turned around and began to walk back up the slope, as though he was returning to the conference hall for something. The two men met head-on.

"Marshal," halting, Mao greeted Peng, "shall we talk a little?"

Peng, flushing crimson, raised his arm above his head in a sweeping gesture, saying angrily, "What's there to talk about? Nothing!"

"Take it easy," said Mao. "If we disagree on something we can talk about it quietly."

"What's there to talk about?" said Peng in a loud voice, dismissing the offer with a wave of his hand as he passed Mao by. "Nothing!...."

---

*A mark of disgrace. This was frequently used to shame and humiliate those who had been denounced as counter-revolutionaries, class-enemies, capitalist-roaders, revisionists and bad-elements during the "cultural revolution." Also a practice traditionally applied to criminals in China.

Peng walked on, his face flushed.

Mao was surprised. He bit his lower lip and continued on his way down the slope. The unpleasant conversation took place in the presence of many leading comrades of the Central Committee.

When Mao returned to his room, he told us to prepare for the trip home. But some leading comrades would not let things go at that. They suggested that the dispute with Peng should be settled once and for all. In the evening I was told that we would not be leaving: there was going to be a plenary meeting of the Central Committee, not to deliberate on the economic situation but to settle the dispute with Peng. Soon those members of the Central Committee and the Politburo who had not attended the previous meeting arrived at Lushan Mountain; Lin Biao was amongst them.

Bitter words were exchanged at the meeting; they talked so loudly that Mao, who was not attending the meeting, could hear it in his room and was unable to sleep as a result. He told me to find out what was happening. As Mao would become irritable if he couldn't go to sleep, I ran all the way to the meeting place. There I found that the participants were quarrelling with Peng Dehuai. When I described the scene to Mao, he grew angry, and wrote out his instructions.

During the plenary session the members of the Politburo met several times in the building where Mao was staying. Their discussions traced Peng's Party record right the way back to the days in the Jinggang Mountains. Lin Biao accused Peng of persistent insubordination and non-cooperation. It was then that I learned that their charges against the general were not merely limited to the issues of the great leap forward and the people's communes, but went all the way back to the Red Army days, and the Korean war as well. The conclusion they reached was that the general had been "thirty percent cooperative and seventy percent uncooperative." By a decision of the Politburo, Peng Dehuai was dismissed as minister of national defence and vice-chairman of the Military Commission, but retained his positions as a member of the Politburo and vice-premier of the government with no changes in income or treatment.

One day after we returned to Beijing, Peng Dehuai presented himself at Mao's residence. He had come by the backdoor of the Juxiang (chrysanthemum fragrance) Study. No longer shaven, he now had a thick head of hair. He asked to be allowed to go to the grassroots levels. Mao tried to talk him out of the idea, saying that he was too old for that now, and that his personal safety would pose a problem if he did, and advising him to do more reading instead. But Peng insisted and Mao finally gave his approval.

As a consequence of rashness and disregard for objective reality, accompanied by attitudes prevalent in 1958, and the natural calamities that followed, China was in deep economic trouble between 1959 and 1961, with nationwide starvation.

Late in 1959, some of the guards who were returning from home furlough in the countryside, where they had been investigating local conditions, brought back some buns made with chaff and wild herbs. The buns had turned mouldy on the way. Mao was shaken at the sight of them. He broke them with trembling hands and gave the pieces to us. "Eat them," he said. "This is what the peasants eat. We should eat it...."

I put my piece in my mouth. I chewed at it for a long time, finding it hard to swallow. In taste, it was a far cry from the bread I had eaten in Henan. I thought of the bun Ma Wei had brought back from home and Mao's "We have to do something about it."

Mao selected a whole bun. When he took the first bite, his eyes turned red, his Adam's apple moving up and down in his effort not to choke; he took a second bite and his eyelashes grew wet with tears, and by the time he took the third bite, his face was streaked with tears.

Mao was crying, crying noiselessly, the cry of someone racked by excruciating grief. At that moment, I believe what flashed into his mind wasn't just the miseries of the peasants: he must have thought of the bread he had eaten in Henan, the stewed pork he had been given in that village by the railroad; what he should have achieved as a leader, the gap between his ideals and harsh reality....

The year of 1960 was the worst of the three years of hardship. For seven months Mao did not touch meat. Often his meals consisted of nothing but a plate of purslane, and that much spinach would carry him through a day's work. When I massaged him, the muscles around his ankles would indent under the pressure of my hands and these recesses would remain for a long time. It was edema. "Eat some pork, Comrade

Chairman," Zhou Enlai pleaded with him many times, "for the sake of the Party and the people." To this Mao would reply, shaking his head, "You're not eating pork either, are you? Let all of us live without it." Soong Ching Ling, widow of Dr. Sun Yat-sen, came all the way from Shanghai, with a net-bag full of crabs for Mao. She took them to him. He accepted them out of his respect for her, but after she left Mao gave the crabs to his bodyguards.

One day, late in 1960, Mao didn't eat anything after getting up, but merely chain-smoked. When the ashtray was almost full, he said to Feng Yaosong, the bodyguard on duty, "Tell Zilong, Yinqiao, Gao Zhi, Jingxian, Lin Ke and Dongxing to come over and have dinner with me today."

It was a dinner without meat or wine, but the food was cooked with a little extra oil and salt. Mao reached for the dishes with his chopsticks, but he put them down without picking up any food. He took a look at each of us, and we, too, put down our chopsticks.

"The people are presently suffering great calamities. I want you to find out just what is wrong, and report your findings," Mao said slowly, his tone grave. After a brief pause he continued, "Find out whether the people's communes and the public canteens are successful and what the people complain about. Report your findings on that."

We all nodded in understanding.

Then he pointed at Ye Zilong and me. "You're going to Shandong to find out as much as you can."

"Yes, Comrade Chairman," we said, nodding our acceptance.

Mao turned to Feng Yaosong, "Do you want to join them, Feng?"

"Sure," answered Feng.

"Good," said Mao, nodding. Then he took a sweeping glance at us, looking stern, his wide eyes gleaming fiercely. "Tell the truth, no falsehood," he warned. "No cover-ups, no cheating."

Feng stayed on duty that night. Later he told us that whilst he was massaging Mao before bedtime, Mao, deeply disturbed, had cried again. According to Feng, Mao had said tearfully, his hand on Feng's back, "I'm worried. They have told me many lies. They're always prepared for my visits. But you can discover the truth out there; that's what I want you to tell me...."

That night Mao couldn't go to sleep. He rose from his bed and wrote a letter to the seven of us in pencil, on xuan* paper, telling us not to go to Shandong, but to the Xinyang administrative region instead, where things were beginning to pick up with shipments of relief grain, so that we would not be "starved." In conclusion he wrote, "I am sixty-seven years old this year, and an old man. The future holds a lot of hope for you. December 26 is my birthday. Signed, Mao Zedong, Dec. 26, 1960."

Why, we had forgotten about his birthday! We might have asked him for permission to celebrate it noisily as we used to do each year, especially when we were in northern Shaanxi.

Mao could not tolerate it when Peng Dehuai told him the truth, but with his bodyguards he was entirely different. Once, during the nationalization of private enterprises, he asked Tian Yunyu, one of his bodyguards, whose grandfather owned a workshop and whose father was a factory worker, "Your grandfather's opposed to the transfer to joint ownership and your father's all for it. What about you? Whose side are you on?" When Tian told him that he sided with his grandfather, Mao said, "I like you for telling me the truth, political viewpoints aside. We can get along well." During the cooperative movement, a movement which virtually replaced private ownership in China's countryside with socialist joint ownership, in the five years between 1951 and 1956, I complained to Mao in my oral report upon my return from home furlough in the countryside. "The district cadres assembled the peasants in a threshing ground," I said, "and said to them, 'Those of you willing to follow Chiang Kai-shek and in favour of private ownership, step to that side. Those willing to follow Chairman Mao and in favour of the cooperative system, step to this side.' That was coercion, wasn't it?" Mao said, "Thank you for telling me this." He immediately wrote a letter to the Party committee of Hebei Province criticizing such instances involving oversimplification and coercion in dealing with things.

So the seven of us went to Xinyang in Henan Province. We spent six months there. When we returned, we truthfully reported our findings, informing Mao that the public canteens were as bad as they were

*A special kind of soft paper specifically manufactured for Chinese calligraphy with brush and ink, to achieve artistic effect.

reputed to be. By the time we arrived in Jiangxi Province, where we spent another six months doing farm work, the Central Committee had ordered the termination of these canteens.

Let me return to that day when I said good-bye to Mao before leaving for Tianjin to begin my new job. Mao, as I have said, held me tightly in his arms; he cried loudly, patting me on the back, his tears merging with mine.

Then I offered to massage his scalp for the last time.

Mao's mind was often overtaxed; massage, which caused the blood in his head to circulate better, would help reduce the strain and refresh him.

I ran the comb carefully through his hair, from the front to the back of his head. As I did so, the tears in my eyes blurred my vision.

Memories of events which had occurred when the three major military campaigns ended flooded my mind. One day, Mao, as much excited as he had been exhausted, leaned back in his chair and said to me in a much relieved tone, "Comb my hair, nice and slow, Yinqiao. Time for a good rest."

I was no less excited and happy than Mao. Picking up a comb, I said, "I'm going to do it really slowly this time, Comrade Chairman, so you can catch up on some sleep."

Those were the days when Mao's hair was thick, strong, jet-black and lustrous. As the comb moved across his scalp, from the front to the back, his hair rose abundantly as it slid between its teeth. I was admiring the jet-black hair as it rose and fell with the movement of the comb, when something gleaming attracted my attention. I bent over and once more ran the comb through the hair at the temple, examining it carefully, and then I let out a cry. "Aiya, Comrade Chairman, your hair's started greying."

Mao, savouring the quiet of the moment with eyes closed, seemed to stir a bit when he heard me. Knitting his brows slowly, he let out a deep "eh."

"Shall I pull it out?" I asked.

After a brief silence, he said, biting his lower lip, "Go ahead!"

Carefully I picked out the grey hair, held it between my fingers and pulled it out. I examined it closely to make sure that I hadn't pulled out the wrong hair before showing it to Mao.

Mao looked at it without blinking, his knitted brows relaxing slowly. Smiling, he murmured, "It's been worth it."

Later, when my wife heard about it, she took me to task. "How dare you pull out a hair from the chairman's head!"

My memory of that remained as fresh and vivid as if it had happened just the day before. It had taken only a few years for that mop of black hair to disappear; what was coming through the comb now was limp, greying, thin hair; the growth at the temples was still thick, but almost half of it had turned grey. Mao had aged visibly during those three years of hardship. Now things had begun to take a turn for the better, but had all that suffering been worthwhile?

"Take better care of your health after I leave you, Comrade Chairman," I said in tears. "Much of your hair's turned grey; you've been working too hard...."

After a long silence, Mao raised his eyelids, revealing red rims around his eyes. "I'm an old man now," he said. "After I die, I want you to visit my grave once a year."

What could I say in reply? Of course I would, but how I longed to see him live a long, long life.

"Could you write something for me, Comrade Chairman?" I said, changing the subject.

"I haven't written any new poems, but here's an old one for you. Come here on Saturday and bring your family. Let's have some pictures taken together...."

The poem he copied for me, complete with his signature, was "The Long March." It was written on a large folder; the empty spaces were later filled in with the writings and signatures of some of the leading comrades of the Central Committee. On the other side of the folder were drawings done by some of China's best artists at my request. After I arrived in Tianjin, the first secretary of the Party committee of Hebei Province took the folder from me, saying that he just wanted to look at it. When I asked him about it some time later, he said he had lost it. I never saw the folder again....

Mao in a Temper

Mao was a serious man, but he possessed a good sense of humour. He occasionally threw tantrums, but not often. As I observed, when he was in a good humour, he would find everything agreeable, even mistakes: he would talk to the offender kindly and playfully so as to make him forget his mistake. But it was an entirely different story if he hadn't slept for several nights or when his nerves were on edge. That was when he would easily become irritable.

In time of war, the leaders were without exception bad-tempered; this was especially true of army commanders; they would call their men names, shut them up in confinement for several days, slap their faces, even treat them to a lash or two. Mao was much milder than any of them; making the offenders stand was the heaviest penalty he would impose.

Nine times out of ten, when Mao threw a tantrum it was connected with sleep. This happened both in Yan'an and Xibaipo: he took it out on the guards when he was aroused from sleep. The last time I remember him making the guards stand for this was when he was living in Fragrant Hills in Beijing.

Mao had not slept for three or four days, having been too busy directing the army in its advance on southern China and preparing for the convention of the political consultative conference. Only after repeated pleading did he go to bed. It took two doses of sleeping pills to ease the strain on his brain and put him to sleep.

I waited until he began to snore gently. Before I left I warned the guard, "Be careful. The chairman's gone to sleep."

What I meant by the warning was that even birds had to be kept away from the house with red strips of cloth tied to bamboo poles. So the guard said to the workers who were installing a bath-tub in a toilet room, "Quit it, quit it! The chairman's sleeping."

The command would have been enough to stop an obedient

peasant even if the work he was doing could not wait. But it was a different story with workers in the cities: they worked when their stomachs were full and slept when they were tired; insomnia was unknown to them. So they said, "Just a few moments and we'll be finished," and worked on even harder.

The guard did not know what to do. He could be huffy with peasants, but how could he treat workers, who were, after all, members of China's leading class, in the same way? Conscious of his own peasant origin, the guard had to think twice before getting tough with them.

His hesitation landed him in serious trouble. A loud clang rang out in the courtyard as a lead pipe struck against the tub. The guard was horrified and the bodyguards frightened. Holding their breath they waited for Mao's reaction, whilst the workers remained blissfully ignorant of what lay in store.

Suddenly the door was thrown open and out strode Mao without any outer garments, heading for the courtyard. He looked worn out and irritated, rage clearly welling up within him, a sight both terrifying and agonizing. Knitting his brows, he stared glumly at the guard. Then, pointing accusingly at him, he burst out in a roar, "You deserve a beating!"

The guard snapped to attention.

Mao breathed heavily, doing his best to control his anger and frustration, the result of his unsuccessful attempt to sleep. He looked pale and his eyes were red-rimmed. Biting his lower lip, he spoke in a slightly subdued voice, "Of course there's army discipline to go by, so I'm not going to beat you or abuse you, but you'll have to stand at attention for some time. The sun will do you good."

Without protest the guard remained standing at attention in the sun.

"Standing there until I get up," Mao said as he walked back to his room, still angry.

Afraid that the guard might not be able to endure the punishment, I went to Jiang Qing for help. Jiang told the guard to leave but he refused. Finding Mao unable to go back to sleep, she entered his room and asked him to let the guard go. Mao looked out of the door and said to the soldier in a loud voice, "You may go now, but you're going to write a self-criticism, and explain why you made such a noise when you knew I was sleeping."

Later Mao regretted the episode. He criticized himself in front of us. "There have been times when you were to blame and times when I was to blame. The guard had to make a self-criticism, and so must I," Mao said. "All I want is a good sleep. I shouldn't have flown into a temper like that, but I need sleep as much as you do. If you had sat up four nights in a row working and then had to get up again before you had hardly slept a wink, wouldn't you have been annoyed? Explain that to the men, and tell them not to hold it against me so it won't interfere with their work."

A man who never loses his temper is not worthy of others' adoration. This what I have learned from life. Not long ago, when many of us who had worked for Mao had a reunion, we recalled fondly the days when we were with him. The sweetest of memories were those occasions when Mao had flown into a rage, for it was then that Mao was closest to us, so much himself, so lovable. We discovered, to our pleasant surprise, that each of these outbursts was connected with sleep. Here are some more such instances which readily come to my mind.

We were at Beidaihe. Mao had been writing continuously for two days and three nights. On the morning of the third day he finally went to bed. Li Liancheng, the bodyguard on duty, massaged his legs and brought him sleeping pills three times before the long-awaited snore began. We in the bodyguard were familiar with the way Mao snored. That day it began as on any other day, like a whisper of spring breeze gently brushing the tree-tops with a soft whistle. Slowly it gathered volume, filling the quiet room with a sound that rose and fell rhythmically, like the ebbing of the sea. Then all of a sudden it broke into a long deep rumble. When the rumble gave way to long regular exhalation, Li crept down from the bed and slowly, very slowly, tiptoed towards the door like a thief.

A beam of light caught Li's attention. Startled, he looked around and discovered that the shutter was open and the sun was glaring through it. Its beam would fall on Mao in less than an hour....

It was summer. The flannel window-curtain had been replaced by a wooden blind to keep out the light and ventilate the room. Standing in front of it, Li told himself: it's wood, the blind is made of wood, heaven bless me.... Holding his breath he began to lower it. He did it a bit at a time, making sure he was not making any noise. But he was doing it so slowly that he could no longer hold his breath. With about one foot left to go, the effort became unbearable. He opened his mouth wide and inhaled noisily. And then the thing he had most dreaded happened.

The blind crashed down. The noise which it made wouldn't have been noticed in a street, but in the quiet room, it reverberated like thunder. Immediately the rhythmic snore stopped, and before his heart had resumed its beating, Li heard the angry and irritated voice behind him saying, "Who's that? What happened?"

Li spun around, looking aghast.

"What happened? Answer me!" Mao was sitting up in bed. He glared at Li, his eyes blood-shot, his chest heaving.

"I ... I was closing the window...."

"Why didn't you do it earlier, you fool? Get out of here! I don't want you on duty here. Go and stand outside!"

Li did as he was ordered. Five minutes later, Mao popped his head out of the door and said to Li in lingering anger, "You may leave now. You're no longer needed here. Go and get Li Yinqiao for me!"

Li came to my office with a long face. After he had told me what had happened, I left for Mao's bedroom immediately. Mao was sitting in the chair, looking glum and tired. I knew it would be useless to tell him to go back to bed; he would be unable to sleep again for some time.

I began to comb his hair; it would relax him and help calm him down.

It was a long time before Mao raised his hand saying, "It's Okay. You may go now. Tell Li I want to talk to him."

Mao was reclining on his side, against the railing of the bed, smoking and reading documents when Li entered.

"I apologize, Comrade Chairman ..." murmured Li, his head bent low.

"Well," said Mao in a husky voice, "it's hard for both of us. You did something wrong, but I did something even worse. I shouldn't have raged like that."

"But the blame's on me, Comrade Chairman...." Li was sobbing.

"Don't blame me. You're blaming me the way you talk. With so much work to do and so many things on my mind, sleep doesn't come easily, and when I feel lousy as a result, I can't control myself very well."

"It's my fault and I mean it, Comrade Chairman...." Now Li was crying loudly.

"I hurt your feelings and I'm sorry for that. Don't hold it against me. I'm only human, I get into a temper sometimes. Try and make allowances for that."

Li cried, not only out of shame for having been so careless, but also because Mao's sincerity touched him. However he was too awkward to make that clear to Mao. So Mao, mistaking Li's reaction for protest, apologized and explained to him as many as three times a week.

Sometimes it could be entertaining to see Mao throw a tantrum, for at such times he would behave just like a child in a fit of pique. In the fifteen years I was with him, he only lost his temper with me once, and on that occasion he acted in just this way.

In 1958, I was with him in Shanghai. We were staying on his special train. One day when he was taking a midday nap, I left him, to pay a business call at the club for government staff employees down town, thinking that he would go on sleeping for four hours until the afternoon. When I returned in the afternoon, the bodyguard on duty called to tell me that Mao had risen earlier than expected and had gone to a meeting in town. When I arrived at the meeting place, Mao had left for dinner. As I knew he was going to see an opera at the club, I waited outside beside his car.

When I saw him coming out, I opened the car door for him. But he halted on the steps. With one hand on his hip, he pointed at me with the other and shouted angrily, "Do you know what your duty is, Li Yinqiao?"

Mao looked glum. I didn't know what had sent him into that sudden fit of pique. I hurried up the steps to meet him halfway, and helped him into the car. He kept on biting his lips, neither looking at me nor speaking, just sitting there in pent-up anger.

Before the opera began I wiped his glasses and put them on for him, loosened his belt and straightened his clothes. All the while he remained moody and silent until the show began.

On the way back I asked him timidly, "What made you so unhappy today?"

Pouting his lips he looked at me. "My mouth go scalded, if that's what you want to know."

Later I learned that his mouth was scalded when he was rinsing it out with water after dinner. The water was too hot; the bodyguard who gave it to him had not tested its temperature, and Mao, out of habit, had taken a large mouthful which he had had to spit out immediately. But it was too late: the damage had been done. I was lucky: I got off with only one angry shout.

Mao was a man of very strong personality and was a non-conformist as far as conventions were concerned. With a life-long vision to realize, he would rage at anyone who stood in his way, and punish him mercilessly.

One sweltering hot summer day in 1956, a strange idea struck him. He said to me, "Let's go to the Yangtse River, Yinqiao, and swim it."

Swim the Yangtse River? I could not believe my ears. All those in his entourage were shocked at the idea and Luo Ruiqing, Wang Dong-xing, Wang Renzhong and many of his staff objected vehemently. With its swift and treacherous currents, the river was much more dangerous than the swimming zones at Beidaihe. If there was an accident, we would never be able to explain it to the Central Committee or the people of the entire nation.

In short, in Mao's own words, there was strong opposition.

"Comrade Chairman," Luo was trying to talk him out of the idea, "I can't possibly let you go and swim in that river. I'm your number-one guard. Your safety is my responsibility. I would never survive the blame if I let you swim in the Yangtse."

Mao insisted, "Keep the Kuomintang under guard, number-one guard, but not the river."

"But this is not a private matter," Luo held his ground, "it's much more important than that. You must have the permission of the Party to do that, and the Party would never give its permission."

"All that worries you," Mao shouted, "is that I may drown in that river. What makes you think I may end up that way?"

Luo was horrified: the idea of Mao getting drowned? The thought had never occurred to him. "I didn't mean that, Comrade Chairman," Luo explained hastily. "I'm accountable to the Party and the people for your safety. I simply can't take chances in your case. None at all."

Mao sneered at the idea. "That's absurd," he said. "You could be killed by an air raid in your own room, or the house might collapse on you."

Seeing it would be pointless to go on arguing, Luo left him, but that didn't mean he had given in. In some instances, restrictions on Mao's movement would not ease unless Luo gave the word.

Wang Dongxing and Wang Renzhong then took turns to dissuade Mao from swimming in the river; they were joined by Mao's physician and others. But Mao was a man who would never budge when confronted with opposition; he would fight until he had his way. Those who stood in his way and made him angry would hear him swear: "You fool!" "You idiot!" or "Bullshit!"

To break the stalemate Mao adopted a tactical approach. He told Commander Han of the First Guard Company to find out whether or not the river was as hazardous to swimmers as it was reputed to be.

Commander Han was one of those who objected to Mao's swimming in the Yangtse. He made an inspection tour of the river, and those he questioned along the way were all unanimous in their response to his enquiries: the river had too many swift whirlpools to be safe for swimming. That was exactly what he wanted to hear. He repeated these answers to Mao.

Mao didn't like what he heard. His face fell, and knitting his brows, he asked Han, "Did you bathe in the river?"

Han was not prepared for that. Flushing, he murmured, "No, I didn't."

"How do you know it's not safe, if you didn't?" Mao was angry. "What did you go there for?"

Han was about to explain but Mao dismissed him angrily. "Cut it! You're dismissed." Then he said to a bodyguard, "Get Sun Yong for me."

Sun was deputy commander of the bodyguard and a good swimmer. The order from Mao was: "Go to the river and find out if it's safe for swimming."

Sun understood what was expected of him. The first thing he did when he reached the river was to swim in it. When he returned he reported: "No problem. It's perfectly safe."

"Just as I expected," said Mao. "The proof of the pudding is in the eating." He might have been talking to the "opposition," saying: "Who says the Yangtse is no place for swimming? Didn't Sun swim in it, and nothing untoward happened to him...."

Now with the evidence in his favour, it was apparent that nothing could stop Mao. Wang Renzhong hurried back to Wuhan. He organized a team of life-guards, found out about the currents and selected a section of the river where Mao was to swim.

Before leaving, Mao said, "That fellow Han, he didn't tell the truth. He never swam in the river yet he told me it's no place for swimming. We're going without him. Tell him to leave."

That's how Han was removed from the First Guard Company, never to be allowed to see Mao again.

In pent-up rage Mao demanded that he fly to Wuhan in defiance of the Central Committee's decision. "You say I'm no longer my own master," Mao said. "I can accept that, but how about making an exception this one time?"

Mao left Guangzhou by air. During the stopover in Changsha he swam in the Xiangjiang River to warm up. From there he flew on to Wuhan. It was a short journey, taking no longer than the time required to eat a meal. That was when Mao wrote the poem that begins with the line: "I have just drunk the waters of Changsha/And come to eat the fish of Wuchang."

With the "opposition" defeated, and in high spirits, Mao just couldn't wait. Talking good-naturedly, he boarded a steamer.

Now the rope ladder was ready. Sun Yong, stocky and proud, led the way with Mao following behind. Down in the river all the men of the First Guard Company were waiting. Sun lowered himself down the ladder and helped Mao to descend steadily. I got into the river after Mao.

"Keep them away, all of them!" Mao ordered, pointing at the rowboats which were closing in. "Don't let them get close!"

The boats rowed away except the one with Mao's physician on board; it followed quietly at an appropriate distance.

Now Sun was in the river. Treading water, he helped Mao down the river. It was the place where the Yangtse River Bridge at Wuhan was later erected.

Mao swam as effortlessly as if he was taking a stroll. Talking light-heartedly with us and the life-guards, he drifted with the current for some sixteen *li*. On the way back to the guest house at Donghu Lake, Mao commented, "Han's a nice man, extremely loyal and devoted. But he was mistaken on this matter." He seemed to regret having sacked Han, but he was not a man to reverse his decisions easily. He continued in a loud voice, "Tian sided with his grandfather, a capitalist. His political stand is wrong, but he told the truth. I like that, and we get along well. Han sided with Minister Luo; he's politically correct but he didn't tell the truth. I don't like that. I hope you'll always stick to the truth."

After having met with the secretaries of some of the provincial Party committees, Mao returned to Beijing for a scheduled meeting with foreign visitors. Before they arrived, he remarked as proudly as a young man who always managed to have things his own way, "Minister Luo wouldn't let me have that swim, but I insisted, and I had my way, didn't I? I swam sixteen *li* at one go! I'm going to do that again next June. I'm going to have him join me in that forbidden adventure." He continued in that vein until the visitors arrived. Then he was the serious-looking Mao once again, as was his public demeanour.

On many occasions I witnessed Mao criticize ranking officials of the Party, government and army in stern, even harsh language. On some of these occasions he almost lost his temper. When that happened, the marshals and generals would listen to him at attention, and the Party and government officals would hang their heads and murmur their self-criticisms nervously. Of all the Party leaders whom I knew, Mao was the most candid about his likes and dislikes and feelings. He would say of himself, "I insist on being myself. I don't want to become my own puppet."

On July 1, 1948, Wang Ming came to see Mao. I was the officer on duty that day. Wang figured prominently in the history of the Chinese Communist Party. He had sidelined Mao as a leader of the Party and the army. His dogmatic practices had cost the Party dearly. He was not striking in stature, had a square face and fair complexion. I met him at the courtyard door. In response to my enquiry, he said, "I'd like to see the chairman." As Mao was not tied up with anything important just then, I nodded saying, "Please follow me."

I was courteous but cold to Wang. Mao had once told me, "That fellow wanted to kill me."

Mao was working on documents. Upon hearing the disturbance, he looked up. When he saw Wang he rose from behind his desk and walked around it to shake hands with him. Wang took his seat on a sofa chair and Mao sat down in his reclining chair. Mao didn't bother about ceremony with those close to him such as Zhu De, Zhou Enlai, Peng Dehuai and Lin Biao. Only with those to whom he was not close would he act courteously.

As they were exchanging greetings I went to make tea. When I returned with the tea, I heard Wang say, "I still don't understand those conclusions the Party came to on some historical issues. I'd like the Central Committee to know what I think about them. I also want to talk to you...."

Mao was listening attentively, looking grave. Realizing this was an occasion from which I should absent myself, I left the room after putting down the tea and returned to my office.

Soon they raised their voices, talking excitedly. I left my office and listened: the two men were arguing over those conclusions, referring to many different people and events, even the Soviet Union and the Communist International. As I remember it, at one point Mao said in his heavy Hunan accent, "You still don't understand? You still refuse to examine your errors at a time when victory is within our reach?"

Mao moved to Beiping on March 25, 1949. As the train in which he was travelling from nearby Zhuoxian County sped past the city walls of the ancient capital, he looked out of the window, saying in a voice filled with emotion, "It's been a good thirty years! I came to this city thirty years ago when I was travelling throughout China in search of the answers which would save China and its people. At that time life wasn't smiling on me, but I had the good luck to meet a really good man, Comrade Li Dazhao. He was my teacher in the true sense of the word. Without his advice and help I wouldn't be where I am today...."

After dismounting from the train at Qinghuayuan, Mao went directly to the Summer Palace by car.

The huge palace garden was empty when we arrived. The monks and the garden employees who lived there had been removed by Li

Kenong who was in charge of civic affairs. Li did that for security reasons. Beiping had just been liberated, the city was thick with Kuomintang undercover agents, and sabotage and assassinations were rampant. This called for the tightest security measures possible. But with everyone gone from the place, there was no food or water for Mao upon his arrival, and he was to review the troops at the Xiyuan airfield that afternoon, on the occasion of the victory parade in the city. Mao was angry. "Look what a fine job you've made of things!" he raged. "What's the matter with those people who got here first?" When the civic affairs people cited security reasons for their actions, Mao shouted, "Rubbish! Are you too stupid to realize that with no water, what can security mean to the fish? This kind of security can only result in death and starvation."

Mao was speaking the plain truth. The civic affairs people had to go to the masses for help. They got cooked rice, three side-dishes and soup from a restaurant just outside the Summer Palace. Picking up his chopsticks, Mao said to me, "You're not coming to the parade. Go to Fragrant Hills and get the house ready for me and prepare some food. Don't make the same mistakes as they have done."

Snow, Money and Mao

In addition to books, swimming, Beijing opera and challenges, the list of things which Mao enjoyed included snow.

Of all his poems, "Ode to the Snow," is my favourite. The white flakes must have touched a chord in the great poet, revealing a breadth of imagination that took in the world in its gigantic sweep.

Mao's own personality was like the snow which he celebrated in his poem: Sparten, proud, pure, sparkling, attractive in so many different ways.

It was during the first snowfall of the winter in 1951. Mao had begun a nationwide campaign against corruption, waste and bureaucracy in an attempt to rid government institutions and economic sectors of corrupt officials and fraudulent businessmen. Mao had been working all night, reading piles of documents and writing instructions on them. When dawn broke, he put down his pen, stretched, rubbed his face and rose to leave the room.

Barely had he stepped out of the door before he stopped. He was entranced by the sight of a fairy tale world and enthralled by the snowflakes whirling and tumbling through the air. Wide-eyed, his gaze traversed the sieve-like sky, from the cypress trees and house-tops laden with snow, to the courtyard beneath its white blanket. He looked long and hard, standing there in complete stillness as if listening to the snow falling, or to the twitter of the birds beneath the eaves.

A guard grabbed a broom, thinking that Mao wanted to have the path cleared in front of him.

"Leave it alone!" Mao shouted hastily, knitting his brows. When he found that there wasn't much snow on a brick-paved path, he shouted at the guard, "Did you sweep it?"

"Yes," replied the guard, hastening to explain, "I did it twice at daybreak, but it kept snowing, so...."

"You shouldn't have. Throw away that broom! How do you have

71

the heart to reopen a wound when it's beginning to heal?"

The guard put the broom away, looking at the faintly visible "wound" in bewilderment.

Now Mao had descended the steps from the veranda. He trod very carefully as if he was afraid of disturbing a beautiful dream. He was just two steps away from the veranda when he halted. He looked at the trail of footprints which he had left behind him in the snow, his eyes shining in childlike ecstasy. Was that man standing in the snow really the same man who had destroyed the old world with his mighty strength, and created a new one? Was he the same man who, in his capacity as leader of the Communist Party, had just resolutely and without hesitation disposed of some corrupt officials? Yet now here he was hesitating, reluctant to make any more imprints in the snow: he backed up, retracing the footprints he had already made.

He began to breathe deeply, his favourite exercise, which he found refreshing. "The air is so beautiful!" he said, inhaling greedily.

Standing with his feet astride, one in front of the other, so as not to crush any more snow, he stretched out his right hand, letting flakes land on it and his arm. He stood there mesmerized, enthralled by the wonder of nature unfolding in front of his eyes.

"Will you move around a bit, Comrade Chairman? You'll catch cold if you stand like that for too long," the guard called out from a distance. Like Mao, he was standing still in the snow, so as not to disturb the scene which held Mao spellbound.

Mao ignored him. The flakes on his hand were beginning to melt, turning into sparkling drops of water, quivering slightly. He stretched out his tongue to one of them; it was gone instantly. He savoured it, satisfied.

He traced his way back by the trail he had already made, placing his feet down extra carefully so that the "wounds" would not grow even larger. He didn't make any more imprints in the snow.

When he got back to the veranda he relaxed. After walking there for a bit he left the house by the back-door. When I caught up with him, I discovered that he was in fact selfish in his love for snow. Away from his house, he trod on the snow with abandon, relishing the crunch underfoot, and avoiding the paths that had been cleared. He would stop now and then to look back at his footprints, or to admire the snow on the pine trees.

Mao had an extremely active mind, too active for anyone to keep track of his thoughts. Turning his gaze away from the snow-laden boughs, he surprised me with a question: "Have you pocketed government money, Yinqiao?"

I was a bit taken aback: it was uncharacteristic of him to ask me a question like that.

"No," I replied with a clear conscience.

"And would you ever do so in the future?"

"Never."

"Good! You were like the snow when you first came," Mao pointed at the snow sparkling on the boughs of a pine tree. "Stay that way. Fight corruption. Don't let those sugar-coated bullets get you. And be thrifty. For instance, when you wash my clothes, only use soap for the collars and cuffs. The other parts don't need much soaping; all they need is a little rubbing."

"Yes, Comrade Chairman."

"My family expenses need planning. Keep the food expenditure within the budget. Don't buy any new clothes without my permission."

"Yes, Comrade Chairman," I said.

At that time, Mao had come off the wartime ration system and received his pay partly in money and partly in kind. His monthly income was around two hundred yuan and Jiang Qing's a little over one hundred yuan. I was the household treasurer. I got a little over fifty yuan a month. Later I informed Mao Chongheng, an instructor of the guard section, of what Mao had said, and worked out a budget to cover our expenses for food, clothing and miscellaneous items, as well as the balance. The budget allowed three yuan a day for food. Mao thought it was a bit too much; but when I explained that it included the cost of extra food for visitors, he wrote "approved" on the budget. We never exceeded it.

As Mao walked on in the snow, he continued with his questions. "Do you like snow?" he asked.

"Yes."

"Peasants like it. It gives them good crops. Pests don't like it. Flies can't survive snow. I like snow, too. We both like it."

That's how I came to know how much Mao liked snow. So I told the guards that from then on, the snow in Mao's courtyard should not

•

be swept, so that Mao could enjoy the sight of it. Mao stayed away from the yard whenever it snowed; he would wait until the snow there had lost its lustre and had been trampled upon by his visitors. Only then would he walk on it, to enjoy the sound of its crunch underfoot.

Comrade Chen Yi, who knew about Mao's love for snow, would skirt round the courtyard when he came on a snowy day. But some of the other leaders were not like that. They would complain loudly as they stamped their feet to remove the snow: "The young guards are so lazy they can't even be bothered to pick up a broom and sweep the yard."

Snow, I discovered, would invariably pep Mao up. It was one of the few things which could lure him away from work.

One winter night in 1953, Mao was returning from a meeting in Huairen Hall in Zhongnanhai. I was following closely behind him carrying an armful of papers. When we were a few steps away from his office, snowflakes, blown by a gust of wind, began to drift from the sky. Mao halted. Looking at the leaden sky, he said to me, "How about a walk? A ten-minute walk. You keep the time."

Mao like a walk. But he was so busy that he could only spare ten minutes each time, so he would ask me to keep the time.

That night he walked faster than usual in the yard, and as the snow fell more heavily, his movement gained in strength and speed. Swaying his shoulders, turning his body from side to side, and swinging his hands to catch the snow, he might have been dancing.

"Time?" he enquired.

"Eight minutes," I answered in all seriousness. In fact he had been walking for more than ten minutes; I didn't want to dampen his spirits.

So Mao went on "dancing" for another ten minutes, which was unusual, for ordinarily his sense of time was accurate to the minute. Finally I announced, "Time's up."

Mao stopped, took a deep breath and went into his office.

"There seems to be something wrong with your watch today," said Mao after he sat down.

"Well ... it's running slowly," I said evasively.

"Too fast, it seemed to me."

"Good heavens!" I cried out, laughing, "I gave you an extra ten minutes."

As regards the question: "What did Mao hate?", different people will come up with different answers. One such may be: "Chiang Kai-shek," another, lies such as: "One word spoken by the chairman says more than ten thousand words spoken by any of us," or such sycophantic slogans as: "Go all out to build the chairman's authority."

However, the thing that Mao disliked most intensely, in my opinion, was money.

Mao touched Chiang Kai-shek's hands when he shook hands with him, but he refused to touch money.

He didn't touch money when he was in Yan'an, nor did he touch money when he was fighting in northern Shaanxi, and after moving to Beijing, his aversion to it only increased.

In the 1950's, Zhang Ruiqi wrote Mao a letter complaining about the financial squeeze he was in. Zhang was a native of northern Shaanxi. He was a member of the guard platoon during the war in northern Shaanxi. After he saw Mao enter Beijing he left the army on account of his age to return to farming. As Mao had a special liking for those he had known for a long time, he asked to have some money sent to Zhang as soon as he received the letter.

Mao was always ready to open his purse for those working for him when they were hard up. The budget, for which I was responsible, set aside a sum of money specifically for that purpose. If the money was to come out of his pay, I would make the payment; if it was to come out of the royalties for his writings, the secretary would handle it.

The money for Zhang came out of Mao's pay. It amounted to several hundred yuan, which I put in a kraft-paper* pouch. As Mao wanted to be sure that the money was sent to Zhang, I decided to let him check it before sending it.

Mao was working at the time. He took the pouch from me, thinking it was an official document and was about to open it.

"It's the money for Zhang, Comrade Chairman. Please check it."

I had barely finished when Mao's face fell. He threw the pouch away as he would have done a toad.

"Take it away! Who told you to bring it to me?" Knitting his brows, he wiped his hands as if they had been soiled. "I never touch money.

---

*A tough wrapping paper made from sulfate wood pulp.

Remember that!"

When Li Erting, also a guard during the war in northern Shaanxi, wrote from home with similar complaints, I sent the money to him as authorized by Mao, without repeating the same mistake again.

When the system of paying a monthly-salary was initiated in China, Tian Yunyu, in the guard, was put in the category of thirty-seven and a half yuan a month, which was a bit too low for him. So he was made a candidate for a two-grade rise in 1956. When Li's case was compared with similar cases of guards of other Party leaders, the leadership decided that Li should have his pay raised by only one grade and not two, because he was Mao's guard. Tian protested the decision, even tearfully, but to no avail. During the anti-Rightist campaign in 1957, a large-character poster in Zhongnanhai said, "Tian Yunyu asked for a two-grade pay-rise because he thinks he is worth ten times more than others." Mao remarked jokingly: "A man cries only when he doesn't get a pay rise," a parody on the line of verse: "a man cries only when his heart is broken." His comment was widely circulated amongst us all.

Tian was on guard duty the next day. The significant look which Mao gave him made him feel uneasy, and he believed that on account of the poster he looked ridiculous.

"I want to talk to you, Tian," Mao spoke kindly and sincerely. "I would like to pay you from my own pocket so that the government won't have to pay you. How much do you need?"

Tian hesitated, unable to decide whether or not it would be correct to accept the offer.

"What's your pay now?"

"Forty-three yuan."

"What would you say to sixty yuan?"

"Well...." As Tian told us later, he was so happy that he was on the verge of thanking Mao, when he had second thoughts. "I wouldn't be on the government payroll any longer then, and should the chairman die...." So he declined the offer with an excuse: "Would that be the right thing to do? Wouldn't I then be hired by you personally, Comrade Chairman?"

"What?" apparently Mao had not thought of that. After a brief pause, he said nodding, "You're right. Money's a lousy thing. But there's nothing I can do about it; nothing anyone can do, not even Lenin. We just can't manage without it. Back in the days when I worked in Beijing, I received only eight yuan a month. I could only afford meat dumplings once; I had them in a restaurant, they tasted better than anything I had ever eaten. Meat dumplings are nothing special to you now, are they? I remember the train trip I made to Shanghai. I borrowed the money for the ticket from a friend of mine. On the train someone stole my shoes whilst I was sleeping. I didn't discover the theft until I was leaving the train at Pukou. A friend whom I met there helped me out. With the money he lent me I bought myself a new pair of shoes and another ticket to go on to Shanghai. You see, money's such a lousy thing, but still you can't live without it."

Mao had helped Tian with money when he heard that he needed it back home. As usual, he didn't touch the money.

In the summer of 1964, after I was transferred to Tianjin, I visited Mao in Beijing. When he learned my folks back home were having a hard time on account of natural calamities, he told his secretary to take one thousand yuan from the royalties for his writings. The secretary brought in the money in a kraft-paper pouch and left it on the table.

"Take it," he motioned to me, keeping his distance from the pouch. "It may help a bit."

"Oh, no, Comrade Chairman," I kept shaking my head. "I can manage. I can't take it." Mao had helped me out with money so many times before, that I found it hard to accept any more from him.

"What do you mean? Do you want me to lay my hands on that money?" Mao reached for the pouch.

"No, no! I'll take it. I'll get it myself." I picked up the pouch containing the one thousand yuan before Mao could reach it.

"That's right," said Mao. "It's good of you to remember that I never touch money. I just hate it."

Mao's Reaction to "Long Live Chairman Mao!"

Sometimes Mao enjoyed the shout: "Long live Chairman Mao!"; sometimes he frowned upon it.

As I recall, Mao once said to us, "You must take me as your leader, but I can't stand it if you always treat me that way." Mao said that in jest, durig a casual conversation with many of us in the bodyguard and the guard, to relax those of us who were ill at ease in his presence.

The first time I heard "Long live Chairman Mao!" was in the summer of 1947. That was the first time I heard it shouted spontaneously in Mao's presence, not shouted as a slogan at mass rallies.

The column of the Central Committee was on the move in northern Shaanxi, pursued by the seven brigades of Liu Kan's army. When the column was twenty *li* from Mizhi, it left the main road and turned east into a gully. After reaching Jing'erping and Chenjiagou we crossed a mountain and reached the flat land between Mizhi and Jiaxian County. The main road was almost deserted, but in the gully there was much activity: Peasants working in the fields, men transporting things on poles carried on their shoulders. Further into the gully, there was a bustling market, alive with pedlars selling their wares. Apparently the enemy had not arrived there.

Mao sensed the danger: the enemy troops were less than thirty *li* away and all hell could break loose there any moment. He instructed the men from the propaganda section, who he had ordered to be brought to him by the guard platoon leader: "Send all your men to these people. Tell them the enemy troops will be here any moment. Tell them to hide everything they have so that when the enemy troops come, they'll have nothing to eat." To the chief staff-officer of the detachment he said, "We're going to make a detour so that the market won't be disturbed."

But the civilians had already seen us and were leaving the market to greet us. Mao Zedong's name had by then become a household word in China, but without modern communication networks, the people in the old liberated areas could only see Mao in drawings, never in photographs, and few of them had ever seen Mao in person. Now, with the assumed name Li Desheng, Mao was not recognized most of the time. In some of the houses where Mao stayed, the host, who would keep on talking about Mao, did not realize that the man who was their guest was in fact the man they longed to see.

But it was a different story on this occasion. Someone in the crowd called out in half-belief, "Can that be Chairman Mao?"

Mao instinctively turned around on his horse, looking in the direction of the shout. Immediately, more people in the crowd joined in, calling out happily, "It's Chairman Mao! Long live Chairman Mao!"

The market exploded with excitement. People began leaving like a teeming current, leaving behind their abacuses, weighing-scales and all their wares. Those already on the outskirts of the market were the first to get close to Mao, their joyous shouts: "Long live Chairman Mao!" reverberating like thunder.

We were surrounded on every side by the excited crowd, unable to proceed. Mao waved at them from his horse, smiling gently, his eyes swimming with tears. Our eyes also filled with tears, and our hearts swelled with pride, as we interpreted the shouts as an expression of popular love and support for the Party, the army and the cause for which we were fighting. The name of Mao Zedong had become synonymous with our ideals and faith and a source of strength. The shouts were not as passionate as those with which the Red Guards were to cheer Mao twenty years later, but the genuine and unaffected emotions which they expressed were more compelling and exalting, enough to move one to tears.

What was unfolding before my eyes was a scene of mass ecstasy: children running about excitedly, jumping for joy; young men raising a forest of arms in welcome; grandmothers and aunts who, pressing each other in the crowd, stood on toes and craned their necks to catch a glimpse of Mao, trying in vain to suppress the happiness beaming in their eyes and visible on their lips, and old men with white head-bands, who, putting down their shovels, elbowed their way towards Mao on his horse, wiping away tears all the while; their wrinkled, sun-tanned faces radiating revived youthful joy as they touched the back of Mao's jacket.

At the time there was no media publicity about "going all out to build the chairman's authority"; the only such publicity Mao received was from the Kuomintang which branded him a "bandit," "gangster" and "demon." Mao refuted such vilifications with facts. He was astutely aware of what was happening in China and what was in the minds of the Chinese people; he explained to them in language they could understand things which would otherwise be too complicated for them to grasp; with his thoughts, revolutionary theories, extraordinary organizational ability and outstanding leadership, he commanded a following comprising the finest men and women of the nation, with whose help he rallied around him the overwhelming majority of the masses. All this culminated in his being accepted as a national leader who enjoyed the unqualified respect and love of the people.

That was the time, as far as I know, when Mao enjoyed being greeted with "long live" and expected to be met in this manner, because the people indentified the name Mao Zedong with the Communist Party and the shout "long live" was an indication that in the minds of the people, the Party's strategies and policies served their best interests for, after all, those who win the world are those who enjoy popular support.

Mao entered the city of Beijing amid shouts of "long live." That day Mao, with one foot in the jeep and the other on the ground, said to Zhou Enlai, "Let's go and test what awaits us in the city. We'll prove we're not like Li Zicheng (whose peasant army toppled the Ming Dynasty in 1644). We'll make the test."

In those days Mao was busy sending the army across the Yangtse River at Nanjing; planning military operations for the liberation of the rest of China; preparing for the convocation of the Political Consultative Conference; reviving the economy; and boosting production. That is to say he was constructively busy. On May 2 he visited the Summer Palace with Liu Yazi, a noted cultural personage, and together they took a boat ride on Kunming Lake in the garden.

The Summer Palace had many visitors that day. At the entrance Mao was recognized. I heard those who had recognized him talking to each other in excitement, saying, "Chairman Mao!" "Yes, it's Chairman Mao." They greeted Mao with applause, but they didn't shout "long live."

As Mao and Liu's boat was approaching the shore, a big crowd gathered there. When I suggested that we land on the other shore, to the southeast, so that Mao could leave the garden by the southern exit, Mao objected, saying, "What's wrong with the crowd? You mustn't be afraid of the masses."

A ripple ran through the crowd on the eastern shore as the boat drew closer in, and once those gathered there were sure the man in the boat was indeed Mao, they burst out in loud greeting:

"Long live Chairman Mao!"

"Long live Chairman Mao!"

The moment Mao landed he was surrounded by the crowd. Eager hands were offered for Mao to shake. Mao, who didn't want to be the centre of attention, walked beside Liu and half a step behind him. As they got into their car, Mao saw to it that Liu got in first.

Inside the car, Mao talked good-humouredly. With a simple gesture, he said, "It's our first visit to the Summer Palace, and also the first time to see so many visitors there. Mr. Liu was happy, and so was I."

On May 12 Mao and Zhu De met with delegates of the First National Youth Congress in a square at the foot of Fragrant Hills. The delegates had arrived in eight trucks; on the way they had sung: "The east is red, the sun is rising, China has given birth to Mao Zedong."

A few days earlier, the national women's representatives had been so happy when meeting with Mao that they just wouldn't stop shouting "Long live Chairman Mao!" So on this occasion, Mao made sure that he and Zhu would share the limelight. As they approached the young people, Mao, who was walking a little ahead of Zhu, made sure that he stayed close to Zhu, and even slowed down a bit from time to time, so that Zhu would not be left too far behind him.

The delegates took the cue. In addition to "Long live Chairman Mao!" they shouted "Long live Commander-in-Chief Zhu!"

At one point their eulogy ran: "In the days of darkness we listened to you, our great chairman. We built our hopes on your voice, and from your voice we drew our strength."

Mao returned from the meeting in a happy frame of mind. Commenting on the eulogy, he said, "The delegates say my voice gave them hope and strength. Their voice means just the same to me."

I did not see anything unnatural about the "long live" shouts, nor

Mao's reaction to them at the time. There was no denying that Mao had done a great deal for the nation. Every single victory scored by the New-Democratic Revolution bore his name. Events in China more than once proved that he was a brilliant national leader. When the people demonstrated their deepest and heartfelt respect towards him, he was careful not to exaggerate his own importance. And when the "long live" shouts swelled, like a rising tide, from Tiananmen Square, he managed to keep a cool head for a considerable period of time. The following account may bear witness to this.

The most dramatic decision made by Mao following the liberation of mainland China, was his decision to send the Chinese People's Volunteers to Korea to fight the American troops in 1950. It was a decision fraught with enormous risks. Many people called it insane, arguing that no one in his right mind would think of going to war with the most powerful imperialist country in the world, along with more than a dozen other member states of the United Nations, when New China had only just been established, and the wounds of a war of more than twenty years had hardly healed. They cited the historic example of Li Zicheng, attributing the tragic end of his revolution to the military losses he sustained at the hands of the Nüzhens.

As I remember, Mao did not sleep a wink for three days and three nights before coming to that decision. Once, he took three doses of sleeping pills, but he still could not sleep. He rose from bed, chain-smoked and drank cup after cup of tea. Then he decided to send the volunteers to Korea.

Once Mao made a decision, those who had formerly been skeptical would unite behind him. So the Politburo and the government gave their unanimous approval to his decision, in itself evidence that events in China had convinced people that they could trust Mao more than they could trust themselves, and even more than they could trust collective wisdom and judgment. Indeed, Mao, who had frequently been in the minority for his views on many issues, had subsequently, invariably been proved right by events.

And the Korean war proved to be yet another example of this: the war ended with the signing of an armistice agreement; the national economy made a remarkable recovery, resulting in rapid progress in just a few years.

However, this same trust heralded the many disasters which were later to rock China. The patriarchal system, which comprised an integral part of Chinese culture, and had held sway over the nation for several thousand years, could not be abolished overnight. Thus Mao alone shouldn't be blamed for the continuation of feudal social structures into socialist society, nor for the monopoly of decision-making by one person, which invariably accompanies such a system.

As someone working close to Mao, I would frequently hear such lavish praise of him as: "great," "brilliant," and "a long, long life to Chairman Mao"; Mao was "genuinely great," "the greatest of men," "a man deserving the greatest of respect," "a seasoned military strategist unrivalled in China," "superior to anyone we've seen," etc., etc. Such praise was uttered by Party and no-Party members alike, including such veterans of the democratic revolution as Zhang Lan, Li Jishen, Shen Junru, Chen Shutong, He Xiangning and Ma Xulun, people whom Mao respected so much that he would help them out of their cars or up flights of steps.

This kind of praise might have turned Mao's head a bit, but he did not lower his guard. About two years after the end of the Korean war, Kim Il Sung made Mao a gift of twenty-four crates of apples. Mao only saw lists of the gifts sent to him by Chinese or foreigners alike, but he never saw the gifts themselves; they were taken directly to a department responsible for handling gifts, where they became public property. But these apples were different; they were from Kim, and were perishable. So Mao told me to give them to the guards.

When I brought the fruit to the First Guard Company, the men were very happy because they came just before Lunar New Year. They opened the crates in excitement, but when they saw the contents their excitement vanished. These apples, each the size of a fist, were perfect in quality, but each of them had been inscribed with a line of characters proclaiming: "Long live Chairman Mao!" It was impossible to erase the characters, since they had been written on the apples, as we learned later, before they were fully grown, and as a result of exposure to sunlight, these inscriptions had become permanent. How could the men bite into a line saying: "Long live Chairman Mao!"? No one knew what to do. Someone suggested, "Why, let's keep them, so that we can enjoy their sweet scent every day."

When I reported this to Mao, he was displeased. Knitting his brows, he shook his head, saying, "I, for one, don't like this slogan. Can anyone live forever? No one can; so eat the apples!"

So all twenty-four crates of apples, each with the inscription, "Long live Chairman Mao!" on it, were consumed by all of us, something impossible to imagine during the "cultural revolution," when Mao Zedong's name became deified.

A man climbing a mountain had to walk up by himself; if he is to be carried up, it is someone else who must bear the burden, not he himself. Mao alone, as I have said, should not be blamed for the continued existence of the patriarchal system in China, nor for the monopoly of decision-making by a single person; and nor should Lin Biao or the Gang of Four, for that matter. After all, the majority of those who shouted: "Long live Chairman Mao!" were not careerists or conspirators. In the beginning, Mao was awake to the danger of "the personality cult." I have cited one such example in my account of the fate of the apples sent by Kim Il Sung. His strong objection to the erection of a statue, cast in bronze, in Tiananmen Square, which he referred to as: "nothing but a piece of sarcasm," was yet another. Examples of this kind are numerous. I may be wrong, but I still claim in Mao's defence, that in a country like China, where the shout of "long live" has been repeated throughout several thousand years of history, a man, no matter how wise, will be unable to keep a cool head for long, when the shout turns into a kind of ritual greeting, but will ultimately come to regard it as a matter of course.

And this ritual invariably transforms the man into a god; and once he has been deified, he becomes increasingly alienated from the masses, and the more he becomes alienated from them, the more he is treated like a god; a cycle which will in due course evolve into tragedy.

In 1952, Mao went on a sightseeing tour in the Gui and She hills in Wuhan, where he visited the Huanghe Tower. Unlike the days when he was in northern Shaanxi during the War of Liberation, Mao was no longer free to mix with the ordinary people. He had to wear a face mask* if he wished to do that, at the insistence of the security people. So fewer and fewer people ever had a chance to see Mao in person, but his portraits were ubiquitous. It was Lunar New Year's Day, and there were many holiday-makers at the tower. Mao was recognized by a child in spite of the face mask he was wearing.

"It's Chairman Mao!" The child's joyous cry was immediately followed by a big commotion amongst the holiday-makers. They swarmed up to Mao, shoving and pressing each other. Luo Ruiqing, Li Xiannian, Wang Renzhong and Yang Qiqing formed a protective ring, with us bodyguards keeping close to Mao within this ring. We swayed as the crowd pressed in on all sides, but we knew that we would not be pushed over; there was no space between us and the pressing crowd to permit us to fall. Bit by bit, sweating profusely, we squeezed our way down the hill, to the river and onto the boat.

Mao removed the mask from his face, and turned to wave at the crowd on the bank, who were clapping in thunderous applause, and shouting "long live" at the top of their lungs. Luo Ruiqing and Yang Qiqing couldn't keep silent any longer: they made a self-criticism in front of the members of the Politburo, apologizing for the loose security measures. But Mao showed no signs of displeasure. With a smile of deep contentment, he said in a slightly intoxicated tone, "Now I know what it's like to be trapped in the Huanghe Tower."

That was all he said.

Mao reached Nanjing, from Wuhan, by boat. There he was joined by Chen Yi and Zhang Aiping, who had come from Shanghai especially to meet him. Mao stayed in Nanjing for two days, and on the day the enemy believed that Mao would be in Shanghai, the Kuomintang aircraft conducted a bombing raid there.

From then on security grew increasingly tighter for Mao, to the extent that he was forbidden to travel by air. This decision was made by the Central Committee in an attempt to ensure that Mao would not become the victim of an air disaster.

Mao didn't like being isolated from the masses in this manner, but

---

*A white cotton gauze mask, covering the nose and mouth, like a surgical mask, commonly worn in northern China in the winter, as protection against the cold and consequent respiratory disorders and bronchial infection. Here the mask is intended to serve the purpose of a disguise, so that Mao wouldn't be recognized by the masses.

in the face of this "collective" wall, there was little he could do. But he would argue. At Beidaihe one time, he had become angry when he was not allowed "go out there." Afraid that getting angry might be harmful to his health, those in charge of such matters conceded to his wish, on the condition that he wear a face mask and sun-glasses. So Mao went to the fields and tried to talk to the peasants. But who would talk to a stranger wearing a face mask and a pair of sun-glasses, with a group of people following in his wake? Angrily, Mao removed the mask and the glasses and instantly the peasants responded, as if by reflex, with loud cheers of: "Long live Chairman Mao!" Their shouts brought the other peasants swarming round Mao. Immediately Mao's guards and body-guards escorted him away, in spite of his angry protests: in a similar situation any guards would have done likewise.

When we discussed such incidents in our private conversations, we in the bodyguard would feel sorry for Mao; for the dreariness of his life and his lack of freedom of movement.

All this may sound incredible, but try to imagine an astronaut in a spaceship; who travels millions of miles without ever being able to leave that hermetically sealed capsule. Mao travelled all over the country, but he couldn't take a stroll in the streets, go to a park, walk into a movie house or a department store as he wished. He was the leader of the people cheered with "long live," wherever he went, but he could not meet with anyone as he pleased. If he was to see someone, the meeting always had to be pre-arranged. This rule applied even to the attendants of his special train: they could not see him without the permission of his bodyguards. Although his imagination knew no limitations, in his daily life, he could not even travel by plane. Before the decisions of the Party, he was just another person. Sometimes a few words uttered by the chairman could change the course of Chinese history, yet this same man did not have the freedom to eat in a restaurant with the masses. What he said within the crimson red walls* could rock the world, yet he had no freedom to step outside these walls; in order to do that he must have permission. How Mao longed for the freedom of the workers, peasants

---

*Traditionally, the colour of the walls of all former imperial enclosures and palace residences in old China, such as the Forbidden City and Summer Palace. Zhongnanhai, where the government leaders presently live, is an extention of the old Forbidden City. It has red walls.

and soldiers!

When Indonesian president, Sukarno, was leaving China after a visit in 1955, I accompanied Mao to the airport to see him off. After Sukarno's plane took off, he unexpectedly said, "Let's find a restaurant and eat there, Yinqiao." I responded, "Let's go to that restaurant that serves buns in mutton soup. I've been there before."

When we got to the place, it had not opened for business. With no customers there, except for Mao and those of us in attendance, guarding the place was no problem. Mao, who did not like mutton, took only a few bites; he just looked at the surroundings in the restaurant, surroundings that must have brought back sweet memories of by-gone days. He also made an unannounced visit, "in disguise," to a private garden to look at the chrysanthemums grown by an old man named Ding. Mao thoroughly enjoyed these visits, but they were few and far between.

On August 13, 1958, Mao went to visit Nankai University and Tianjin University. When he left the latter it was lunch time. At his insistence, we went to a restaurant called Zhengyangchun on Changchun Road. We did not expect to see any other customers in the restaurant, because the management had been informed that Mao was coming, and guards had been posted around it. Mao, who felt hemmed in inside the restaurant, walked to a window to take a look at the street outside. It was only a brief look, but he was spotted by a woman who happened to be hanging out washing on an upper floor, in a house across the street. She let out a cry of pleasant surprise: "It's Chairman Mao! Long live Chairman Mao!"

The two phrases, "long live," and, "Chairman Mao," had by now become so inseparable that the shout "Chairman Mao" would always be preceded by "long live."

The woman's loud greeting instantaneously drew huge crowds from all directions. They poured towards the restaurant like water rushing through a sluice gate, their shouts of "Long live Chairman Mao!" increasing in volume. Many of them just cheered, without actually seeing Mao. The scene of this mass acclaim was, however, different from the one that I had witnessed in northern Shaanxi. On that occasion, the cheering had varied in emotion, depending upon the age and sex of the person cheering; whereas here such individuality seemed to be absent:

the emotion was undifferentiated; and some people cheered just because everybody else was doing so.

The excited crowd surrounded the restaurant, blocking all the street exits and stopping all the traffic. Even the traffic policemen joined in with the cheering crowd and were trying to catch a glimpse of Mao. Mao tried to go to them, and was of course blocked by us: what useful purpose would it serve under the circumstances? This was not northern Shaanxi, where he would have been able to collect manure with a rake or push a mill-stone* and talk amicably with the peasants to find out what they thought. The relationship between man and "god" is one of prayer, and the answers to prayer; there can be no exchange of thought between them on an equal footing.

For more than six hours, from a little past eleven o'clock in the morning, until well past five in the afternoon, we were trapped in the restaurant, until a Polish sedan, a Warzawa, came to our rescue. A platoon of soldiers from the Garrison Command had pushed the car through the crowd to the restaurant with great effort. A group of them, all husky young men, escorted Mao to the car. The Warzawa was really too small for a man of Mao's build, but nevertheless, the soldiers managed to squeeze him in. With the soldiers clearing the way and pushing the car, we managed to break through the crowd. Later, when the place was cleaned up, the shoes, hats, fountain-pens and wrist-watches found there, filled seven and a half large-sized baskets.

At Beidaihe, Mao had grown angry when the "long live" cheers had made it impossible for him to carry on a conversation. But this time, he seemed to enjoy the sight of a vast number of people following him, carried away by ecstacy. On this he commented briefly: "A repetition of the experience in the Huanghe Tower."

Did he intend it as a compliment or a criticism?

From then on, Mao would be reminded of what had happened at the Huanghe Tower and the restaurant in Tianjin every time he said he want to "go out just for a walk." After all, there was public order to consider in addition to Mao's personal safety. Mao was a winner all his life, yet he had to make concessions so that scenes like those at the

---

*A mill-stone, using for grinding corn in rural areas, which is rotated by a wooden pole attached to it horizontally. Peasants push this by hand, walking round in circles to rotate the mill-stone. These mill-stones are still in use in the Chinese countryside today.

tower and the restaurant would not recur. This was the beginning of a life of seclusion to which Mao later grew accustomed.

In 1949, I had overheard Mao say to Liu Yazi, during the boat ride on Kunming Lake: "Now that Chiang Kai-shek's gone, you can write and speak freely without having to hide your identity. Your safety is guaranteed and your opinions will be respected." Ten years later, at Lushan Mountain, when he commented on the letter which Marshal Peng Dehuai had written to him, in which he freely expressed his views, I heard Mao say, "Peng doesn't realize that if the army doesn't want me any more, I shall raise a new army." These were the words of a man who had total confidence in himself. Indeed, Mao's confidence in himself exceeded the confidence he had in Peng, or even in the collective, by a wide margin, and, more importantly, it was justified by later events. Mao was the man who could rob the Party of all its power with just a few words, and who was charismatic enough to command a mass following at any place, any time.

Sometimes Mao enjoyed being cheered with "long live," and sometimes he didn't. Later he grew as much bored by the cheering, as he was carried away by it; he could never entirely get rid of this mixed feeling. I was no longer with him in his later years, but I noticed, so did many others, that his objections to being cheered with "long live" and to the buildup of this personality cult came to mean less and less. He chose both knowingly and unknowingly to allow the cult to gain in momentum, thereby fostering the inclination of the masses to turn him into a god, which led ultimately to ten years of national tragedy, in the form of the "cultural revolution."

Mao — the "Rustic"

In Mao's case the word "rustic" can be used to describe some of his living habits which had their origins in his early life as the son of a Chinese peasant, as well as his Spartan life-style as a revolutionary. In these one can see both the history and culture of a nation, these qualities which go to make a revolutionary and constitute his hopes and aspirations.

Let me begin by relating some stories about Mao in connection with the way he dressed, since the clothes one wears show most readily whether a person is "sophisticated" or "unsophisticated" in taste.

Mao never wore shoes when they were new; he would ask the guards or bodyguards to wear them in first, and would take them back and wear them himself when they were no longer new.

During the war, on more than one occasion, Mao gave his shoes to the men who needed them. He did that so as to set a good example to the other cadres, in order that they should "take good care of every man in our ranks." Giving new shoes to the men to wear first was, however, a "matter of a different nature"; it was a matter of personal preference. Some people like their clothes, hats and shoes new, believing that they look good in them. Mao was the opposite. Like the peasants, he was a practical man; to him the best clothes were the ones in which he felt the most comfortable.

"You young people look good in new clothes. But I'm an old man and find old things more comfortable," Mao would say when he gave new shoes to the men or took them back, adding, "To each according to his preference."

Mao's habits and his attitude to the way he was dressed, originated partly in the early years of his life in the countryside, and partly as a consequence of the shortages he endured during the years of war. These habits and attitudes enabled him to adapt easily to the social conditions which prevailed in China, which were determined by a predominantly rural economy and the environment of war.

Mao was quite familiar with farming, as was clear from the numerous inspection tours he made in the countryside. When we looked at the paddy fields together, at Xinli Village in Tianjin, in 1958, a leading comrade of the Central Committee and the local officials told him that one *mu** of land could yield as much as 100,000 *jin*** of rice. Mao did not believe them, dismissing what they said as mere "bragging." To prove that it was indeed possible, they had resorted to using artificial lighting, ventilating the fields with blowers, and even laying children on top of paddy to demonstrate the abundance of the growth,*** but Mao refused to be taken in. He said, "I don't believe you can grow so much. The higher you go the harder you fall." He remarked to that leading comrade of the Central Committee, "You've never done any farming. All you do is talk big. I've been a peasant myself and I know 100,000 *jin* is impossible; you can't even heap that much rice in that amount of land. So don't take me for a fool." Would anyone wear fine, crisp clothes when his job often took him to the countryside, where he would sit in the fields, work the ploughs, cut the crops or join the peasants in collecting manure, and talk with them?

History has created an image of Mao wearing clothes covered with patches. In fact, the patches on Mao's clothing were mostly on his underwear and coarse cotton socks, which were hidden from view. They came in all shapes and sizes; and odd bits of cloth, in blue, yellow or grey, that came to hand, would do. When these were not available, old bandages would be substituted. Mao's comments on patches varied with the times, ranging from: "Don't worry. They'll be on my underwear and won't be seen from outside. They're okay as long as they don't bother me"; "All I ask is that they don't reveal the skin underneath and keep the wind out"; "One piece of clothing I save means one more bullet for our men at the front"; "We musn't be wasteful and set a bad example when the country is still poor"; "It's easy to pay scant attention to what

---

*One hectare equals fifteen *mu*.

**One *jin* equals half a kilogramme.

***Indicative of a trend on the part of peasants during the great leap forward, to vie with each other for the highest harvest yields, and even exaggerate their production figures. They would lay children on top of the crops, to prove that they were indeed abundant and strong enough to bear their weight.

you wear when you can't get anything better"; to "It's not easy to ignore what you wear when the country's economy improves and you can afford good clothes"; "A communist should do what it's not easy to do."

However, Mao paid a lot of attention to patches on his outer garments. He insisted that they must be the same colour, or as close as possible to the colour of the clothes they were to mend and must look presentable. "Find a piece of cloth," he would say, "that matches the clothes. What you wear on the outside is for people to look at; it's not polite to have patches on your clothes that look outrageous."

Not long after moving to Beijing, Mao met with the leaders of the democratic parties, representatives of various circles and well-known figures. One of them was Zhang Lan, a founder of the China Democratic League and vice-chairman of the Central People's Government of China. Before the meeting, Mao said to me, "Mr. Zhang Lan's done a great deal for the liberation of the Chinese people and is highly respected by democratic personages. I want to meet this senior gentleman in better clothes, as a mark of respect for him."

I rummaged through all Mao's clothes, but I couldn't find a single item that was neither badly worn nor patched. Mao had nothing new to wear when he moved to Beijing. As he had compared his entry into Beijing to that of an impoverished scholar travelling to the capital, to take the imperial examinations,* I said, "We're like that scholar you mentioned, Comrade Chairman: none of your clothes are presentable."

"Dandies never made good grades in those examinations," Mao commented. "Success belongs to those who do not cry over being poor. Nothing is impossible if, when you're reduced to eating vegetable roots, you don't complain about it. We'll get good grades."

"It's too late to have some new clothes made, but shall I borrow something better for you?"

"It's not necessary. Patches are all right, as long as the clothes are neat and clean. Mr. Zhang isn't the type of man to feel displeased on account of a few patches."

So Mao wore the patched clothes when he met with Zhang, and later, he was to meet with other well-known figures like Shen Junru, Li Jishen, Guo Moruo and Chen Shutong, wearing the same clothes.

---

*This was the examination system set up by Confucius, for entry into officialdom.

Still, I couldn't help feeling a little dismayed by the fact that the leader of the Communist Party, which now governed the whole country, didn't have so much as a single item of clothing that was not patched. Only when Mao was to declare the founding of the People's Republic at the Tiananmen rostrum, did I have a new suit made for him, by Wang Ziqing, in Wangfujing Street.

Perhaps Mao was naturally reluctant to part with anything he had used for a long time. Anyway, he never threw away old clothes. When they were beyond mending, they would become material for patches.

One day, in Yangjiagou, in northern Shaanxi, I was showing Mao a grey army uniform that had become threadbare in many places and was as hard as cardboard in others, and was covered in patches. "Look at the uniform, Comrade Chairman," I said. "You can't wear it any longer; you'd look ridiculous in it. If you wear it to address a meeting, any movement you make with your hands will cause it to come apart at the seams."

Mao took the uniform from me. None of his clothes could be thrown away without his permission. He placed the uniform carefully on his lap, and ran his hand over the crinkles as if stroking a wounded soldier.

"It's what I wore at the Luochuan meeting," Mao said, his eyes suddenly moistening around the rims. For a while he just stared blankly at the uniform, nostalgically recalling the enlarged meeting of the Polituro held in Luochuan in northern Shaanxi in August 1937. Then, after recounting some of the "services" it had performed, he said with a deep sigh, "Let's agree on this: we'll use it for patches so that it can still serve some useful purposes and I can still see it."

Mao might have been talking about an old comrade-in-arms with whom he endured hard times.

As he advanced in age, Mao gained in weight, outgrowing many of the old clothes he possessed. He handed these clothes down to Mao Anying. That's why Anying was never seen wearing good clothes, but only those with patches on them. Jiang Qing didn't mind having patches on her clothes either until the 1960s when she became clothes-conscious. But Mao never changed. The holes in his uniforms were darned in a laundry shop in Wangfujing Street, but those in his underwear were patched and re-patched repeatedly. Before he met with a foreign guest, I would each time remind him: "When you sit in the easy chair, Comrade Chairman, remember to tuck in your feet or you'll reveal our 'secrets.'"

These "secrets" were the patches on his socks which would show beneath the ends of his trousers when his legs were stretched out. Later on, I used to remind him about that in a borrowed phrase: "Remember to 'keep the family skeleton in the closet.' "

To "keep the family skeleton in the closet," was what was expected of all Mao's bodyguards.

When weighing up the pros and cons of a matter, political, military or personal, Mao was always sure where his priorities lay.

One day, not long after I became his bodyguard, I discovered that Mao only had one towel, which he used to wipe both his face and his feet, and which, with all the pile gone, resembled sack cloth.

"Comrade Chairman," I said, "shall I ask for another towel issue? You can keep this one for your feet. You can't use the same towel for both your face and your feet."

"That wouldn't be fair," Mao said after thinking for a while. "With a war to fight and a lot of walking to do every day, as we do now, the feet have to work much harder than the face. If the treatment's different, the feet will complain."

I laughed. "Use the new one for the feet and the old one for the face then."

"You're forgetting your arithmetic," said Mao, shaking his head in disagreement. "A new issue of towel doesn't seem very expensive, but if each one of us gives up a towel, the money saved would be enough to fight a battle like the one we fought at Shajiadian."

Mao liked a good bed. "You spend one-third of your life in bed," he once said, "and perhaps I spend even longer in it. So my bed has to be comfortable."

Mao didn't mean he spent more time sleeping than others; in fact, he slept only half as much as anyone else, as evidenced by my later recollections. He was talking about his habit of reading newspapers and documents in bed.

What kind of bed did Mao regard as comfortable?

First of all, such a bed must be "hard" and "cool." Mao didn't like the heated *kang*, a mud platform for a bed, in northern Shaanxi; he endured cold better than he did heat. Wherever he went he would ask to sleep on doors for a bed. Once he had to spend a night on a heated *kang* in a village in northern Shaanxi because his hostess couldn't remove the doors from the door-frame. When her son, a county government official, returned and learned of this, he criticized her, and got the doors off the frame by sawing off their tenons. A Chinese-type door opens and closes on two reounded tenons that fit into recesses or holes in the door-frame. When Mao was told of what had happened to the doors, he was surprised and kept on saying, "That was a crazy thing to do!" He immediately examined the doors. Only when he was sure that they were not damaged, could he set his mind at ease. That night, with doors for a bed, he took one dose of sleeping pills fewer than the previous night, and fell asleep. After moving to Beijing, he always slept on beds which had a wooden board for a mattress, both at home and on inspection tours. He never used a spring mattress.

In summer he used a minimum of bedding to keep cool, and in order to prevent the pillows from being soiled by sweat, he would cover them with old newspapers, which would soon become tattered and wet with perspiration.

Mao also liked his bed to be big. In northern Shaanxi, the doors he slept on were so large that they covered a large-size *kang*. His bed in Beijing measured 5.4 feet across. Why so big? Because a large bed made it easy for him to read in it. As Mao liked to read lying down, half of the bed was reserved for books. The bed in his former residence in Zhongnanhai is still loaded with books, but there aren't as many as when Mao was alive: then they were piled in stacks more than one foot high. Mao couldn't go to sleep if he didn't have something to read, and wouldn't get out of bed until he had read the day's newspapers.

Not any kind of bedding would do for Mao. He preferred cotton to feather or camel-hair padding for quilts, and cotton cloth to Dacron for the covers; he had an intense dislike of synthetic materials. As for colour, he liked very light colours. His mattress was covered in white cotton cloth, and so were the buckwheat-husk pillows.* These and some

---

*Pillows filled with buckwheat husks, instead of feather.

pyjamas, patched all over, along with some towelling coverlets comprised Mao's personal bedding when he moved to Beijing and until he died.

Mao possessed an old army blanket which he was so fond of that he never travelled without it. When he worked in bed, reading official documents and writing instructions on them, as I have already mentioned, was his habit, he would lean against the pillows which were covered with the blanket hanging from the railing at the head of the bed. When Soong Ching Ling learned about this, she made him a gift of a large and very expensive pillow. Since it came from someone he held in special esteem, Mao accepted it; but after it had lain on his bed for some time, he sent it to the storehouse: it was too much of a luxury for him. He put the blanket back in its former position, and placed the buckwheat-husk pillows in their white cotton covers underneath it. "I'm just too used to them to want any changes," Mao said.

The following may sound unbelievable but it is true: right from the end of 1953 until the end of 1962, Mao didn't have any new clothes made. He never washed his face with scented soap. In order to remove ink-stains or grease from his hands, laundering soap was good enough for him. He never used any kind of face-cream or oil for skin protection; he didn't use toothpaste: he preferred tooth-powder. "I don't object to people using toothpaste or even expensive toothpaste," he said. "It's produced for comsumption. If no one used it, how could we increase production? But tooth-powder serves the purpose just as well. That's what I brushed my teeth with in Yan'an. I'm used to it." He never asked for a new toothbrush until the old one had lost all its bristles, like a piece of wasteland. For chopsticks, he preferred those made from bamboo. He refused to eat with ivory chopsticks, like the ones one find in a posh restaurant. "They're too expensive," he would say. "I'm not comfortable with them."

Perhaps Mao's drinking and eating habits say more than anything else about his "unrefined" habits.

Mao drank tea heavily. He did not generally get up when he woke up; but rather, after wiping his face and hands with a wet towel, he would remain in bed, drinking tea and reading the newspapers for about an hour. He did that every day if there wasn't any urgent business to attend to. Before every change of tea leaves, he would shovel the old ones into his mouth with his fingers, chew them and swallow them. He never left them in the cup. Apparently that was how he disposed of used tea-leaves when he was peasant boy living in the countryside.

Coarse grain and vegetables were Mao's favourite foods; sometimes he would crave wild herbs. These things continued to make up his diet after he moved to Beijing. He always ate brown rice cooked with millet, black soya beans or taro roots. He developed this preference during the war, when he was in northern Shaanxi.

If Mao ate at mealtimes, the food generally consisted of four side-dishes, two of which would always be dried hot peppers and preserved toufu*, and a soup, which sometimes just consisted of plain water with which he would rinse his dishes. But Mao rarely ate at mealtimes; he was not "disciplined" enough to do that.

Mao's behaviour was often unconventional, and he would not allow convention to inhibit his personality in any way. He did not work according to a schedule; he ate when he was hungry, which could be any time. Often he had two meals a day, and sometimes only one. And when work kept him busy for several dsys and nights at a stretch, he would eat five or six meals a day. He did not always eat at the dinner-table but wherever was convenient, as was his custom during "the years of tumult." The bodyguards kept an electric stove and a large enamel mug in their office, in which they would cook oatmeal or noodles for him, which Ye Zilong, his attendant, would bring to him. That was often all he ate for a meal, an eating habit which he had developed during the war years.

Mao's eating habits often bring to mind the way Mao wrote. He never wrote his characters inside the squares. The strokes flowed freely, gracefully, looking at once elegant and bold, with infinite variation in structure and style, and ingeniously arranged, the finished work would be a testimony to the calligrapher's personality and something to marvel at.

During the fifteen years I was Mao's bodygurad, he never ate in any other manner than that which I have just described: anything would do for a meal: a handful of roasted soya beans, a few taro roots, a mug of

---

*Bean curd.

oatmeal or a plate of purslane. Let me cite one ready example of this.

Mao was going to speak to an enlarged meeting of the Eleventh Session fo the Supreme Conference of State Affairs, on February 27, 1957, on "the correct handling of contradictions among the people." At the instruction of Zhou Enlai, the guard-section called its weekly meeting earlier than scheduled, to discuss ways to ensure that Mao would eat properly and sleep well.

"Do you mean," I asked Tian Yunyu, with a frown, at the meeting, "that the chairman hasn't slept for two days and has had only one decent meal?"

"And two mugs of oatmeal," added Zhang Xianpeng.

I glanced at the faces of some of the bodyguards and then looking at Feng Yaosong, I enquired, "You're on the next shift, aren't you, Feng?"

"Yes," Feng looked worried, anticipating the pressure on him.

"We've got to think of a way, we've got to," I kept on repeating, but in fact, I couldn't think of anything we could do. Surely we couldn't force Mao to eat or sleep, or he would get angry. "Be tactful, Feng," I said. "Seize every opportunity and make the best of the circumstances. We're counting on you, whatever you do."

On each shift there were two guards, one to remain on duty for twenty-four hours and attend to Mao, the other to assist him. Reluctantly, Feng went on the twenty-four-hour shift that day. For seven or eight hours, he was silent, bringing Mao cups of tea. He was watching, looking for an opportunity.

At two o'clock in the morning, Mao put down his pen. He stretched his neck and massaged his forehead, breathing deeply with his mouth wide open. Feng saw his opportunity. He went up to Mao and asked him in a low voice, "You haven't eaten anything for more than ten hours, Comrade Chairman. Shall I bring you something?"

Mao stretched hard. When he lowered his arms, he looked at Feng with blood-shot eyes; fatigue written all over his face. He had barely begun to speak, before he yawned twice. Then, sighing deeply, he first shook his head and then nodded, saying, "Not a meal, just a few roasted taro roots."

Feng wanted to say something else but Mao stopped him with a wave of his hand and picked up his pen once again. Feng knew better than to say anything more.

He went to the kitchen to prepare the food for Mao. Now, as was his practice in northern Shaanxi, when Mao wanted to eat something during the night, he never asked his cooks to prepare the food, but would tell his bodyguards to roast a few wheat or cornflour buns for him, so as not to disturb the cooks.

But that night, Hou, the cook, was roused from sleep. Blinking sleepily he shouted at Feng, "You're crazy! Is this what you're going to feed the chairman when he hasn't eaten anything the whole day?" Feng shook his head, and with a wry smile, retorted, "This is what the chairman wants. Make something better and take it to him yourself if you're not crazy." Hou was left speechless. "Do what I say," was what Mao always demanded of us. Hou knew that it would be "crazy" to do otherwise.

Feng put the six small roasted taro roots on a plate and left the kitchen. Just as he entered Mao's room, he heard a loud snore. Mao, who made a loud noise when he snored, had fallen asleep, leaning against the railing of his bed, with the blanket for a cushion. He was still holding the document he had been working on in his left had and his pen in his right hand. Mao was often to be seen sleeping like that and no one could afford to wake him up. Since he was a light sleeper and was not to be disturbed when he was sleeping, Feng put the food on the radiator and retreated to the door to wait. When he sat down, he was instantly overcome by drowsiness. So he moved outside of the door where the cold air would keep him awake.

Mao was a man of superhuman energy. No one could keep a record of how many hours he worked a day, because the difference between night and day did not exist for him. The guards on duty only recorded how much time he slept a week. As I recollect, Mao slept not more than thirty hours a week. If the record showed thirty-five hours, it was an occasion for celebration with wine. None of the leading comrades of the Central Committee could stay awake as long as Mao. Even Luo Ruiqing, who was known for his extraordinary vigour, had to concede defeat. "I'm exhausted," he would say. "I've been staying with the chairman." Once he said to us, "I know your job is extremely strenuous. It's hard work attending the chairman. He's a man with superhuman energy. None of us can rival him in that."

About a quarter of an hour later, Feng heard Mao cough. Immediately he went back into the room, treading lightly. Picking up the plate, he said, almost in a whisper, "The taro roots are ready, Comrade Chairman."

Mao put down the document and the pen. Rubbing his face, he said, "Oh, yes. I do feel like eating now. Bring them here."

Feng put the plate down on his desk. Mao walked over and sat down. He picked up one of the taro roots and began to peel it carefully, his body rocking gently as he recited one of his poems: "Soon dawn will break in the east/Do not say 'you start too early.'"

Feng looked out of the window. Day was breaking. When Mao had peeled the skin off half of the root, he took a bite from it, and as he chewed, he went on peeling the other half and reciting the poem. With Mao enjoying himself thus, Feng quietly left the room to refresh himself in the cold air outside.

Another fifteen minutes or so passed before a light snore was heard coming from Mao's room. Feng tiptoed in and found there was only one taro root left on the plate. Mao had fallen asleep, his head resting on his right shoulder.

Feng tiptoed over. He picked up the plate and was about to leave, when he noticed that the snore sounded strange. He leaned over to take a closer look at Mao, and then he rubbed his eyes.

Good heavens! Half an uneaten taro root was clenched between Mao's teeth, quivering as he breathed, and the other half was in his hand. Immediately Feng's vision blurred with tears. He rubbed his eyes again, and putting down the plate, gently, very gently, slide his fingers in between Mao's teeth.

The half-root was removed and Mao was awakened.

"Who's that?" Mao stared at Feng, his eyes misty, blood-shot from lack of sleep, displaying annoyance. Then he shouted angrily, "What's going on here?"

"Comrade Chairman!" Feng uttered a loud cry and choked back a sob, tears streaming down his cheeks. He held the half taro root in his hand, his lips trembling, no longer able to speak.

"I'm sorry," Mao said with a sigh. "I shouldn't have shouted at you."

"No, no, Comrade Chairman. It's not that.... I took this taro root out of your mouth. You need sleep. You must go to bed. Please do, I beg of you."

Mao smiled half-heartedly. He raised his right hand over his head and drew two circles in the air above it, saying, "The world's turned upside down, it's turned upside down." Then looking at Feng, he added, "All right, Feng, don't cry. I'll do what you say. I'm going to bed."

Stewed Pork: Mao's Favourite Dish

According to Mao, someone who loves hot pepper is a good revolutionary. Mao liked his pepper roasted, not fried, so that the original flavour, which he relished, would not be lost.

But it is his enthusiasm for stewed pork and live carp which I most vividly remember.

Mao never took tonics, with the exception of stewed pork, if that can be called a tonic.

As I recounted earlier, during the battle at Shajiadian, Mao did not leave his room for three days and two nights, nor did he sleep a wink. When victory was won, with the annihilation of the enemy's thirty-sixth division and more than six thousand enemy troops captured, Mao said to me, "Try to get me a bowl of stewed pork, Yinqiao. And make it fat."

"That's the least you deserve for such a big victory," I said. "I'll get it right away."

"I don't mean that," said Mao, shaking his head wearily. "My brain's been overworked in the past few days. Some fat meat will help refresh it."

When I brought the meat to him, he smelled it long and hard, and with eyes half-closed, he said with satisfaction, "It smells really good." He picked up the chopsticks, and in just a few minutes it was gone.

He put down the bowl. When he found me watching him in surprise, he smiled bashfully like a child. "Couldn't resist the temptation," he said. "I didn't ask too much, did I, compared with the victory we won?"

Suddenly I felt tears welling in my eyes. More than six thousand enemy troops had been captured and all he had asked for was just a bowl of stewed pork. "Not at all," I shook my head vigorously. "In fact, you asked for too little, far too little."

"I don't agree. There isn't any stewed pork for our men at the front. They can only slaughter horses for meat."

That is how I came to know why Mao liked stewed pork. After that I would do everything I could to obtain it for him during a big battle, or when he had to stay up for several nights on end writing.

In the latter part of that year our food supplies ran out. For two months, it was black soya beens every day, which upset our stomachs. To make things worse, those were the months when Mao was extremely busy, no longer differentiating between night and day. At intervals of three to five days, he would engage in a seventy-two-hour "work day," which was "Mao's concept of a day." In addition to directing operations in the various war zones around the country, Mao wrote a large number of monographs, including "The Strategy for the Second Year of the War of Liberation" and "The Manifesto of the People's Liberation Army." The sight of Mao rubbing his forehead hard as he would often do then, disturbed me deeply, but with all the food supplies gone, how could I get him a bowl of stewed pork? Surely I couldn't steal piglets from the peasants, could I?

Then, to my great relief, General He Long sent Mao a chunk of preserved pork from east of the Yellow River. Preserved meat does not make good pork stew, but it tastes good when fried, and a small plate of fried sliced pork would give Mao the nutrition his brain needed.

Mao told me to take the meat away when he saw it on the dinner table. "You're trying to feed me with something good," he said, "but how can I eat it?"

"It's for your brain, so that you can work better," I protested loudly. "It's not meant to be luxury."

"My brain needs nutrition, but you can only do what existing conditions permit; when they change, what you eat to build up your health also changes. Now, how about combing my hair?"

Mao sat back in his chair and closed his eyes. As I massaged his scalp, he told me what nutrition black soya beans contained, which he said, had all the protein his brain required, and what the effects of a good scalp massage were on the brain, such as increasing blood circulation, thereby providing it with sufficient nutrition. But I wished he wouldn't say those things: they only made me all the sadder.

So no one touched the preserved meat again until General Chen Yi came from East China for a meeting before New Year's Day; we treated him with it.

Food supply was no longer a problem after we moved to Xibaipo. But Mao would often work several days and nights at a stretch, directing operations for the three big military campaigns. Concerned about his health, I discussed with the others what we should do to make sure that Mao was properly fed. When Mao learned of this, he said to me, "You're not doing the right thing. I wouldn't have time to eat the kind of food that your're trying to get for me. All I want is a bowl of stewed pork every three days. With that you can be sure I'll defeat Chiang Kai-shek."

I did as Mao instructed, and sure enough he sealed Chiang's doom.

Stewed pork remained Mao's favourite dish after he moved to Beijing. He had no interest in expensive food, and found banquets extremely boring. With respect of entertaining foreign VIPs, he once said, "It doesn't have to be expensive food every time. It's not only wasteful but unnecessary." One day he said to me, "We live in this world, not to eat what it offers us, but in order to make it a better place. That's man's function, and that's what makes him different from animals."

Dr. Xu Tao, Mao's physician, tried on many occasions to persuade him to change his diet, by eating more nutritious food. But each time Mao would shake his head in disagreement. No one could make Mao give up what he insisted on, and he had sound reasons for his insistence. I can never forget what he said on three occasions, on the subject of food.

One day, tapping a bowl of poor quality cooked rice, he looked at Dr. Xu and said, "It'll be a great thing when every peasant in China can afford rice like this. Then you can come to me with all those suggestions of yours."

On another occasion, finding Xu's talk about nutrition tedious, Mao stopped him with a wave of his hand, saying with a frown, "Cut it out! I'm a peasant's son, and have always lived like a peasant ever since I was a child. I'm used to that. So don't try to force me to change my ways, please don't!"

On still another occasion, Mao, looking disapprovingly at Xu from the corner of his eye, said, "Do you think you're the only one who knows anything about dietetics? You may not be in such a good physical shape as I am now, when you reach my age. As far as I know, the not very rich landlords live longer than the very rich capitalists." Then, turning to me, he added what he intended for the doctor: "You can't ignore a doctor's advice, but you shouldn't do everything he tells you either. If you turn a deaf ear to him, you'll pay dearly. But what if you do the opposite? Even I would be finished."

One day after working for more than twenty hours straight, as he often did, Mao went to sleep. When he woke up, I said to him, "You haven't eaten properly for several days, Comrade Chairman."

"Is that so?" Mao blinked his eyes as he drank tea. "Yes, I do feel a bit hungry now. Bring me my meal."

"Dr. Xu has worked out a menu for you, but I haven't been able...."

"Forget the menu. Give me stewed pork."

"But...."

"You can leave now," Mao dismissed me with a wave of his big hand and took up his pen. "Let me know when it's ready."

I left quietly. When I was about to tell the cook to prepare the food, Jiang Qing saw me. She was holding a book in her hand and was strolling in the courtyard near her room. She beckoned to me and I went up to her.

"The chairman wants to eat now?" she asked in a low voice.

"Yes," I said, nodding. "He wants stewed pork."

"No more stewed pork for him. Why always stewed pork when we can feed him with something better, like chicken or fish?" She looked at me, and I noticed a suggestion of reproach in her eyes. "The chairman hasn't had a decent meal for several days. What did he eat yesterday?"

"Yesterday.... Only two mugs of oatmeal."

"The day before yesterday?"

"Zhang said he cooked a mug of noodles for him."

"You're not doing your job properly. That electric stove and enamel mug of yours! They belong to the garbage heap!" She said angrily. Then pointing at me: "Tell the cooks to follow the menu recommended by the doctor. Dr. Xu has complained the weekly menu is seldom followed, not even for three meals."

"But the chairman says to forget it. He asks for nothing but stewed pork."

"I won't hear any more of your nonsense! Don't give him stewed pork. What's so wonderful about it? I wonder if this country bumpkin will ever change his ways."

I could say no more. When Mao was fighting in northern Shaanxi, Jiang Qing had once driven him into a rage when she called him a country bumpkin. But she was our boss and I couldn't afford to argue with her. Besides, I, too, wanted to feed Mao with something better.

Mao came to the table when I told him the meal was ready, I stood in waiting.

Mao sat down without taking his eyes away from the newspaper he was reading. He had the habit of reading whilst he ate. With his eyes on the newspaper, he reached for the bamboo chopsticks, picked them up from where he knew he would find them, stood them on end and was about to dig them into his bowl. I watched nervously, but when I saw Jiang Qing reach out from across the table and put a piece of fish in his bowl, I relaxed a bit, believing I could count on her for an explanation.

"What?" Mao looked from behind the newspaper at the table. "Where's the stewed pork?"

I didn't make any response; I just stood there motionless, looking straight in front of me, silent.

"Where's the stewed pork?" Mao turned to me. I couldn't remain silent any longer, but I couldn't look in Jiang Qing's direction either, still less refer the question to her. So I stalled for time by swallowing loudly. Three seconds passed, and Jiang Qing still remained silent. At last I stammered: "I, I didn't get it."

"Why not?" Mao asked in a loud angry voice. "Why didn't you do what I told you?"

I lowered my head in silence. I still had to keep my eyes away from Jiang Qing, or she would have been made the target, but I still hoped that she would come to my rescue.

She never did.

"Speak! Why didn't you do what I told you?" Mao was angry now. "All I asked for was a bowl of stewed pork. Did I ask too much?"

Now I realized that Jiang Qing had betrayed me, leaving me to face the music alone. It was a painful realization, made worse by my inability to say anything by way of explanation. Large tears trickled down my cheeks, tears of bitterness and resentment. But I didn't make any move and was determined to keep my mouth shut.

Mao, who didn't like to see a man cry, grew uneasy. "Forget it! Just remember: do what I tell you in future," he murmured. "Now stop crying if you don't want to spoil my appetite."

He only took a few mouthfuls before putting down the chopsticks. When he rose to leave he said, "Come with me."

"Tell me what happened," Mao asked as soon as we returned to his bedroom. He must have sensed something was wrong; he could tell it from my tears and the fact that Jiang Qing never said a word all that while. So what did he want to know?

"Why ask me? You know what happened." I began to cry again.

"I want to hear it from you," said Mao, growing impatient. "Come on! There's only you and me here. You're not going to refuse me, are you? Tell me. Everything."

I did.

"That's good! I'm glad you've stopped crying. If you have a grievance, air it to someone. It makes you feel better. If you hadn't told me all that, you'd still be crying."

Mao's words eased my mind and made me feel embarrassed at the same time. I must have looked silly when I moved my lips. Suddenly Mao's countenance fell. With an air of finality he said angrily, "She's right; I am a country bumpkin. I'm a peasant's son, and I have the habits of a peasant. If this city bumpkin of a woman doesn't want to share the dishes with me, she doesn't have to. From now on, she will eat from her pot and I from mine. I won't permit any more interference from her. That's final."

Mao always meant what he said, and expected it to be carried out to the letter unless he changed his mind. Whatever he said had to be done, and it had to be done exactly "as told" or the offenders would "be punished pending investigation." His reasoning being: "It has to be that way or I'd set a bad example."

That's when Mao and Jiang Qing stopped sharing their food. Even when they ate at the same table, as they sometimes did, Mao would never touch her food, but Jiang Qing would, from time to time, help herself to Mao's peppery dishes. Mao loved hot food, and Jiang Qing didn't want to be left out.

The other thing Mao liked to eat was carp. Once, in Yangjiagou in northern Shaanxi, Zhou, the cook, prepared a dish with two of the carp which General He Long had sent to Mao. Jiang Qing, who had brought her daughter, Li Ne, back from east of the Yellow River, gave the largest fish to Mao, saying that with his brain overworked, he deserved it after eating black soya beans for so long. She kept the small one for herself and Li Ne.

During the meal I waited on Mao whilst Han Guixin, Li Ne's nurse, who later became my wife, took care of the girl. Like her nurse, Li Ne had eaten nothing better than boiled black soya beans for every meal, so the sight of the fish made her mouth water. Jiang Qing picked a piece of the fish for her and with the other ends of her chopsticks picked another piece for Han. Han tried to decline the offer, but when Li Ne insisted she complied. Jiang Qing went on serving them until the fish was finished. I saw tears in Han's eyes; at that time there was *camaraderie* between them.

Mao helped himself to the fish and black soya beans whilst reading documents, deep in thought. He didn't offer me any of the fish, and the thought of sharing it with him never even crossed my mind.

When he rose from the table, he pointed at the carp, saying, "It's for you, Yinqiao."

"Oh, no, thanks...."

"I'm not a sick man, and I didn't touch the other side."

"I don't mean that. I was thinking of keeping it for your next meal...."

"Don't keep it. I don't eat leftover fish."

He left.

Jiang Qing finished her black beans in a few quick mouthfuls, and left with her daughter and Han; they wanted to stay out of the way so that I wouldn't feel too shy to eat what Mao had offered me.

Mao had not touched the other side of the fish. It was the best fish I've ever eaten. He didn't save it for me for the reason which he gave; I had seen him eat what was left of a fish before and I was to see him do the same thing again at a later date. He just intended that part of the fish for me, because he knew the food situation was deplorable at the time.

Mao never left a morsel of food in his bowl, or on the table uneaten. In his youth, he had eaten cooked rice, cold, or not fresh enough for others, or after it had turned acrid. He did that in order to toughen himself up physically, in preparation for hard times. But with respect of fish he could be very particular.

In late 1948, Anastas Ivanovich Mikoyan was sent to Xibaipo, on a secret mission, by Stalin and the Central Committee of the Soviet Communist Party. He met with Mao many times and the other four members of the Politburo: Zhu De, Liu Shaoqi, Zhou Enlai and Ren Bishi. These meetings took place in Mao's room. Stalin, it was said, was trying to dissuade Mao from sending the People's Liberation Army across the Yangtse River, for fear of U.S. armed intervention, which he believed would be the consequence of such an action. But Mao, a fiercely independent man, never allowed anyone to lead him by the nose. His decision and firm resolve on that issue are well known to all. What I am about to relate are some side-lights of Mikoyan's visit.

Mikoyan looked quite impressive in his fine clothes and fur cap. By comparison, the five most important members of the Chinese Communist Party wore nothing better than shabby old cotton-padded military uniforms and Mao even sported a few patches on his apparel. The Mikoyan party had brought a lot of canned food and alcoholic beverages in fancy bottles with them, whilst all we could offer them were the chickens which we had raised and fish, stewed or stir-fried, from the nearby Hutuo River. During their week-long stay at Xibaipo, they dined with Mao and the other standing members of the Politburo twice. Mikoyan guzzled spirits from large glasses, as if it were water. Mao couldn't drink or he would become flushed. Zhu De had a sore throat. Ren Bishi was suffering from hypertension. Liu Shaoqi drank, but not much, and from tiny cups only. Zhou Enlai was a heavy drinker by Chinese standard, but he would never dream of downing spirits in large gulps like Mikoyan. At table they talked amicably, but, as I noticed, Mao, a man imbued with a strong sense of national pride, didn't want to see the Soviets steal the show even on matters like drinking. Soon he asked for the last course to be served.

At one point, Mikoyan said, "We all like Chinese cuisine, but we don't know how to prepare Chinese food. When you win your revolution, we'll send our men here to learn Chinese cooking so there'll be more variety in our food."

To this Mao responded with a smile: "I believe the world will find that China has given it two great gifts: Chinese medicinal herbs and Chinese food."

At another point, one of the Soviet guests, holding his fork above a plate of stewed fish, asked, "Is it fresh? Is it live fish?" Only when he was told that it was, did he sink his fork into the food.

Mao glanced at him casually and said nothing. A year later when he was in Moscow on a visit, the order he gave to the Chinese cook who had accompanied him was strict: "The fish which you cook for me must be live fish. If they give you dead fish, throw it back at them."

The Soviets did come along with fish. It was brought to the cook by a colonel of the special guard, in the company of his aides. It was a dead fish. Acting on Mao's order to "throw it back," the cook rejected it. The colonel was surprised, but didn't know the reason, until an interpreter explained to him that Mao only ate live fish.

"We'll fetch one right away," the colonel promised.

Soon it became known in Kremlin that Mao was very particular about the fish he ate: it had to be carp and live carp.

What Plagues Mao

Two things troubled Mao almost all his life: bowel movement and sleep. The habitual constipation from which he suffered was so acute that sometimes he only had a bowel movement once a week.

Less than two hours after Mao and I came to that agreement about having me loaned to him for six months, we reached another agreement, that being to assist him when he relieved himself.

That night Mao was studying a military map, marking it with a pencil and thinking, when he suddenly grimaced. After waiting for a while, he took a piece of paper and left the room. I followed him, my hand on my Mauser pistol, and as he headed for the open fields, I kept a watchful eye on the surroundings, but I didn't know what he was going to do.

It was a quiet night. The rain had made the fields soggy. Mao stopped at a small mound and loosened his belt. When I knew he was going to relieve himself, I relaxed a bit.

Mao squatted down. I kept a watch round-about, concealing myself in the darkness. I don't recall how long he remained in that position. When he rose at last, he did not walk away immediately; squatting down too long must have numbed his legs, and when he moved away his steps were unsteady.

"Why didn't you use the toilet, Comrade Chairman?" I asked.

"It stinks. The smell there hurts your brain," Mao grumbled.

"I've seen you break lumps of manure with your hands, wipe off the bits and smoke, when you were talking with the peasants. The smell of manure didn't seem to bother you then."

"Times are different," he said. Then he asked me, "Shall we reach another agreement? Every time I want to relieve myself, you grab a shovel and dig a hole for me. What do you say?"

"Agreed," I said. That's what I did from then on, even after Mao moved to Zhongnanhai in Beijing: I would dig a hole and fill it up again.

It was only after Zhou Enlai had a toilet designed and built especially for Mao, in his bedroom, that I was relieved of the shovel duty.

Mao conceived the idea of wiping out the enemy's thirty-sixth division at Shajiadian, on one such occasion after relieving himself. He told Zhou Enlai of his idea and very soon they had worked out the plans for the campaign, which were taken to General Peng Dehuai by Ma Hanrong and Shao Changhe of the guard; they could not wait for the telephone lines to be set up. It was a decisive battle in Northwest China, "a turning point," as Mao called it.

The constipation from which Mao suffered was, according to the doctor's theory, caused by the excessive amount of hot peppers Mao ate. So Mao was not allowed to eat any more hot pepper. After a few days, Mao, who loved hot food, began to crave it. One day, when a young man, new to the bodyguard, announced to Mao that lunch was ready, Mao enquired, "Is there any hot pepper?"

To the young man, "hot pepper" pronounced in Mao's heavy Hunan accent, sounded very much like "candle." So he answered, "No."

"Give me some hot pepper," Mao was a bit displeased, "or I'm not going to have any lunch."

Soon the bodyguard returned with a candle, wondering why Mao wanted a candle in the daytime. "The candle's here, Comrade Chairman," he reported timidly.

"Is it roasted?" Mao asked, without removing his eyes from a document he was reading.

"Roasted? How?" the young bodyguard was even more puzzled.

"Do it over fire, that's what I mean," Mao was growing impatient.

Too afraid to ask any more questions, the young man turned to leave. But since he couldn't understand why it had to be roasted, he halted at the door, and summoning all his remaining courage, asked, "But it will melt, won't it?"

"Don't let it melt. Roast it dry, whole, no oil...." Now Mao saw the candle the young bodyguard was holding in his hand. He was surprised, and then burst out laughing. "I mean hot pepper, the thing with a sharp tip that grows in the fields."

Now the bodyguard understood what Mao wanted. He laughed, too.

So Mao went on eating hot pepper and suffering from constipation. The doctor recommended bees' honey, which, he said, would relieve him of the discomfort.

But Mao didn't follow his advice; he liked peppery, salty food too much to change to sweet things. But the experience he gleaned from his long "struggle" with constipation taught him a few things about how to combat the disease, such as eating a lot of vegetables stir-fried whole, so that their long fibres, which aid digestion, would remain intact. That's why his vegetables were not sliced, and why he could sometimes pick all of them, either small cabbage or spinach, from a plate with one sweep of his chopsticks, and eat them in big mouthfuls. As it happens, vegetables prepared in this way are an effective cure for constipation, and the nutrition which they contain is not lost. Even the doctor became convinced of its effectiveness: he passed it on to his children.

If constipation plagued Mao, insomnia troubled him even more.

All his life Mao struggle "to get to sleep"; he could never do without sleeping pills.

There were times when Mao respected the natural cycle of a day, following a twenty-four-hour schedule for work and rest. And there were times when he did not. Then he would sleep in the morning and work in the afternoon and at night, a habit he developed during two decades of war, when he had to deal with an enemy much superior in strength, and was forced to operate only by night, in order to avoid bomb-raids by enemy aircraft, a habit which was difficult for him to break.

Thus, most of the time, Mao defied the natural cycle of a day, and went by "Mao's concept of a day," a twenty-eight-hour day. I don't know who invented that term, nor do I know when and where it first came into use. Anyway, it was like this: Suppose you go to bed at seven in the morning and get up at eleven; then you start to work and keep at it until about ten o'clock the next morning when you go to bed again; at three in the afternoon you get up again and another day begins. The four-hour overlap stretches the day to twenty-eight hours.

When there was a major battle to fight, an important meeting to call, a much-needed article to write, an emergency or a crisis to attend to, Mao could work two or three, even four or five, days without sleeping a wink. The superhuman energy he displayed on such occasions was quite incredible.

To ease the physical and mental strain caused by constant over-work, Mao needed to be able to rest better than anyone else, when he did go to sleep, but often he was too excited to sleep. This disturbed both Mao and those of us in the bodyguard, and a joint effort by his doctor and nurses, those of us in the guard and bodyguard and Mao himself, would be required to put him to sleep. Such an effort, involving so many people, was in a certain sense the most important aspect of our work, as well as the most important aspect of Mao's life.

Before Mao retired, he would first put down his pen and whatever document he had been reading; this was sometimes followed by a ten-minute walk and sometimes not, and then he would say to the bodyguards on duty, "I'm going to bed."

Mao's low, but deep voice always lent significance to that verbal message. Immediately the bodyguards would inform the guards: "The chairman is going to sleep."

Instantly the courtyard would fall silent. No footsteps were to be heard, no visitors allowed. During the war years, Zhou Enlai shared a courtyard with Mao. When he met Mao's bodyguards, the first thing he asked was: "Is the chairman sleeping?" He would usually clear his throat loudly when he got up, but if he was told that "the chairman is sleeping," he would cover his mouth with his hand and wait until he had returned to his cave-room and closed the door. In Zhongnanhai, Zhou had to pass by the road behind Mao's residence on his way home. When Mao was sleeping, that road was closed to motor traffic. Zhou's car had to slide noiselessly by with its engine cut and the lights turned off.

Mao used to take a tub-bath before going to bed: with his muscles relaxed thus, he could go to sleep more easily. He did that until 1956; until it was feared that with his blood vessels hardened due to advancing age, hot baths might present a health hazard for him. So then he washed himself by having his body rubbed down with water. He enjoyed having his back rubbed in this way, especially after working for two or three days at a stretch. He liked it to be rubbed hard, believing this was good for his health, since it made the blood circulate better and took away his fatigue.

Mao enjoyed talking with the bodyguards during these rub-down sessions. Some of the bodyguards were good conversationalists like Mao, others were not. These were moments during which Mao could relax and was cheerful and very much himself. He talked about everything under the sun, cracking a joke or two from time to time; when a bodyguard broke wind, there would be a round of laughter.

"Did I hear something, Feng?"

"I'm sorry, Comrade Chairman. I, I broke ... wind."

"You didn't, did you? You complained. I should apologize to you, not you to me. It's my fault for making you so tired during the last few days."

"No, I didn't complain, Comrade Chairman. I broke wind."

"You didn't. You complained. You were right to complain." Then, in his thick Hunan accent, Mao would continue rhythmically, "When people have a complaint to make, there is wind to break. Break it boldly to the chairman so you'll live happily."

They would have a good laugh at this.

In such a happy frame of mind, Mao would return to his bedroom, take sleeping pills from the bodyguard on duty, and get into bed. Then, propping himself up against the blanket on the railing, he would continue with his work, reading documents and writing instructions on them, whilst the bodyguard, sitting on a chair or on the edge of the bed, would massage his legs and feet. He would rub them hard as it would still be some while before Mao could fall asleep. There was no need to do the back, for it had already been thoroughly massage during the rub-down.

After about thirty minutes to an hour, the sleeping pills would start to take effect, and Mao would begin to show signs of relaxation. He would then put the documents away and take a second dose of pills from the bodyguard.

No longer working, Mao would slide slowly from the railing until he lay supine on the bed. He would start reading a newspaper or a book from amongst the stacks of books that ran the entire length of the bed on the other side. Sometimes it would be a picture-book—he liked picture-books. If he was not reading anything, he would chat with the bodyguards. During these conversations Mao, no longer cracking jokes, would listen to them when they told him of their family woes, or what was on their minds; ask them their opinions about something or someone; or tell them about his past. Often, with eyes half-closed, and speaking softly, Mao would tell me and the other bodyguards about his childhood and youth, his parents, his feelings. Once, touching the back of my hand, he asked, "Are you afraid of me, Yinqiao?"

"No."

"What about the others? The other bodyguards?"

"Generally speaking, no. There may be a few exceptions, but I'm not sure."

"They needn't be. Tell them Mao Zedong is not a man to be afraid of. Tell them it never occurred to him that he would one day become the chairman of the Communist Party. He was just like any of you when he was your age. All he wanted to do then was teach in a school, and he found teaching a tough job.... So why should he be feared by anyone?"

As Mao said that, his voice began to trail off. When that happened, it was a sign that he was ready to fall asleep. The massage should continue but the touches should be light. Then Mao would close his eyes and begin to breathe evenly. At this moment, whether or not Mao sank into sleep depended upon the bodyguards. One time, I did the wrong thing when I stopped massaging and edged away from the bed quietly. Just as I was going to tiptoe out of the room Mao seized my hand.

"Don't go away yet. Stay with me for just a little while longer...."

When I saw his eyelashes quiver between the slits of his half-open eyes, I realized that I had misjudged. A sense of guilt gripped me: I had stopped too soon and delayed his sleep.

The moment when Mao was on the verge of sleep was the moment when the bodyguard massaging him had to be extremely careful with his touches. Once, Feng rubbed so hard that he hurt Mao just as sleep was creeping over him. As expected, Mao raged.

"What's the matter with you?" Opening his eyes, Mao kicked in a great annoyance. "Go away! Get your chief here. I don't want you."

I hurried to Mao's bedroom and massaged him in Feng's place. It was a long time before I succeeded in putting him to sleep.

When I left Mao, Feng came to me with a long face. "The chairman's sacked me," he told me.

"Don't worry," I said. "I'll talk to him. He's sleeping now. He'll change his mind after he's had a good sleep."

After Mao got up, I said to him, "Feng is a good bodyguard, Comrade Chairman. Shall we let him stay on and see what happens?"

As Mao was now in a better frame of mind, he nodded his consent. "Okay. Let him stay."

Ordinarily two doses of sleeping pills would be enough to put Mao to sleep. If something important had happened and kept him awake, he would need one more dose. But sometimes even three doses were not enough. That was when he would easily become irritable and the bodyguards had to be extra careful so as not to annoy him.

Generally, when Mao threw a tantrum, it was because he had been unable to get to sleep. But insomnia was not always the cause of his anger; usually, it just left him moody. Once the strain on his mind, which was causing his insomnia was lifted, he could easily fall asleep.

During the years I was his bodyguard, there were many occasions when Mao took three doses of sleeping pills, but still could not go to sleep.

One day, in 1949, after taking the third dose, he got up from bed and began to pace the room: he was trying to decide whether he should send the army across the Yangtse River. After he had informed the other standing members of the Politburo of his decision to send the troops across the river, he went to sleep without taking any more pills.

Another such incident occurred in 1950, when he was considering whether or not we should join the Korean war to resist the U.S. and aid Korea. After taking three doses of sleeping pills he was still unable to sleep. Finally, he got up and called a meeting in the east room of his residence. The meeting, joined by Comrades Peng Dehuai and Peng Zhen, and Lin Biao and Gao Gang, in addition to the five standing members of the Politburo, lasted from five or six o'clock in the afternoon until midnight, in a smoke-filled room. After it was decided at the meeting to send our men to Korea, and which armies were to be dispatched and under whose command, Mao got to sleep.

For several days during October of that year, just before the Chinese People's Volunteers crossed the Yalu River, Mao was unable to sleep. One day, General Nie Rongzhen came to the east room, asking to see Mao. He did not take the seat which I offered him, but walked up and down the room whilst he waited. When I entered Mao's bedroom, I saw

117

him tossing in his bed: the third dose of sleeping pills had failed to take effect on him.

"Comrade Nie Rongzhen's here, Comrade Chairman," I told Mao. "He's in the office room waiting to see you."

Mao got up immediately, saying, "Let's go!"

I helped him on with his clothes and followed him to the east room. When Nie saw Mao, he took a step forward, clicked his heels and saluted Mao. "I've come to report to you, Comrade Chairman," he said, "that the Volunteers have reached the other side of the Yalu River."

When Nie left half an hour later, after reporting to Mao on the details, Mao said to me briefly, "To bed."

As soon as I put him to bed, he lay down on his back, and when I turned to give him water and sleeping pills, I found, to my surprise, that he was already lying in perfect repose. I heard a light snore, and then in record time Mao was sound asleep.

That day in 1956, when Zhou Enlai was expected to return from a trip abroad, Mao was in bed the whole morning, but was unable to sleep, although he had stayed up working the previous night and had taken sleeping pills. Nine times he opened his eyes and asked, "Has Zhou Enlai returned?" "Hasn't the premier returned yet?"

In the afternoon, when I told Mao that the premier had come home, Mao turned over in his bed and fell asleep. He did not go to the airport to meet Zhou. That trip Zhou made was said to be a secret one.

On September 30, 1959, when sleeping pills once again failed to put Mao to sleep, he got up and drank cup after cup of tea whilst chain-smoking. In the afternoon, he ate a mug of oatmeal which he told the bodyguard to prepare for him and ordered hot pepper and preserved toufu to go with it. In the evening he held talks with Nikita Khrushchev in Zhongnanhai. Khrushchev had just finished talks with the U.S. president at Camp David.

I have the impression that deep in his heart Mao must have felt lonely sometimes. He had a family, but he didn't see them very often. We were the only ones he saw every day. He treated us like his children, but as bodyguards, we were not able to give him the love and care that only a family can give.

Mao Declares the Founding of New China

The several decades of armed struggle, waged by Mao Zedong and his comrades-in-arms, ended victoriously with the birth of New China on October 1, 1949.

At about half past six that morning, Mao said to me, "I'm going to bed, Yinqiao." He seldom went to bed that early.

He took a bath, and when he got into bed, said, "There's nothing more I want for the moment. You may go now." So I left him and returned to the bodyguards' office without massaging him.

An electric bell on Mao's bed connected his bedroom with the office. In the office, besides chairs and desks, there was a bed. As I said earlier, there were two bodyguards on duty for each shift; for the one attending Mao it was a twenty-four-hour shift with no sleep; the other one, his assistant, who attended Jiang Qing, could sleep when he was not needed. I was on the twenty-four-hour shift that day, so I had sat up all night, and had to stay awake throughout the morning.

Although Mao had gone to bed earlier than usual, my experience told me that he would toss sleeplessly in bed until noon. So I would have to wake him up before he pressed the bell-button: missing the founding ceremony of New China would be a "historic mistake."

At one o'clock in the afternoon, upon hearing no bell, I went to Mao's bedroom.

"Comrade Chairman, Comrade Chairman," I tried to wake him up.

"What?" Mao opened his eyes, and when he saw me, let out an "ah" and inhaled noisily.

"It's one o'clock now." I put the blanket on the railing, shoved the pillow underneath it and helped him up so that he could lean on the cushion. After wiping his face with a wet towel which I brought him from the bathroom, he looked refreshed. Then he took another deep breath.

With his left hand he picked up the cup of hot tea which I had placed on the bedside cupboard, and as he sipped the tea he reached habitually for the newspapers in the bed with his free hand, picking up one that had been published the previous day. As I did not want to disturb him whilst he was reading, I left quietly, in order to prepare the "formal dress" which he was to wear for the big event.

It was a uniform; the material, from Ye Zilong, was woollen khaki, the colour used for U.S. army officers. It had been made by the tailor Wang Ziqing, a student who had returned from France. He was then working in what was later to become the Leimeng Tailor Shop, in Wangfujing Street. Wang was Mao and Jiang Qing's tailor, and I also had him make a few clothes for Mao's children, Li Min and Li Ne.

"It's now half past one, Comrade Chairman," I reminded Mao, getting him to put down the newspaper. When he got up from bed, I helped him on with the uniform, stretching and smoothing it down here and there until I was satisfied. Then I told him lunch was ready.

Mao, who was a fast eater, finished the meal in just a few minutes, and after a short rest, he left for Qinzheng Hall in Zhongnanhai, arriving there at two o'clock, to join Zhu De, Liu Shaoqi, Zhou Enlai, Ren Bishi, Zhang Lan, Li Jishen, Soong Ching Ling and Gao Gang in the Hall, for the first session of the council of the Central People's Government. At the meeting they were inaugurated as members of the council and the founding of the Central People's Government was declared. Beaming and in high spirits, they chatted with delight for about ten minutes after the meeting.

At ten to three, the leaders of the country got into their cars in front of Qinzheng Hall. Their motorcade left Zhongnanhai by the east gate and arrived at the back of Tiannanmen in five minutes. After they assembled, they started for the rostrum with Mao leading the way. As the tunnel to Tiananmen had not been built then, I assisted Mao up the one hundred steps. At three o'clock, they appeared atop Tiananmen as scheduled.

The open space, now known as Tiananmen Square, was then in the shape of a huge cross and could hold 200,000 to 300,000 people. It lay between the Imperial Ancestral Temple to the east, and Zhongshan Park to the west, linked by an avenue running down the middle, beginning at Tiananmen Gate in the north, and ending at Zhonghua Gate, at the southern tip. That day the place was a heaving sea of red flags, and with the crowds dressed in green, blue, yellow, grey and white, although a little drab by present-day standards, at that time, looked like a multi-coloured flower-bed immaculately laid out. Flanking the marble bridges in front of Tiananmen were two large platforms, one for the directors of the parade and the other for the Soviet delegates.

After Mao had taken his place, Secretary-General, Lin Boqu, declared the beginning of the ceremony. Mao walked up to the microphone, taking in the scene down below in that vast cross, where paraders stood quietly under fluttering red flags, waiting for the great historic moment to come. Then with a slight heave of his shoulders and chest, Mao declared in a solemn, resonant voice that echoed and re-echoed like spring thunder throughout every corner of the 9,600,000 square kilometres:

"The Central People's Government of the People's Republic of China is now established!"

The declaration was immediately greeted with thunderous shouts of joy up and down Tiananmen. Mao, his eyes shining brightly, looked solemn and composed. Then as scheduled, he pressed a button, and a huge five-star red flag began to rise up a pole, which stood tall in front of the foundations of the Monument to the People's Heroes, watched by thousands of eager, upturned faces.

Mao watched the flag being hoisted with a heaving chest: the People's Republic, of which he was the founding father, had now been born. Looking at the hoisted flag, Mao found himself saying, in a loud voice, "It looks great!"

Mao's comment was immediately followed by earth-shaking salvos from fifty-four guns, the highlight of this great and solemn occasion, expressing national unity. The fifty-four guns were intended to represent the fifty-four groups which constituted the Political Consultative Conference, and the twenty-eight salutes which they fired, symbolized the steel-like strength of a united nation.

Mao read out the First Proclamation of the Chinese People's Government, to all parts of China and the entire world. This clearly declared the Central People's Government to be the sole legitimate government of the people of China, willing to establish diplomatic relations with foreign countries on the principles of equality, mutual benefit and mutual respect for one another's territory and sovereignty.

Next there was a military parade. Commander-in-Chief Zhu De, flanked by the commanders of the four field armies, He Long, Liu Bocheng, Chen Yi and Luo Ronghuan, gave the order for the parade to commence.

Four divisions of troops, headed by General Nie Rongzhen in his command car, marched past the reviewing stand in front of the marble bridges beneath the Tiananmen rostrum, in company formations from east to west. The infantrymen that led the march were followed by cavalrymen and tanks, heavy artillery and military trucks. As they passed, the huge space was silent, apart from the flutter of red flags, the music of "The March of the People's Liberation Army" and the reverberating steps of the soldiers. Then came the air-force fly-over, at which point the leaders in the rostrum and the crowds below, burst into deafening cheers, greeting the airplanes with thunderous applause.

The parade went on for three hours, until dusk.

When night fell, the place was lit by numerous colourful lanterns and torches; their burgundy, red, pink, gold, orange and bright yellow flames resembling silk threads criss-crossing each other in a huge brocade; a brocade woven from the people's aspirations and joys. The night air was filled with songs and the shouts of slogans, the loudest of which was: "Long live Chairman Mao!"

From three o'clock in the afternoon, when he arrived at the rostrum, until ten o'clock that night, Mao remained standing, declining the offer of a chair brought to him by one attendant, Yin Xinsheng. He kept his arms uplifted the whole time, alternately acknowledging the cheers, in all solemnity, or waving vigorously. He looked composed and genial, but when the shouts reached a crescendo, he grew so excited that he leaned over the railing in front of him and waved at the crowds. Then he shouted into the microphone: "Long live our comrades!" "Long live the people!"

When those in the parade realized that their leader was still up there, and was speaking to them over the PA system, they changed their minds. Instead of leaving Tiananmen by the east and west exit routes, they returned and swarmed onto the marble bridges beneath the rostrum, shouting out their best wishes to Mao with all their might:

"Long live Chairman Mao!" "Long live Chairman Mao!"

In response, Mao called out from the rostrum: "Long live our comrades!" "Long live the people!"

This heralded the climax. The crowds, dancing or just jumping, were wild with joy. Chen Yi commented loudly in his excitement: "This is what I call the experience of a lifetime!"

After the founding ceremony I put away the uniform which Mao had worn that day, reserving it for special occasions.

At that time, our army apparel was not uniform in style. The uniforms which our men wore for the ceremonial march into Beijing were replicas of U.S. army uniforms captured from military depots of the Kuomintang. To us, any khaki uniform was a military uniform; so the one which Mao wore for the founding ceremony was also regarded as such. Later on, I had Wang Ziqing make three more such uniforms for Mao in material of the same colour as that provided by Ye Zilong.

After the signing of the armistice at the end of the Korean war, Mao said to us, "It's time we stopped wearing army uniforms. I'm not going to wear them any longer, and neither are you."

So we shed our army uniforms, and Mao never put on the one he had worn for the founding ceremony again.

Early in 1954, several months after Mao told us to change out of our army apparel, Mao said to Jiang Qing, "I don't have any more use for those khaki uniforms. You can give them to anyone you like."

One day Jiang Qing sent for me. When I entered her office I saw the four uniforms on a table. She said, "These clothes are yours now, Yinqiao. The chairman doesn't need them any more."

I thanked her and picked them up to look at them. As I was about to leave, Jiang Qing said, "You may give two of them to Sun Yong if you like."

Sun was a deputy commander of the bodyguard in charge of those on compound duty. Jiang's words made me think of something, and I decided to keep the one Mao had worn for the founding ceremony for myself. My decision was not based on its historical value, of which I was not then aware; I had only a vague idea that there was something special about it, something special which the other three uniforms did not possess. Besides, it was made with American material, whilst the other three were made from Chinese wollen fabrics, and it was the only one with black-and-white striped sleeve linings. So it had to be the best of the four in quality.

I picked out another one from the remaining three and took them home, giving the rest to Sun Yong.

But the uniform which Mao had worn for the founding ceremony was several sizes too large for me, and I would look ridiculous in it. So I decided to have it taken in. When my wife heard about this, she said half-jokingly and half-seriously, "You can't do a thing like that! That uniform's as sacred as the dragon-robes worn by the emperor* on the day of his enthronement."

"But this is New China," I retorted, "and the chairman has said many times that he's the chairman of the government, a servant of the people, and not an emperor. What do you mean by such talk?"

So I had the uniform, which was of such great historical significance, remade to fit my size. At the time I was glad that I did it because I looked really good in the altered uniform.

In 1967, the Tianjin Museum of History contacted me. They were collecting items of historical importance and offered me a new suit in exchange for the uniform Mao wore on the day he declared the founding of New China. As I was still unaware of the value of that uniform, I thought it was a good bargain and accepted their offer.

It was not until the Central Museum of History was looking for that uniform, after Mao's death, that I realized how foolish I had been: I shouldn't have had it altered, nor swapped it for new clothes. I asked the Tianjin museum to return it to me as requested by the Central Museum, but they refused. So the Central Museum had to make do with one from Sun Yong. It is the uniform now on display at Mao's mausoleum; the accompanying information says that it is what Mao wore for the founding ceremony, which of course is not true.

---

*These were bright yellow silk, embroidered robes, handed down by the ancestors, and worn by the emperor in imperial China, for his enthronement. Later, they would be worn on other grand ceremonial and state occasions. Thus, yellow came to be regarded as a sacred colour, and so it was forbidden for ordinary citizens to wear yellow in the old society.

Mao's Life with Jiang Qing

As far as I could tell during the fifteen years I was Mao's bodyguard, there was intense disagreement as well as love between Mao and his wife, Jiang Qing. Most of the time they lived happily together, but the many clashes between them overshadowed their marriage.

No one is born wicked; wickedness is something which is acquired. Such human degradation can be a slow process with some people, and a fast one with others. There have been many cases where, as the saying goes, "a hero turns into a criminal overnight." Jiang Qing should be judged in the light of this process, if the judgment is to stand the test of time.

I am not going to give an account of how Jiang Qing became a wicked woman; for I don't know anything about that. I worked for Mao for only fifteen years, and I think it was during the "cultural revolution" that Jiang sank into depravity. By that time I had left Mao, and I have never met Jiang since. What I am going to relate here are the few things that I do know about her.

With the whole country entering a war against the Japanese aggressors, following the Marco Polo Bridge Incident* on July 7, 1937, Yan'an** attracted a lot of patriots. But life there was so hard, and the work so demanding, that quite a few of them, finding it too much to endure, left shortly afterwards. Jiang Qing didn't; she stayed on, a fact that should be viewed positively. But of course, that didn't mean she

*Lugouqiao (Reed Gully Bridge) in Chinese; Marco Polo Bridge in English, in western Beijing, was the scene of the first exchange between Japanese aggressors and Chinese forces of resistance, marking the beginning of the War of Resistance Against Japan.

**Yan'an, in Shaanxi Province, was the revolutionary headquarters of Mao Zedong and the Communist Party, directing operations during the War of Resistance Against Japan, and during the civil war with the Kuomintang, whose headquarters was the ancient capital of Xi'an.

was a staunch revolutionary. Mao said to her face, many times, "You're a bourgeois egoist, period," and "You will never rid yourself of the mentality of the exploiting class." These criticisms impressed me deeply: Mao wouldn't have talked like that if Jiang had not been inspired by the revolution, nor would Mao have said it, if Jiang had indeed been a seasoned revolutionary.

At the time there were many young women in Yan'an*. Quite a few of them were outstanding in character, ability and physical appearance and later married high-ranking cadres and army officers. As the leader of the Party and the army, Mao was undoubtedly the most eligible; in fact, he had many admirers amongst these young women. This being the case, Mao would not have picked one that was not eligible to be his wife, as some later articles would have us believe.

Jiang Qing was quite pretty then. She wore a ribbon in her thick, jet black hair. The fringe she sported had a casual kind of beauty about it, and the hair beneath the ribbon was either braided or cascaded all the way down to her shoulders. Her large eyes shone brightly underneath pleasantly arched brows. She had a straight and elegant nose, and her mouth, although a bit on the wide side, still added beauty to her face when it was closed.

Then Jiang was a movie star to us, and she was also good at Beijing opera. Her acting in "The Fisherman's Revenge"** was very well liked by the leaders of the Central Committee, including Mao. Li Ne learned theatre arts from her, and she would often entertain Mao and the men in the army with her performances. When our men were fighting in northern Shaanxi, Li Ne's performances provided a welcome break in a life of intense struggle.

Jiang Qing's handwriting was excellent, especially when she used the regular script.*** Speaking of Li Ne learning calligraphy, Mao once said, "I'm not a calligrapher, her mother is. She qualifies to teach her

---

*Many young patriots volunteered to go to Yan'an at this time, either to fight alongside the Communists, or to entertain or service the troops. Thus the influx of young women as well as men.

**A very famous Beijing opera.

***Here the author is referring to the old style of Chinese calligraphy, using more complicated characters than the modern, simplified version, which was not introduced until much later on.

penmanship." So Li Ne owes her training in calligraphy to her mother, and she is now a good artist, too.

Jiang also liked a fiery horse and enjoyed taming it; there was no horse too wild for her. When we were in northern Shaanxi, her steed, a gift from General He Long, was a dark grey one and was extremely vicious. She was said to like challenging others to horse races when she was in Yan'an. That was just like her: she was a woman determined to win and given to showing off. Once she was seeing Zhou Enlai off on his way to the Central Party School where he was to give a lecture to the students there, after he had seen Mao for instructions. On their way from Yangjialing, in just such a race, Jiang's horse charged and Zhou was dislodged from his frightened steed, breaking his right arm. This occurred in 1939. According to one theory, this was a conspiracy against Zhou plotted by Jiang. However, this was sheer speculation to which I never gave any credit. Ironically enough, it was precisely this kind of speculation which Jiang and her cohorts engaged in during the "cultural revolution."

Jiang had no interest in guns. Her hobbies included playing cards and knitting. She was very good at knitting; the wollen sweaters she made were rich in beautiful patterns. She was a dress-maker, too. All the dresses and skirts worn by Li Ne were her own hand-work, and they were beautifully cut.

During the war in northern Shaanxi, Jiang wasn't really involved in anything important nor did she do anything evil. Her job then was to look after Mao. To be fair to her, as our boss, Jiang did her job quite well. She managed to stay close to us, giving us haircuts, a few lessons in general knowledge, elementary science and needle-work; and when we were on a march, she would cheer us on a bit and would sometimes ask us a riddle or two. One of her riddles was:

> When do you walk a thousand *li* without ever leaving your room? When do you see an assembly of emperors, ministers and generals? When do you have a son that has a different family name? When do you have a wife whom you love, but don't share the same bed with?
> The answer: when you act on the stage.

Jiang liked to look well-groomed, and she knew how to present herself that way. During the war in northern Shaanxi she stopped wearing her hair loose, but instead put it up in a bun at the nape of her neck. Young girls sought her advice on hair-style, and Jiang, feeling honoured, was always glad to help them. In winter, she wore an army uniform most of the time, but she would sometimes change into a blue cotton-padded jacket that was cut to reveal her figure. In summer she sported a double-breasted cotton jacket which fit well in the waist. She was proud of her fair complexion and slender waist-line. And yet, in spite of all this, Jiang was quite different from other women. She was, after all, a woman conscious of her strong points.

However, her attempts to show off her talents betrayed the flaws and weekness in her character. She was never able to rid herself of these. They seemed to be innate in her, and as they developed from bad to worse, a rupture in her relationship with Mao became inevitable.

Jiang had lived in Shanghai in an open environment, which is not necessarily a bad thing. She desired to be accepted as one of the masses of workers, peasants and soldiers by mingling with them, but she was so haughty, so bossy, so eager to show off, so exceedingly self-centred and selfish, that she never succeeded in doing this; she even failed to understand her husband or share his feelings.

During those days in northern Shaanxi, when we were constantly on the move, with several thousand, sometimes even tens of thousands of enemy troops in persuit, threatening our very survival, Jiang never quarrelled with Mao. After all, it was a time when unity within our own ranks was essential if we were to survive the danger. But when this pressure was lifted, and life became comparatively easier after we moved to Yangjiagou, where we stayed for about six months after winning the victory at Shajiadian, disagreement between Mao and Jiang began to surface. The first such instance that I witnessed was over Li Ne's nurse.

Jiang had made the nurse a gift of all her favourite jackets and red leather shoes upon the very first day of her arrival. The effect which this would have upon their relations later on, was not hard for me to predict; for as far as I am aware, when a woman shows excessive care for another woman the first time they meet, you may expect trouble between them soon.

That was exactly what happened between Jiang and the nurse.

Besides taking care of Li Ne, the nurse mended clothes for Mao. One day, looking at what she had done, Jiang said to her with a sneer, "Look at these stitches! They're terrible."

The nurse was a seventeen-year-old girl and had never done needle-work before. She hung her head in humiliation. But Jiang wouldn't let the matter drop. Pushing her in front of Mao, she said, "Look at the stitches she did, boss. Look at them!" In those days Jiang called Mao boss.

Mao, who was at that moment too preoccupied with his work to be interested, just raised his head a bit, but when he saw from the nurse's face how much Jiang had hurt her feelings, he grew angry.

"What do you mean?" Mao yelled at Jiang. "You fool!" Then, turning to the nurse, he said kindly, "Thank you, nurse. I don't see anything wrong with the stitches."

After the nurse left, Mao lashed out verbally at Jiang: "You're a downright bourgeois egoist...."

Later, Jiang apologized to the young girl: "I didn't mean to hurt your feelings, nurse. I wish I weren't such a rash person. Please don't take it to heart."

Jiang wasn't lying when whe told the nurse she hadn't meant to hurt her: that kind of response was part and parcel of her nature.

Soon after picking on the nurse, she offered to teach her needle-work; a few days later, when she was not satisfied with the nurse's work on a fur-lined jacket, she lashed out again at the poor girl: "Do you call this sewing? It's terrible! Do it again!" But the next day she again offered her apology: "I'm sorry for talking to you like that yesterday. I wish I weren't such a rash person. Please don't take it to heart."

Jiang's apologies rang hollow to me; they were intended to forestall the nurse from taking out any grudges she might hold against Jiang, upon her daughter, Li Ne.

One day during the rectification movement* I was attending Jiang at the dinner-table. She kept on shoving the fish from General He Long into my bowl. She was so insistent that I couldn't possibly refuse her offers. Besides, fish tasted much better than the black soya beans we usually ate at that time.

In the middle of the meal she stopped eating, and, looking at me,

---

*A series of campaigns launched over the years, to rectify incorrect styles of work within the Party. Rectification means the whole Party studying Marxism through criticism and self-criticism. The most famous of these took place in 1942.

gave vent to her ill-feelings.

"Bastards!" she said. "Not believing what I say about my past record. It was in 1932 that I joined the revolution, there can be no doubt about it. But they insist it was 1935. It's absurd!"

I said nothing. As a veteran bodyguard I knew that whenever the leaders were unhappy about something, they would find someone to vent their feelings upon; not another leader who might be embarrassed, but a bodyguard. So I pretended to be all ears and sympathized as I listened to her.

"Investigating *my* past record, of all past records! What a cheek!" She gave me another piece of fish. After a short pause, she continued, "Now I remember: they say you're my favourite and get your clothes from me. Have I given you any clothes?"

"Of course not!" I protested loudly. "Who made that one up?"

"You see? Nothing but fabrication!" She didn't tell me who had said it, but instead changed the subject, asking me in great detail about the life and health of Mao, giving me the impression that she was trying to establish some sort of connection between Mao's frame of mind and something which had happened around that time, or that she was looking for an opportunity to talk to Mao, when he would be likely to be receptive to her.

The following morning, after escorting Mao, who had worked all night, to his bedroom, I left him. Jiang was still in bed, sitting wrapped up in the quilts. As I was standing guard outside the door, I overheard bits of their conversation, from inside the room. They were talking in low voices: It was Jiang complaining to Mao; she seemed to be telling him that someone was trying to persecute her, and was asking Mao to come to her assistance by speaking out in her defence. Mao refused, saying, "Nothing can change one's past record," adding, "if you're a true revolutionary, as you claim to have been when you were in Shanghai, why do you need me to speak on your behalf?"

Soon, they raised their voices. "Do I have to remind you," Jiang shouted, "that the Kuomintang reactionaries have told a lot of vicious lies? Their newspapers printed a lot of stories claiming that both you and Zhu De were killed in action, and these stories were accompanied by not just one, but several photographs. Was there any truth in those?"

Then she added, "These people are doing exactly what the Kuomintang did. What's their game?"

Then I heard Mao yell at her: "You muddle-headed fool!"

"I'm nothing but a junior secretary," Jiang wouldn't stop crying, "and they needn't make such a big fuss about me. They're trying to get rid of me, because they want to get rid of you. It's you they're really after...."

"Get out of here! Out!" Mao roared.

I hurried away from the door so as to put some distance between myself and the room. Hardly had I halted, when Jiang, crying, flew out of the room, passing me by like a gust of wind, heading for Zhou Enlai's cave-room. Whenever something like this happened, she would go straight to Zhou, who was a skillful mediator. That day she talked with Zhou from early in the morning until noon. When she left, she looked calm.

That afternoon, after waking up, Mao chain-smoked in bed. We had a long talk, during which he aired his grievances to me in a grave and sad tone. Here is a summary of what he said:

> Since I'm a member of the Party group under your leadership, I would like to confide to you what is disturbing me. If Jiang weren't my wife but one of my attendants, I would have sent her away a long time ago. I married her in too great haste. What can I do now? In my position I can't divorce her. She hasn't done anything bad enough to deserve that; a divorce would be viewed unfavourably by the comrades and would give rise to all kinds of rumours. But if I don't get a divorce, she'll become a political embarrassment to me. So there's nothing I can do, but try to put up with her.

The military victories which we won soon after that quarrel lifted Mao out of his bad mood. One day when Jiang sent the nurse to Mao to get a sample of his handwriting for Li Ne, who was learning to write Chinese characters, Mao said, "Ask her mother to teach her to write. I'm not a calligrapher, her mother is."

That relieved Jiang of her worries: she knew the storm had blown over.

Once Jiang had a plate of the preserved meat from General He Long prepared for Mao so that Mao wouldn't have to eat black soya beans for once. But Mao thought otherwise.

"Save it for the comrades from the frontline," Mao said.

"But where's the frontline?" Jiang was displeased. "Is it east or west of the river? We're closer to the enemy troops than any of them are. They aren't seeing any action and don't have to keep moving from one place to another like we do; they can always get what they want to eat."

That drew Mao's sharp criticism. Frowning, Mao said, "You have the wrong attitude. Even if you don't complain about having to eat those beans or having to keep on moving from one place to another, it doesn't mean that you can begrudge others, your comrades, if they don't have to eat beans and keep on the move."

In Jiang's case such an attitude was her undoing. It is not uncommon amongst most people, but important people should guard against it. Unfortunately, in Jiang's case, the situation was exacerbated by her unmistakable jealousy.

Starting in 1953, the leaders of the Central Committee would visit the beach at Beidaihe in the summer. Jiang was a poor swimmer, but she was not ashamed of this in presence of other women crowding the beach, who could or could not swim. But with Liu Shaoqi's wife, Wang Guangmei, it was a different story. The sight of Wang doing breaststroke, sidestroke and backstroke in the water, would always bring a sneer to the corners of her mouth.

When things were starting to pick up for us, and final victory was no longer a mere hope but was beginning to materialize, some subtle, barely noticeable changes occurred in Jiang.

She began to pamper herself. She derived increasing pleasure from summoning the bodyguards to her room, with the electric-bell, and ordering them to do this and that for her, even when she could quite well do it herself. She seemed to love always having someone at her beck and call, interpreting that as a status symbol, and acknowledgement of her new position in life.

Once Zhang Tianyi, one of the bodyguards, was summoned to her room by the electric-bell. When he hurried in, Jiang said, "Give me the hand warmer." It was right in her bed, within easy reach if she bent forward a little. But instead of getting it for herself, she had brought the bodyguard all the way to her room to fetch it for her. It made Zhang very sad when he recalled that previously Jiang had never acted like that, but used to decline our offers of help, saying, "No, thanks, I think I can manage."

She also became very choosy about her food, and increasingly so as supplies improved. In Yangjiagou, in northern Shaanxi, when she had to endure privation, all she could demand was that her food should taste right, but later on, when we could get pork and chicken, and especially once the supply of pork no longer presented a problem in Xibaipo, she demanded far more than just right taste; she grew very fussy about the fat content and nutritional value of her food. Her recipe for stir-fried pork slices included pickled cabbage, which she said helped digestion. If fresh cabbage was not available, she would ask for dried vegetables, saying that they contained vitamins essential to one's health. Looking back, I must admit that Jiang was not wrong in this respect, but at that time we found her ideas a little difficult to accept, Mao included. Once, Jiang had stewed pork prepared with more lean meat and less fat than Mao was accustomed to, mixed with dried vegetables. At the table she explained to Mao: "The dried vegetables help digestion." Mao didn't make any comment; he ate all of it.

After the victory of the revolution, Jiang became even more difficult to please. In the morning, the bodyguards were expected to greet her with, "Did you sleep well last night, Comrade Jiang Qing?" The body-guard would be given the cold shoulder for the rest of the day if he forgot to say that.

Jiang had her breakfast in bed. A crank at one end of her bed raised the top half so that she could sit up in it. After she had wiped her face with wet towels and rinsed out her mouth, a small table would be placed in front of her, with her breakfast on it. I have seen some people have their breakfast like that in Western movies.

Jiang had a good appetite when she was not sick. Her breakfast usually consisted of bread or small steamed buns, butter, some pickled vegetable, which was usually potherb mustard, and kidney beans boiled with salt. Sometimes she would ask for preserved toufu. She seldom drank milk; for soft food she liked rice porridge.

Her midday meal was served with a few regular dishes. Her favourite dish was fish with fine bones and meat, such as certain species of carp. Mackerel was also one of her favourites, but it was not included in her regular dishes. She would have eaten shad more often, but it was too expensive. For Jiang, fish was a must for lunch or dinner.

Young chicken, not much larger than a pigeon when cooked, was another of Jiang's favourite foods. For soup, it was spare-ribs cooked in an earthenware pot, or fish soup. The vegetables she liked best were leaf-mustard, large leafed spinach, amaranth, and celery. She liked them finely chopped. When she was not feeling well, they would be made into a paste which she could eat with a spoon. She shunned lard; her food was always cooked with vegetable oil and was not greasy. It might sometimes be mixed with a bit of minced meat or mushrooms or fungi.

For a woman in her position, Jiang's daily menu did not exceed proper limits; sometimes it could even be very simple. The trouble with her was that she was too fastidious about the taste of her food. No cook could satisfy her requirements in this respect, not even Mao's cook; Liao Bingfu was the only exception.

Apparently Jiang was widely read on matters of nutrition. As she grew more particular about her food, she tried her best to change Mao's diet. But Mao, being very "conservative" on this matter, simply refused to listen to her or his physician. What he liked most, was exactly what Jiang hated: his dishes had to be hot and salty, and stewed pork had to be oily. To be fair to her, Jiang was not wrong on this matter; it is sad to recall that her insistence about what Mao should eat ended in the quarrel which I recounted earlier,* and from then on they never ate from the same pot again. It is hard to say whether rancour between them led to that conflict or vice versa; perhaps it was a bit of both. But at any rate, if a married couple refuse to share each other's food, it is an indication that their marriage is "on the rocks."

As I said earlier, Jiang was a woman with regular habits. She never changed her schedule for work and rest, even during those days of the three major military campaigns. By contrast, Mao followed a completely different schedule, working twenty-eight hours a "day." As a result, when Mao was working, Jiang would often be sleeping, and when Jiang was up, it would be Mao's "dinner-time." They seldom slept at the same time. And when Mao had some important business on hand, he would work for several days at a stretch without sleep, until he was exhausted, and would then be put to sleep by the bodyguards and was not to be

---

*See page 107.

disturbed. This meant that Jiang only stayed with Mao once every few weeks, or even months. What does that imply?

Jiang was full of complaints, complaints about anyone for anything, important or unimportant. And on many occasions she would add fuel to a dispute. This also incurred Mao's displeasure and put him on guard.

Mao gave me the impression that he could easily be swayed. He would believe what those closest to him said if they repeated it often enough. During work breaks Mao liked to joke with us, at which times he felt just like the next person. These were the times when we would say whatever we liked to him for fun. Once, we teased one of the bodyguards, saying that he couldn't sleep because he had run into trouble wth his girl-friend. Mao took it as a joke when he heard it the first time; when he heard it again, he still believed that it was said in jest, but the third time he heard it, he took it seriously and offered to mediate. So we told him that it was only a joke, but he wouldn't believe us until we told him so three times. That's how we were spared, to put it jokingly, "the crime of disabusing the sovereign."

Once, Mao was told by Shi Zhe, a well-known translator, that Gao Gang was a very capable and trust-worthy man. After hearing this evaluation of Gao a number of times, Mao was heard saying on more than one occasion that Gao was a fine man. Two years later, Gao was denounced together with Rao Shushi, at the Fourth Plenary Session of the Party's Seventh Central Committee, on account of their disruptive activities against the Party. When the session closed, Mao said to Shi, "You told me Gao was a good man, but he engaged in disruptive activities against the Party." Shi replied, "What was he when I said that? He was then vice-chairman of the Party." Mao said nothing more.

As Mao's wife, Jiang Qing could easily have put in a good word for someone whom Mao was angry with, and calmed things down, like a good wife should. But instead of doing this, she would merely exacerbate the situation, speaking ill of whomever Mao was angry with, or whatever he was unhappy about. And she did that far too often. I remember on two occasions Mao just looking at her when she did that, and when she had finished, his saying with a frown, "You're just incapable of getting along well with other people," and "You can never learn to treat others like friends. You're turning everyone you know into your enemy." I shall never forget what Mao said about Jiang to those of us attending him: "Jiang's always hurting people with that vicious tongue of hers. She's a trouble-maker. She'll come to a tragic end after I die." Mao's prediction proved true.

Nevertheless, Jiang knew her limitations. Sometimes, when she had something she wanted to tell Mao, but knew that Mao wouldn't listen to her, she would ask someone to speak to him for her, someone she believed Mao would listen to. That's why she ganged up with Mao Yuanxin during the last few years of the "cultural revolution."

At one time, with her talent for entertainment, Jiang was a help to Mao. She provided all of us with some recreation and relaxation, during those years when life was extremely hard for us. The best moment of the day was in the evening, after we had finished the day's march and eaten our ration of black soya beans for supper and were either squatting on our heels, or just standing around or slouching on stools against a wall, listening to Jiang sing an aria or two of Beijing opera or trying to answer her riddles. Jiang would often play Mao some Beijing opera on a phonograph she had brought from Shanghai, whilst I massaged Mao's scalp with a comb. There were only a few such records, which were played over and over again, but Mao never seemed to find them any the less enjoyable for that. After hearing them each time, he would smile lovingly at Jiang, or would say good-humouredly, "Nice records. Play them again."

During the first few years after Mao moved to Beijing, Jiang concerned herself with trying to maintain a balance between work and rest for him. When Mao had been working too long, Jiang would tell her daughter to get him out for a walk or get him to play a bit of mahjong,* or she would have a movie shown for him. She would say to Mao, who didn't like movies, "Come to the movie. If you don't, the boys in the bodyguard will never see it." In the exhibition hall Mao would say to us, "I wouldn't have come if it weren't for you."

I can't recall now just what caused them to drift apart on matters of entertainment. Maybe it came about imperceptibly, maybe it had to do with Mao's advancing age, maybe it was the result of Jiang's personality and "the change of life," maybe....

Anyway, it happened, and this is what I saw happen.

---

*A traditional Chinese game for four people, played with pieces called piles.

As Mao gained in age, his physician's concern for his physical well-being increased. In addition to swimming and walking, he made it a rule for Mao to dance once or twice a week so that he would get enough exercise to keep fit.

Mao liked to swim and dance in the noisy company of young people; the fun he shared with them would make him forget, temporarily, the loneliness which he felt when he worked, ate and slept, for he did all that alone. On such occasions, aware of Mao's needs, we young people would shed all inhibition, talking, laughing, and shouting with abandon, with no respect for age or position.

By contrast, Jiang was deadly serious, looking at us disapprovingly, taking all the fun out of these occasions. Beginning in 1957, she became increasingly irritable. The doctor attributed this to the "change of life," saying that this was when a woman tended to become edgy, and easily provoked, even by such things as wind and noise. We were then too young to understand what the "change of life" meant. All we knew was that Jiang was in poor health, and the bodyguards would say privately, "Her position's changed. She's now an important secretary with the rank of vice-minister," and "the higher your position is, the more complicated your malady becomes."

In 1957, when Mao and Jiang were on vacation in Hangzhou, Mao was invited to a dance one day, hosted by the Party provincial committee at a hotel. Mao went without Jiang. It was a lively gathering, filled with laughter, and we danced until our shirts were wet with sweat. Tian Yunyu met a girl at the dance who was later to become his girl-friend. She was a member of a song and dance ensemble. We had a lot of fun that evening. Subsequently, the leaders of the Party committee, encouraged by the credit Mao's doctor gave them for providing Mao with the rest and relaxation he so badly needed, invited Mao to another dance two days later, at another hotel.

All the partners at that dance, members of a song and dance ensemble, already knew us. The moment Mao appeared, in the company of his bodyguards, his doctor and his secretaries, they came up to us, greeting us noisily like old friends, promising a jolly beginning to another pleasant evening.

But this free and easy atmosphere disappeared as quickly as it had arisen. The dance-hall suddenly fell uneasily silent, and the young people, who would otherwise have been standing around Mao, chatting with him, had now retreated to two sides and were standing there in all seriousness, clapping dutifully.

Walking pompously behind Mao, was Jiang Qing. She looked haughty and standoffish, making everyone in her presence feel nervous, and keep a cold and respectful distance from her. Mao tried to dissolve their inhibition by cracking jokes, but to no avail. The casual and abandoned atmosphere Mao had hoped to recapture was lost. Mao observed all this with visible displeasure. Sitting in an easy chair, he grumbled to me, "She's spoiled everything."

The band had started playing, and just as the dancers were beginning to take to the floor, someone was heard shouting: "Stop the music! It's terrible! Play another tune!"

.It was Jiang. With the air of a hostess, she went up to the band, to her satisfaction, drawing everyone's attention to herself as she did so. The leader of the band named a number of tunes for her to choose from, and she dismissed each one of them as "no good," in much the same way as a maestro would reject an inferior piece of musical composition. Whilst those in the band and those of us waiting for the music to recommence were surprised by Jiang's knowledge of music, Mao was left breathing heavily in anger. It was a long time before she finally "authorized" several tunes for the evening and the dance began.

Jiang had the first dance with Mao. To do her justice, I must admit that Jiang was an excellent dancer: she was all elegance and grace, but she danced too formally and lacked vitality. Mao dropped me a hint, and I immediately lined up the other bodyguards. When the music started again, Li Liancheng went up to Jiang, so that Mao could switch partners.

Just as the young people were bringing the dance to a kind of climax, Jiang, who enjoyed taking people by surprise, was suddenly heard shouting again, and this time she held her hands over her ears: "Too loud, it's too loud! The noise is deafening! Don't you know anything better than playing so loudly? Can't you play it softer?... Still softer!"

The whole evening Jiang was on everyone's nerves, leaving Mao in dismay. When he returned to the guest house, Mao said, breathing heavily in anger, "What a kill-joy! She spoils all the fun wherever she is.

I just don't want to see her again."

After Jiang behaved like that several times, Mao began to shun her. Many times Mao said to me, or Tian Yunyu, or Feng Yaosong and the other bodyguards: "Jiang's a kill-joy" and "She makes everybody suffer." Mao would leave any place he was stopping off on a journey, when he learned that Jiang was coming to join him. That is what he did when he was in Guangzhou in 1959. He said, "She'll make us miserable when she gets here. We'd better leave now."

Mao's unexpected departures naturally infuriated Jiang, so she would take out her anger on her attendants. She did this several times without warning. One such unwarranted outburst of anger was even felt in Beijing. This is what happened.

One day Li Liancheng had just entered Jiang's room, when he was greeted with an angry shout from Jiang: "Get out of here! Take off your shoes before you come in." Li retreated as ordered, took off his shoes and entered in stockinged feet.

Jiang, combing her hair in front of a mirror, said in a bad temper, "I just can't stand your heavy steps. It's uncivilized the way you walk."

Li looked at the floor. The carpet was more than one inch thick; a glass wouldn't have made any noise if it fell on it. Earlier that year, Jiang, accompanied by Li and myself, had visited Lin Biao to ask him for his advice on ways to recuperate health. Lin told her to avoid three things: the sun, noise and cold wind. To achieve this, Lin said the window curtains must be black in colour, the air moderate in temperature, and carpets be fitted from wall to wall. From then on Jiang would ask to have her room fitted with wall-to-wall carpeting wherever she was, to ensure quiet.

"Is it cold outside?" Jiang looked at Li in the mirror.

"No, it's not cold, Comrade Jiang Qing."

After she did her hair, Jiang rose, announcing, "I'm going out for a walk."

Just as she stepped out of the door, Li heard Jiang cry out angrily in a shrill voice: "But it's so cold! What do you mean, it's not cold?"

"I'll get you some more clothes." Li was nervous. "It's such a fine day, and it'll do you good to move around a bit in the sun...."

"Is that what you really mean? Of course it's not; what you really want is to see me catch cold!" Thus saying, she slammed the door shut and returned to her room: she was not going to take a walk that day.

Li, smiling wryly to himself, was suddenly filled with pity for Jiang. With everyone trying to shun her, Jiang grew increasingly irritable and lonely, and the more bad-tempered she became, the more everyone tried to avoid her.

Soon Jiang sent her nurse to fetch Li. "Jiang wants to play cards now. Hurry up!"

Since time hung heavy on her hands, Jiang would often spend all day doing nothing but playing cards. She was a bad loser; she always wanted to win, not easily, but the hard way. Playing cards with her could be a nightmarish experience.

During that game, when Li followed with a wrong card, Jiang flew off the handle.

"Get the hell out of here! I don't want you!" Jiang threw the cards down on the table, and just as Li was going out of the door, she shouted again: "Not that easily! Stand there! That's the punishment you deserve."

The door closed and Li was left standing in the corridor. An hour later, Jiang's doctor came and quietly told Li to leave, as Jiang had fallen asleep, and come back later, when she got up.

But Li obstinately refused.

The doctor got Su Hanhua, director of the Guangdong provincial public security bureau, to mediate. Su, not believing that he could talk Jiang into dropping the matter when she was angry, asked Li to apologize to Jiang. Li refused: making a mistake in a card game was no reason for an apology. So he remained standing there until Jiang got up.

Li's feelings were so deeply hurt that he cried. He called long-distance, to tell me about the incident. Mao was unhappy when he learned from me what had happened. After a short pause, he said with a frown, sighing sadly, "I'm sorry Li's been made to suffer in place of me. Recall him and take him away from Jiang. If he can't afford to make her angry, he can at least afford to stay out of her way. When she has no one around her, she'll have no opportunity to throw her weight about."

Li left Guangzhou for Beijing by train that same evening.

When he saw Li, Mao said, "I'm sorry Jiang Qing raged at you. Please don't take it to heart for my sake. She's not feeling well. Forget it."

Since Jiang Qing spared no one, Mao said to everyone in the bodyguards, "Please don't take it to heart for my sake."

But Mao took it to heart himself: he grew increasingly reluctant to see Jiang. Such was the married life of this couple: they ate, slept and worked apart; they couldn't even spend an evening of entertainment together. By the time I left for my new job in Tianjin, I had the feeling that there wasn't much affection left between them.

Mao the Mediator

"If Jiang Qing throws a tantrum at you, try your best not to take it to heart for my sake."

Mao said that to us bodyguards many times, but when a dispute between his wife and his bodyguards was referred to him, as "acting" head of the family, he would find it difficult to settle.

Quarrels between myself and Jiang were not unusual, but they were negligible. Only on two occasions did they become violent, disproportionately violent, because they were over mere trifles that arose when we played cards.

In the 1950s and early 1960s Jiang did not have much work to do as Mao kept her out of political affairs. She passed her time by playing cards. Unlike Mao, who was a good loser in games, Jiang was a bad one.

Mao seldom played cards; only once in a while did he have a game of "go," and most of the time he was the loser. He didn't mind losing, but he would be unhappy if his opponents made things easy for him. So those who knew this would play aggressively, and when Mao knew the game was lost for him and that he couldn't do anything to save the situation, he would accept his defeat with a deep sigh, as though such experience provided him with a rare opportunity to experience defeat, and made life all the more worth living. Each time this happened, he would grudgingly admit to me: "It looks as though Mao Zedong is not infallible, or he wouldn't have lost the game."

Jiang was not that philosophical. Like Mao she wanted to win a game the hard way, but if she lost, she would raise hell and make everybody miserable.

I was her card partner. My feelings at such times could be summarized in the words of Su Dongpo, a Song Dynasty poet: "It is unbearably cold up there." I was very careful lest I should follow with a wrong card and be given a scornful look by Jiang. It was not too bad if our opponents were poor players like the bodyguards in my charge: they could never win, no matter how hard they tried. But with the nurses, who were clever and played better, it was a different story. Not that they always won, which they could have, but they would give us a chance to win, and do so without Jiang's noticing it, for we would have been landed in even bigger trouble if she had found us out. With so many worries, it was easy for me to make a mistake, and each time I followed or led with a wrong card, she would give me a cutting look. So playing cards with Jiang was an agony.

One spring day in 1952, I was subjected to just such an agony. As soon as we sat down at the table, I noticed that Jiang was in a bad mood. That made me nervous, and the more nervous I grew, the worse I played, and the worse I played, the moodier she became—so much so that the nurses found it hard to let us win.

At one point I followed with a wrong card again. Before I could withdraw it, Jiang had thrown her cards down in front of me.

"I quit! Now, what makes you think I'm dodging the campaign?"

My heart sank and I grew pale with fright. As if responding to a military command, I shot up from my seat and stood at attention, wondering how on earth she had come to know that.

A nationwide campaign against corruption, waste and bureaucracy had started the year before. Back in Yan'an, Jiang had never liked any of the rectification campaigns in the Party, and had grown afraid of them, resented them even, after the violent quarrel she had had with Mao over her past history. So any political campaign, whatever its purpose, would find her trying to evade it. Many times I heard her talk resentfully about such campaigns: "Those people should know better than spending their time framing others," and "Be careful! You may persecute others this time, but you won't be spared next time."

So when this campaign against the three evils* began, she absented herself from the activities of her Party group for some time. When Xu Yefu, a confidential secretary, asked me, "Why is it that each time there's a political campaign we will find her away?" I replied casually, "To dodge it, that's why." Later Jiang learned of what I had said, and now she was throwing it back at me.

Her accusation left me speechless, and I grew a bit afraid.

---

*Corruption, waste and bureaucracy.

"You young bastard!" Filled with anger, she was a frightful sight, and was breathing noisily as she paced around her room, and since I was too nervous and afraid to say anything, all I could do was follow her around.

In mounting anger, she left for the courtyard and continued to walk. I followed her out, keeping closely behind her.

"What makes you think I'm dodging the campaign?" There were tears in her eyes. "Answer me if you're not dumb! Did you say that?"

"I, I'm sorry, Comrade Jiang Qing." I made an effort to explain: "I didn't mean to hurt you. I was just answering Xu...."

"How ungrateful you are!" Tears were swimming in her eyes. "Slandering me in return for all the political protection I have given you...."

"Please believe me: I didn't mean to hurt you, still less to slander you...."

"No use denying it! It's only one bad thing I'm told you have said about me; you must have said a lot more than that behind my back. What else is there?"

"Nothing more, absolutely.... I said nothing more."

"No? Now tell me: why did you try to turn Li Min against me?"

"I've never done anything like that!"

"Will you repeat that denial? I dare you to repeat it! I told you to send a car to take her home that day, but you didn't do it. Why?"

"I did. I went in person, but she didn't want to come back."

"That's because you turned her against me. You know that a step-mother is vulnerable, so you attack me where it hurts the most. You're not interested in helping us get along; all you do is gossip and generate ill feelings. Is that true?"

"Absolutely not!"

"You've even tried to turn the chairman against me!" Now she was hysterical, stamping her feet and in tears. I hung my head in dejection, at a loss to say anything. I shouldn't have told Mao that it was Jiang's idea not to serve him the stewed pork he had asked for that day, or Mao might not have gotten so angry as to decide not to share his food with her any longer. Jiang had good reason to be so upset.

I looked at my watch: it was four o'clock in the afternoon, time for Mao to get up. With an effort I managed to say to her calmly, "It's time for the chairman to get up, and I have to attend to him. You can have my self-criticism when I've finished."

I returned to my office just in time to hear the bell. I straightened out my clothes and went into Mao's room with a heavy heart.

After wiping his face, Mao sat up in bed with his back against the railing, reading the day's newspapers and smoking, as he usually did. After some hesitation, I said to him in a low voice, "I've just had a quarrel with Comrade Jiang Qing, Comrade Chairman."

"Why did you quarrel with her?" Mao asked nonchalantly, without taking his eyes off the newspapers.

"I didn't start it; she did," I was choosing my words carefully. "I accused her of dodging the campaign, and she accused me of political slander."

"Dodging the campaign?" Mao raised his eyelids, apparently growing interested. "Did you say that?"

"Xu was asking me about her the other day, and I said that without thinking."

Then I told Mao what had happened. When I had finished, I explained: "I never intended to slander her, Comrade Chairman."

"I see," said Mao, nodding.

"She has also accused me of sowing discord between Li Min and her, and creating ill feelings between yourself and her. Have I ever done anything to turn you against her?"

"Well," said Mao after thinking for a while, "you may go now. Tell Jiang I want to talk to her."

I left Mao, and when I saw Jiang still walking in the courtyard, I went up to her timidly.

"The chairman wants to see you, Comrade Jiang Qing," I said.

"How smart you are!" she looked at me out of the corners of her eyes. She might have said, "It's wicked of you to steal a march on me." I hung my head in silence: any explanation would only make things worse at such a time.

Soon the bell in my office rang again. I arrived at Mao's room in no time. Jiang had gone.

"It looks like a difficult problem," Mao said slowly, looking at me. He was still reclining in bed, smoking. "Something more than my help alone is going to be required. You'll have to write a self-criticism, I'm afraid, if you want to get it over with."

"What am I to write?" I was worried.

"Just what you said."

"She calls it a political slander, but I didn't intend that."

"Say you didn't intend it."

"She says I turned Li Min against her, but I didn't do anything like that."

"Say you didn't do anything like that."

"She says.... But would you call that a self-criticism?" I didn't believe that would work.

"You didn't listen to me," Mao smiled, "when I advised you to study. Now you end up not knowing how to write a simple thing like a self-criticism. This should teach you not to study."

I smiled awkwardly.

"Now let me tell you how to do it." Moving his index finger in the palm of his left hand, as if they were pen and paper, he said, "Address it to Jiang and I. Put two dots after our names, the two dots are called a colon. Then begin the first paragraph. In this paragraph say that you regret saying that she was dodging the campaign and apologize for that. Follow that with a 'but'; this will begin the important part of your self-criticism. In this part, deny her charges of political slander and those of sowing discord between her and Li Min, saying that you never did anything of that kind. Say that you did go to fetch Li Min, but that Li Min didn't want to return, and that you were at fault, not because you didn't do what were told to do; you did, but because you failed to carry it out, and then wind it up with your guarantee that failures of that kind will not happen again. Show it to me when you've finished."

"Thank you very much, Comrade Chairman."

I hurried back to my room, and began writing at once, before I forgot what Mao had told me. When I had finished I took it to Mao.

"That's it," Mao nodded his approval. Putting my self-criticism on the bedside cupboard, he continued, "But the problem remains. It's a terrible thing to say that she's dodging the campaign. What shall we do?"

I looked at him vacantly.

"The only thing you can do," Mao said, smiling and winking playfully, "is for you to do a bit of dodging yourself."

So I left Mao.

A few days later Mao sent for me. The moment he saw me he said with a smile, "The thing has blown over, Yinqiao. Jiang Qing's been hospitalized in Beijing Hospital. You're going to see her. I've got a few things here. You're going to take them to her when you visit her. Do you understand what I mean?"

"Yes, I do." My spirits rose.

"I don't mean right now. Go back to your room and wait there."

I returned to my room, not understanding why I had to wait. In about a quarter of an hour, a nurse called me from Beijing Hospital, telling me that Jiang had asked for cigarettes and fruit. I made a note of what she wanted, and when I looked at the things Mao had got ready for her, I discovered that they were exactly what Jiang was asking for. I left for the hospital with them at once.

There was no one in the ward when I arrived there. Hearing the sound of running water in the wash-room, I waited. Soon Jiang appeared, rubbing her hands together. She greeted me with a smile and shook hands with me.

"How are you? Sit down, please."

I sat down courteously and put the things on a table.

"I don't mind if you complain about me, but you shouldn't have said those things behind my back." Jiang had softened in her attitude. I told her again that I hadn't had any bad intentions, and that I wouldn't talk like that again.

"Complain to me if you have to, but don't do it behind my back. Then I won't hold any grudge against you for your complaints."

Having said that she changed the subject, discussing what improvement might be made in my work so that Mao would rest and eat better.

"I'm not in very good health, so I have to leave the chairman primarily in your care. I'd appreciate it if you'd do a good job of it."

Later on, I learned that Mao had called Jiang whilst I was waiting in my room. "Don't behave like a narrow-minded woman," Mao had admonished her. "Yinqiao was very anxious when he learned that you're ill. He's got a few things for you and wants to see you. Why don't you ask to see him and show him that you can be magnanimous?"

So Jiang told the nurse to call me, and asked for the things that she knew Mao had got for her. Mao had settled that dispute almost effortlessly. Soon I was promoted to deputy-commander of the bodyguard.

But I could never have imagined that this incident would later land me in trouble.

Before I went to the hospital to see Jiang, Mao returned the self-criticism to me, saying casually, "Take it back and keep it yourself."

I should have known better than to keep it. In 1967, during the "cultural revolution," the Red Guards found the self-criticism in my house when they searched it. They took it as evidence of my opposition to Mao Zedong, alleging that my opposition to Jiang was really intended for Mao. They threw me into jail, tormented me and ransacked my house several times. Only when Mao learned of my imprisonment, when he stopped in Tianjin on his inspection tour of the southern provinces, was I set free.

The self-criticism is now in the Tianjin Archive, collected perhaps for its historical value.

With Jiang picking quarrels with us so often, we grew accustomed to them and ceased to take her seriously; sometimes we would even show open defiance. This was especially true of those of us who had been with Mao long enough to be counted as members of his family. I am not going to recount the flare-ups between her and the other bodyguards here, but I shall recall a violent quarrel which I had with her.

I accompanied Mao and Jiang to Beidaihe in the summer of 1960. We stayed in Building 1, a one-story house in a grove of trees.

One day, before retiring at ten o'clock in the morning, Mao told me to wake him up at three in the afternoon, for a meeting scheduled for four o'clock. After I left Mao's room, I went to the bodyguards' office and began to read. At two o'clock, Jiang sent the assistant bodyguard, on duty, to fetch me.

"Come and play cards, Yinqiao," Jiang said, in high spirits. "Let's be partners as usual."

I didn't like the idea. Playing cards with her every day bored me to death, but since I could not refuse her, I showed my reluctance by sighing and looking uninterested.

It didn't take her long to notice how I felt. Displeased, she pulled a long face, and with great effort asked me in mock humour, "What's the matter with you, Yinqiao? Thinking about your wife? Look alive!"

"No, nothing the matter," I replied in a bored tone. I looked at my watch: it was half past two. I sighed again: how boring the game was.

"Your turn to follow." Jiang was beginning to look annoyed.

I did not respond immediately, but looked at the cards in my hand absent-mindedly. It was some time before I mechanically picked out a card from my hand and threw it down on the table. It was a wrong card. Jiang stared at me, but I pretended not to notice.

"What's the matter with you, Yinqiao?" Her tone suggested that she was doing her best to control her anger, which was treatening to explode at any moment.

"Oh, nothing," I sounded uninterested. I took another look at my watch. "The chairman's going to a meeting in the afternoon."

"Tian Yunyu will take care of that, he's on duty today."

I moved the corners of my mouth a bit, too lazy to speak, not even to tell her that the chairman expected me to accompany him to the meeting. People become lazy in summer. I kept on sighing.

We lost two straight games, and shortly after the third one began, we knew we were going to lose that one, too. But I didn't stop sighing.

"I quit! What a lousy game!" Jiang slammed the cards down on the table, yelling: "Just what do you want to do today?"

"I'm going to a meeting with the chairman if you want to know. But you want me to play cards with you. What do you think I want to do?"

"How dare you!" shouted Jiang, pointing a finger at me. "Who do you think you're speaking to?"

"I'm speaking to you. You started all this."

"How rude! Are you supposed to serve me or am I supposed to serve you? Answer me!"

"I serve the people by serving the chairman. We're equal politically. Playing cards with you isn't my job."

"How, how ..." she was trembling with anger, "how dare you! You're nothing but a bodyguard! Get the hell out of here!"

Jiang committed a grave error when she talked to me like that in the presence of the other bodyguards and the nurses: for she hurt my pride. She could say all those things to the other bodyguards, but not to me, the commander of the bodyguard, a thirty-eighter who had been with Mao for more than a dozen years and had the rest of the bodyguards under my command. Such humiliation would make me look ridiculous in the eyes of those under me. Enraged, I shouted back: "You can cut out all that arrogance! You're just a secretary. You're not someone people shout 'long live' to."

"Do you mean me? Repeat that! I dare you to say that again!" Jiang was about to rush at me when she was restrained by the nurses. And breaking free from the bodyguards who were trying to pull me out of the room, I yelled, "I mean you. So what? I'm the bodyguard commander, not your card partner!"

The squabble escalated, with both of us trying to outdo the other by raking up the past, quite unlike the way we had behaved at the time of that quarrel in 1952, when she had accused me of slandering her and I had known myself to be in the wrong. So we continued to bicker, becoming so embittered that we were all crying, accusing each other tearfully like two kids, and refusing to stop, paying no heed to the nurses' and bodygaurds' attempts to stop us. By now, however, I had realized the gravity of the situation and was feeling a bit scared; besides, I was expected to accompany Mao to the meeting. So with the bodyguards trying to pull me out of the room, I left Jiang and made for Mao's room, crying all the way.

Mao, who had already gotten up, was reading documents when I rushed into his room. In a loud sob, I said, pointing outside, "Jiang Qing's swearing and raving at me.... She says I'm her servant and have got to work for her...."

"Can't you ever stop bickering like that?" said Mao, frowning as he rose. "How did it start?"

"We were playing cards. I played badly and she blamed me for that, but I've got to accompany you to the meeting this afternoon, and didn't feel like playing. So she lost her temper and threw the cards down like this...."

Before I could finish, I heard confused voices at the door and Jiang came running in, crying loudly. Immediately we started yelling at each other again. Mao walked over, stood between Jiang and I and ordered us to stop, but we were so upset that neither of us would stop first. Mao, who must by now have gathered that the squabble was over mere trifles, tried to pull me into the room with one hand and push Jiang out with the other, shouting, "Cut it out! Shut up, all of you! Just shout one more time! Fools! How nasty!"

Silence. Then, pushing Jiang out of the room, Mao said to her, "You're his senior, why can't you shut up?" But just as Jiang was about to leave, I shouted at her again. Jiang, unable to ignore that, turned around and rushed at me, crying and swearing. Mao spun around and stared at me angrily. "What's the matter with you? Why didn't you stop when she did?"

So I stopped, but this time Jiang didn't. She was so mad she wouldn't let Mao shut her up, and with me finding it hard to restrain myself any longer, I yelled back in retort once again.

By now Mao was genuinely angry. He thundered: "Shut up!" The room fell silent immediately. "I'll hold whichever one of you starts it again, responsible for the whole thing."

That stopped both of us.

"Do you mean to say that you think I'm not busy enough doing what I have to do, that you want to give me something extra to worry about? Do you mean that you have so much spare time that you don't know how to spend it except by bickering with one another? Just imagine what people would say: Mao's secretary and his bodyguards getting into a row over a game of cards, crying, raving at each other, and refusing to stop. Wouldn't it look ridiculous? Wouldn't it be shameful?" Mao drew in his lower lip, and cutting a line in the air with his hand, added, "From now on you two will not play cards at the same table, if you can't. You can do some reading instead."

That put an end to my being Jiang's partner at cards.

The incident, however, did not leave much for me to worry about. It was a violent quarrel, but like all family quarrels, it remained a family affair, and left no ill feelings after it was settled. Indeed, all Mao's long-term bodyguards would say that they were members of his family, because Mao treated them as such, and Mao knew that they wouldn't hold it against him, nor did he need to worry about "leaving a bad impression" on the occasions when he raved at them. There was no barrier between him and his bodyguards.

Mao's Treatment of Those Whom He Knew

Mao's attitude towards those whom he knew varied in accordance with his relationship to them, in a manner which was in keeping with his character.

With members of the Party, Mao was reserved, even dignified, but not ceremonious. When he spoke to them, he would be terse, to the point, candid and sincere. He never made any special effort to greet them or see them off, even if they were generals or high-ranking government officials. If their arrival found him working in bed, as was his habit, he would not rise to greet them, but would continue with his work. Sometimes he wouldn't even offer them a seat until they had begun their briefing. Nor would he rise from his chair; he would merely motion to them to a seat, and get straight down to business as soon as they were seated.

If a visitor was someone in the Party who had called after a long absence, Mao would rise upon his arrival and departure, and would shake hands with him, but he would not leave his room in greeting unless the visitor's arrival found him out of it. He made no exceptions with visitors from fraternal parties.

One morning in the early 1950s, the telephone in the bodyguards' office rang. I picked up the receiver. It was Zhou Enlai calling.

"Has the chairman gotten up?" Zhou asked.

"Not yet," I said.

After a brief pause, Zhou asked, "What time did he go to bed?"

"Eight o'clock in the morning."

"Wake him up, Yinqiao. Ho Chi Minh's here. He has some urgent business...."

Ho Chi Minh, chairman of the Vietnamese Workers' Party, was then in Beijing on a secret visit.

I went to Mao's bedroom and woke him up. After wiping his face, Mao left for the reception hall together with me. Less than two minutes after we arrived, Ho Chi Minh was to be seen conversing with Zhou on their way to the hall. When I informed Mao of their arrival, from my position by the door, Mao rose from his seat, walked towards the door and stopped just one step short of the threshold. He did not take that one extra step which would have taken him over the threshold. Mao did not shake hands with his visitor until he was inside the door. In response to Ho's warm greetings, in Chinese: "How are you?", Mao replied, "I am well, thank you. Are you enjoying your stay here?" They walked to the easy chairs exchanging greetings and sat down. I brought them tea.

When they had finished, Mao accompanied Ho Chi Minh to the door and saw him off, without leaving the hall. Ho left in Zhou's company.

One day in 1948, when General Su Yu, who had come from the front for a military conference in Chengnanzhuang, came to visit Mao, the chairman strode out of his room to greet him. They shook hands for a long time, during which I overheard them say "... it's been seventeen years." I am not sure whether they meant that they had not seen each other for that long. Since Mao seldom showed so much warmth towards anyone in the Party, that meeting left a very deep impression on me.

Mao seemed to restrain himself from developing personal friendships with anyone of high position in the government, Party or army. He saw to it that his relationship with such people was one of business and not much else. Zhou Enlai was his aide for decades. He attended to the details of his daily life. Most of the houses Mao lived in were selected by him. During the war, or in unusual times, it was Zhou who would travel the length of a road to find out whether it was safe for the chairman to use. He was also the man whom Mao would entrust with decision-making authority on extremely important matters. One would have thought an intimate relationship would have developed out of this, but in the fifteen years I was with Mao, I never heard him say anything to Zhou of a personal nature.

This attitude had to do with the history of the Party. During the long periods of war the liberated areas were cut off from each other by the enemy. In order to survive and expand territorially, they were forced to fight on their own. Many factions emerged as a result, a situation that Mao took for granted when he said, "It would be strange if the Party did not have factions in it." But as chairman of the Party, he had to treat everyone within the Party equally, and avoid giving the impression that he maintained any close relations with anyone to the exclusion of others. This is perhaps the reason why no one in the Party could claim to be Mao's close friend.

However, something else resulted from Mao's effort to keep an equal distance from everyone within the Party. Many people in the Party, including some in very high positions, showed so much respect in Mao's presence that they would appear nervous and find themselves unable to express themselves as they wished. As Mao's prestige grew, such inhibition became even harder to break and was, I think, a factor governing the emergence during the late 1960s and the 1970s of a certain degree of monopolization of power by one single person.

There were exceptions, however, the most outstanding ones being Peng Dehuai and Chen Yi.

Relations between Mao and Peng were like those between close friends. With no barriers between them, they were quite at home in each other's company. They would talk to one another candidly, laughing and arguing with abandon. With Peng speaking rapidly, like a machine-gun, in a voice loud enough to bring down the house, gesticulating wildly, and Mao joining in with no less enthusiasm, his interest aroused to whatever subject was under discussion, they were just like two old friends, having a good time together, talking.

Long before the war in northern Shaanxi, "Chairman Mao" had been adopted as the form of address for Mao, by everyone in the Party, everyone except Peng, who was still to be heard calling the chairman "Lao Mao"* sometimes. He was perhaps the last one in the Party to drop that term of address.

All that came to an end after Peng "accused" Mao at the conference of the Central Committee at Lushan Mountain. From then on Peng was reticent, even ill at ease in Mao's presence.

Chen Yi was different. When he visited Mao, the first thing he

---

*"Lao" is traditionally a term of intimacy or respect, used to address someone of seniority in years. Here, its use implies intimacy.

would do was to click his heels, salute the chairman at attention and say, "Chen Yi is reporting for duty, Comrade Chairman!" or "Chen Yi is here, Comrade Chairmao!" Then Mao would motion to him to a seat, saying, "Why don't you sit down? Sit down and talk." Chen would then break into a smile and "relax," and immediately the room would come to life.

Chen was perhaps Mao's only poet friend in the Party. He was a man without inhibition and was endowed with a deep, resonant voice and the unrestrained enthusiasm of a poet. He had such easy manners and was given to such laughter and gesticulation that when he warmed up to a subject in conversation, his charm was simply irresistable. Throughout the 1970s, Mao attended only one memorial meeting, and it was for Chen. He was a man whom Mao liked.

On public occasions, such as swimming, or at a dance, Mao liked the company of young people, and the more and merrier they were the better. In his private life, Mao's friends were mainly elderly people, especially those whom other people referred to as "museum pieces" —those who had experienced a great deal in old China and were conservative in their views. Mao thought highly of those amongst them who were known for their faith in democracy.

Mao treated his personal friends with courtesy and was loyal to them. Soon after the victory of the revolution, in the company of Zhou Enlai, Mao called upon some of his close friends, including Zhang Lan, Li Jishen, Shen Junru, Guo Moruo and Chen Shutong. He treated them quite differently from the way in which he treated those in the Party. When any one of them arrived or departed—Zhang, Li, Shen, Chen, He Xiangning, Ma Xulun or Liu Yazi—Mao would go all the way outside of his room, either to greet him or see him off, help him into or out of his car or up or down a flight of steps. When he strolled with them, he would keep very close to their side.

Mao once said that he didn't like to be regarded as the national leader all the time. I remember one elderly gentleman who, as I learned from the newspapers, was a native of Hunan Province, like Mao, "a scholar of international fame" and had "experienced many ups and downs in life." In the first few years after the founding of New China, this gentleman, like many other well-known democratic personages, was

Mao's frequent visitor. Once, he and Mao were sauntering along the lake in Zhongnanhai. He kept a short distance behind Mao and bent his body forward a little. In the middle of the stroll, with his neck stretched out in front of Mao and his face upturned, he stuck up his thumb saying, "You're a really great man, Chairman Mao. You're really great...."

Mao frowned. With a wave of his hand he said, "Please don't talk like that. It's not the way friends talk to each other."

Mao's criticism left him blushing.

But when it came to state affairs, this same elderly gentleman was bold enough to stick to his views, which Mao found unacceptable. So there was argument between them, and heated argument at that, with Mao directing sharp criticism at him and him refusing to give in. According to Mao, ideology and friendship are strangers to one another, and he would often say, "We argue only on matters of ideology," and "Disputes concerning ideology are not to be avoided." So Mao, who was invariably the winner in an argument of this kind, would drive on relentlessly.

Once, Zhang Lan tried to mediate one of these disputes, suggesting that Mao should not be so persistent. I learned from the newspapers recently that Zhou Enlai had also done likewise, and had asked the old man to make a self-criticism so that the whole thing would be forgotten. But their mediation efforts were unnecessary, for Mao did not bear any grudge against the old man for that argument; the only change in his attitude towards this elderly gentleman was that he no longer listened to his expositions regarding his "political faith." Indeed, as Mao said, "I had to argue and be firm because the dispute arose from differences in ideology, and not from personal ill feelings. Arguments of this kind are quite common, and can I think be settled through compromise."

Mao's contact with those in the Party was largely limited to business. Chen Yi was the only exception: they exchanged poems. But Mao had many good friends amongst democratic personages who were not Party members. These contacts had little to do with business.

Mao was constantly in correspondence with Zhang Shizhao. Zhang had been a member of the delegation sent by the Kuomintang government to the peace talks in 1949, and later became a member of the Standing Committee of the National People's Congress. One day after reading a letter from him, Mao tapped lightly on the table with his fingers and then, turning to me, said, "Get two chickens and take them to Zhang Shizhao. Now."

I started out immediately. It was already seven or eight o'clock in the evening; I went to many grocery stores before I could get the chickens.

Zhang lived in a courtyard house which was in shocking condition. I showed him the chickens. "They're from the chairman."

"Many thanks," said Zhang, nodding in appreciation.

"The chairman has received your letter," I said.

Holding up the chickens, Zhang said, "Yes, I know. These birds are his reply. How is the chairman?"

"He's very well," I replied.

I left Zhang, wondering what the two chickens could mean by way of a reply. I did not know what he had said in his letter, and I had no way of finding out. When I repeated what he had said to Mao, the chairman gave a mysterious smile, leaving me with a question, the answer to which I shall never know.

That was in 1955.

In the same year, He Xiangning made Mao a gift. It was a picture of a standing tiger which she had painted. It came mounted in a picture-frame. He Xiangning was an outstanding member of the Kuomintang's Left wing, a leader of the people's government and an artist. Mao set the picture against the wall and stood looking at it for a long time, thinking. Then he said to me, "Now I know what I am going to do with it. It belongs to the east room."

So I put it in the east room, but I never got to know the reason why it had to go there.

In 1959, Mao resigned as the Chairman of the People's Republic and was thus spared the day-to-day responsibilities of that position. In his leisure time he practised calligraphy, in the manner of one given to the cultivation of the mind. During this period his contact with such democratic personages increased.

Huang Yanpei, another democratic personage, had an album of calligraphy by Wang Xizhi in his collection. Wang Xizhi was a famous calligrapher who lived from around A.D. 321 to 379 (or A.D. 303 to 361) in the East Jin Dynasty. Mao borrowed the album from Huang and promised Huang that he would return it a month later. Mao liked it so much that he studied it all month whenever he had time. When I brought him tea, I would see him pondering over the calligrapher's art or copying from him, not mechanically, but in an effort to embellish his own style with the inner beauty of Wang's handwriting, through practice. Sometimes he would become so absorbed that he would not stop for meals.

Huang, however, was anxious to have the album back, perhaps because it was a genuine piece. During the first week Mao had it in his possession, he called the bodyguards' office many times asking if the chairman had finished studying it or when he would finish.

Yin Jingshan, a bodyguard, informed Mao of one of these calls as he was pouring tea for him: "Huang called again, Comrade Chairman."

"What?" Mao raised his eyes and knitted his brows.

"He ... can't wait."

"Another debt collector! Didn't he say one month? I'm counting the days." Mao threw his cigarette-holder down on the desk. Huang was giving the impression that he was doing the same thing as Khrushchev, who was then pressing China for the repayment of debts.

"He's not pressing, Comrade Chairman. He's just asking. Asking if you still need it."

"I certainly do!" He took a mouthful of tea and picked up the cigarette-holder once again, adding in a calmer voice, "If I don't return it within a month as I promised I'm in the wrong. If he wants it back sooner than the time specified, he's in the wrong. Either way, it's a breach of agreement."

But Huang called again, and this time he spoke directly to Mao. At the end of the conversation, Huang asked about the album. Mao replied, "Is one month too long for you to wait, Mr. Huang?"

I did not hear what was said at the other end of the line.

"So mean!" Yin commented.

"Should show more respect to the chairman than talking like a debt collector," I said.

The expression of annoyance on Mao's face disappeared when he heard our comments. With a smile he remarked that although Huang was "not a good friend, he was bold enough."

On the day the album was due to be returned, Mao placed it carefully between two boards and gave it to Yin. "Take it back to Huang. Be sure it's returned before zero hour."

"But Mr. Huang had said that you can keep it a few days longer if you wish," said Yin.

"Take it back to him," Mao said with a wave of his hand. "I said one month. Friends should keep faith with each other."

The principle of "drawing a line between business and personal life," which Mao insisted upon, also applied to his relatives.

One day, in the spring of 1950, he said to his son Anying "I want you to visit your mother's grave back home in my stead. Take her mother something as a brithday present from me. Your mother* was an intelligent and sympathetic woman, and a woman of great vision, too. She was a great help to me. Her father, Mr. Yang, held progressive political views. He gave me a lot of financial help...." Mao paused, and his eyes became a little moist. In a low, hoarse voice, he added emotionally, "I miss them very much...."

Mao supported Mrs. Yang for a long time without fail and helped his friends and relatives out when they were hard up, with money from his salary or from the income which he received from his writings. But he refused to do any of them any favour when it came to business matters. Shortly after the founding of New China, he received dozens of letters from them asking for such favours. Mao's replies were fine examples of his adherence to principle. In his letter to Yang Kaizhi, his brother-in-law, he said, "Don't expect me to do anything of this nature. Don't come to Beijing," and advised him to obtain what he wanted "through the proper channels." In another letter, to Mao Senpin, who was an old school-friend of Mao's, he said, "Your offer of service in the government is highly valued. Perhaps it would be advisable for you to earn your position in the government naturally, as a reward for your devotion to the well-being of the people and in acknowledgment of prestige thereby established. My recommendation might do harm to your good name. I would be glad if you share my views on this matter."

---

* Mao's first wife, Yang Kaihui, the daughter of his professor, who died a martyr at the hands of the Kuomintang, when, during China's civil war, she refused to disclose Mao's whereabouts.

The opening line of his poem in memory of Yang Kaihui, Anying's mother, and Liu Zhixun perfectly encapsulates his enormous affection for Yang, Liu, and Liu's wife, Li Shuyi. The poem offended Jiang Qing. Commenting on her reaction, Mao remarked to me, "Jiang Qing still remains petty-bourgeois in mentality. She's got a vicious tongue and is a trouble-maker." When Jiang learned of this, she refused to speak to Mao for several days. After the founding of New China, Mao continued to correspond with Li Shuyi. But when Li asked Mao for help to get her to Beijing to study, Mao refused.

During the fifteen years I was with Mao, I was never aware of his allowing his friends or relatives to exploit their connection with him for personal gain. But on more than one occasion I witnessed how extraordinarily warm he could be with them.

On one such occasion an old lady came to see him. She was somebody Mao had known back home. She came to tell Mao about her village. The manner in which Mao treated her was quite unusual. He helped her both into and out of her seat, and kept on saying, "Easy, easy" as he helped her up and down the steps, and all the while she was saying, in the same tone as Mao, "Easy, easy. I'm an old woman and can't walk properly."

As far as I'm concerned, the scene is unforgettable, for the old lady took the treatment which she received from Mao entirely for granted, as though it was her due.

As I observed, throughout the years I was his bodyguard, Mao behaved just like anyone else when he was in the company of those of us "close to him."

One day, early in the 1950s, a new ambassador from one of those countries friendly to China, was going to present his credentials to Mao. The procedure was to commence with the ambassador reading the credentials out loud to Mao, who, as chairman of the government, would remain standing whilst listening to him, after which the ambassador would hand Mao the letter of appointment.

As required by elaborate etiquette, Mao had to shave and have a haircut before meeting with the ambassador. The barber was Wang Hui, an old man with bald head, white beard, and lean face with a pair of outsize presbyopic glasses straddling his nose. He had done nothing other than cut people's hair all his life, and now probably hoped for nothing more than to be able to continue in his profession for a couple of more years.

But even these glasses were not much help to his failing eye-sight. With his eyes straining behind them, his head cocked to one side, and his neck stretched this way and that, in a painful effort to find the angle from which he could see best, each shaky movement of the razor was a long time in coming. On this occasion, he was no faster. With his left hand on Mao's head holding it still, and his right hand holding the razor above Mao's head, as if threatening to execute the chairman, he would aim long at Mao's face each time before applying the instrument, and each time he had finished, he would step back and admire his work, as though it were a work of art. With him working like this, even those of us watching him were beginning to lose patience.

Mao looked at his watch. "Faster, please."

"Keep quiet, keep quiet!" He mumbled. When he changed position to work on the other side of Mao's face, with the razor poised above Mao's head in exactly the same manner, he still worked no faster.

"Aiya! Can't you go a little faster, Wang?" Mao was growing impatient. He moved in the chair, only to be stopped by the barber, who said unhurriedly, "Why can't you sit still, as I say? You won't be late, I assure you."

When he finally finished with Mao's face, the chairman wiped his brows—perhaps he had been sweating. Just as he was about to rise from the chair, the pressure of Wang's hand on his head prevented him. "You're not doing what I say. I told you to sit still and take it easy...."

"I want you to go faster," Mao protested feebly.

"Hold it! Do as I say! I haven't finished yet." So saying, Wang patted Mao twice on the back of the head as he would do a child. All the bodyguards present were stunned.

But Mao did not take offence; he only sighed in resignation. As if emboldened by Mao's passivity, Wang began to "admonish" the chairman as he shaved the back of his neck: "You're the chairman of the government and you should look the part. You see, you bear my work, and I don't want to hear people say that I don't know anything about my trade; I would be ashamed."

Wang Hui was the only person I can remember who carried himself with great self-esteem in Mao's presence and never failed to demonstrate his belief that he was equal in political status to the leader of the nation.

The world does not lack people who are eager to help others attain happiness, and Mao was such a person.

Han Guixin was eighteen years old when she joined Mao's staff. As our work brought us into frequent contact, we became friends and grew to like each other. But we stopped at that. One day, during the war in northern Shaanxi, Mao asked me, "What do you think of Han?"

"She's a nice girl," I replied casually.

Mao looked at me, smiling mysteriously and significantly. "What you two need is more contact and a better understanding of one another."

Mao's words were heartening, but I flushed, hanging my head in silence. I knew I had found an intimate friend in Mao.

"Talk to each other more often," Mao advised, like a tender father, "show more concern and help one another more. That's what you should do."

Once we were no longer constantly on the move, after reaching Xibaipo, my contact with Han increased. One day, when we were taking a walk, Mao asked me intimately, "Going strong with her?"

I smiled bashfully and said nothing.

"There's nothing improper about it," Mao took my hand in his and patted it encouragingly. "You have my approval...."

As a matter of fact I was worried, for in Xibaipo single men outnumbered single women, so the former all vied with each other for the attention of the latter. Han was approached by quite a few matchmakers, whilst I was too bashful to let her know of my feelings towards her, or to ask for the help of a third party.*

Then an opportunity presented itself.

My folks back home wrote to me, telling me that they had found a girl for me. I showed the letter to Mao.

"What do you think I should do, Comrade Chairman?"

---

*A third party or match-maker, traditionally used as a "go-between" to arrange marriages in China. Such a system is still not uncommon in China today, where social opportunities for young people to meet each other are perhaps fewer than in the West.

After reading the letter, instead of answering my question, Mao asked, "What do you think you should do?"

I hung my head in silence.

Mao laughed. "You're too shy! Why don't you go and ask Han for help? Ask her to write a reply for you; she writes better than you do."

My face immediately brightened. There couldn't be any idea better than this.

"Read this letter, Han," I told her. As she read it I watched her reaction, and than asked by way of testing her, "What do you think? Should I ... say no?"

"Say, say it then...." As she spoke her breath grew shorter and her face crimson.

Now I saw my chance. "Would you write a letter for me to tell them so?"

"That's a smart thing to ask," she mumbled bashfully. "But you've been so dumb. I refused the whole lot of them. I was waiting.... I would say yes...."

I gave a long sigh and smiled. "I would still be dumb if the chairman hadn't tipped me off. He told me to ask you to write the letter for me."

When I returned, I told Mao what had gone on between Han and myself. He was so happy, as though he had been rewarded for his good deeds, that he took my hand and said, "Let's go for a walk, Yinqiao."

In the courtyard, with his hand on my arm, Mao said to me softly, "Be persistent, Yinqiao, be persistent. It seems as if you were brought together by an invisible hand: two from the same county, working for the same person."

Han and I sent in our request for permission to get married in December 1948.* In two days the letter of request was returned to us. It was filled in with the written comments of my superiors: "Full approval for this happy marriage," "Unreserved approval," "Approval and congratulations," "No reason to withhold approval for this perfect marriage," "The Party branch gives its approval." We have treasured this letter of request ever since it was returned to us.

I was not the only bodyguard who was indebted to Mao for his marriage. He helped others, too, and in doing so, he was both enthu-

---

*In China today, it is still necessary to obtain letters of permission, authorizing a couple to marry, from their respective work units.

siastic and cool, principled and realistic, and above all, he saw to it that the suitor didn't lose his dignity.

Feng Yaosong met a girl at a dance. He fell in love with her. Very soon he fell out of it. She was a member of a song and dance ensemble. When Mao heard about this during a trip, he tried to talk Feng out of his feeling of frustration.

"You shouldn't have taken a fancy to a girl from a song and dance ensemble in the first place," Mao said. "A girl like that wants to look chic and enjoy life. On your salary of just over forty yuan a month, you could hardly make her happy. We're not living in a communist society yet, and you have to be realistic."

He gave similar advice to the other bodyguards: "Be realistic when you look for a wife. Don't make use of your connection with me; if you do, you'll end up miserably. The social circumstances in our country still make it necessary for both sides to be realistic. Love alone won't get you anywhere."

Feng, perhaps wanting to try again, met another girl from a song and dance ensemble at a dance in Hefei, in Anhui Province, and fell in love with her. When Mao learned of this, he said to Feng in jest, "Are you testing the theory of decisive warfare?"

Mao said that when Zeng Xisheng, secretary of Anhui provincial Party's committee, and his wife were visiting him. Mao asked them to find out about the girl. In the evening, they informed Mao that they did not think she was the girl for Feng, since she was nearly three years older than he was.

"Her age isn't much of a problem, is it?" Mao said to Feng. "Get a wife three years your senior, and you get a gold-mine, as the saying goes.* Besides, she looks younger than her age."

"But she's a divorced mother with a child," the Zengs added.

"What do you say, Feng?" Mao looked at Feng. "Would you like to be the child's step-father? Be honest."

Feng shook his head in dejection.

"These young men working for me are all fine lads," Mao explained

---

*The traditional Chinese saying goes: "If you marry a woman three years your senior, you are holding a golden brick in your arms...." An older woman was considered to be more responsible in terms of domestic duties, maternal responsibilities and household management.

to the Zengs. "Girl-friends for them should be satisfactory both in looks and other respects. I'm sorry for this song and dance ensemble actress in your province."

After the Zengs left, Mao said, jabbing at Feng with his fingers, "The theory of quick decision didn't work, did it? But don't give up. Try protracted warfare instead."

At Lushan Mountain Mao solicited the help of Shui Jing, the wife of Yang Shangkui, who was then secretary of the Jiangxi provincial Party committee. Soon Shui found a nurse for Feng. After Mao returned to Beijing, he helped Feng with his love letters to the nurse. On the day of their wedding, they brought Mao wedding candies.* Popping one which the bride had unwrapped for him into his mouth, Mao offered them his best wishes with a smile: "I'm so glad. I wish you a long-lasting and happy marriage!"

Tian Yunyu's first girl-friend was also an actress. When they split up after going steady for two years, Tian asked for the return of a wrist-watch and some woolen fabrics which he had given to her as presents. Mao didn't like that. He said to Tian, "It's not manly to do a thing like that," and "Stop asking her for the return of these things. They make good mementoes of the happy days you spent together. It's not manly to treat a former girl-friend like an enemy." Later Tian found a wife with Mao's help.

Yao Shuxian, a girl attendant of Mao's special train, once missed a date with her boy-friend on account of work. She had not been able to let him know that she would be unable to meet him as promised. Mao was a bit worried when he heard about this. "That's not good," he said. "If he waited for you the whole evening and you never showed up, he must be very unhappy." Yao said, "Don't worry. I'll explain to him."

But Mao couldn't set his mind at ease. He wrote a verse for Yao and told her to give it to her boy-friend. The verse, which Yao still has, reads:

"Fair is the young lady
Who waits for me in the corner of town
But never steps out

---

*It is traditional in China to distribute candy at the time a couple marry, to friends, acquaintances and relatives.

Leaving me wonder all day"

The bodygaurds' office kept a list of names of people who had worked for Mao. Mao said to us more than once, "Whenever anyone who used to work for me in the past comes to see me, be sure to let me know. If I'm not working, I'll see him. If I'm too busy, you can receive him in my stead."

One day, in the fall of 1954, the guard-house at the west gate of Zhongnanhai called to tell me that a man by the name of Zhai Zuojun was asking to see the chairman. I checked the name-list and found the name there. So I left for Mao's room.

Mao was working. When I told him of the request, he nodded his assent. "You don't know him. He's from Henan Province. Used to be a Red Army officer, lean and tall. Show him in."

I saw Zhai in the guard-house. He was about forty years old, lean and tall and from Henan, as Mao described. I escorted him to Mao's study.

Mao rose from behind his desk when Zhai entered. He offered him his hand, and Zhai, after saluting him, took it in a handshake.

"Welcome," Mao was relaxed and kind. "Sit down, please. What do you do now?"

"I'm in the air force."

"Good! Sit down, sit down and talk."

I brought them tea and left. Mao's visitors could always expect to be offered a cup of tea.

Half an hour later the telephone rang in the bodyguards' office. When I returned to Mao's study I found them talking still. Zhai, who apparently knew Mao's ways, rose as soon as I entered the room. "I must get going now, Comrade Chairman. Thanks!"

Mao accompanied him to the door, stopping short of the threshold. Zhai left Zhongnanhai in my company.

Later on, when Mao was in Wuhan, Zhai visited him again, and once more left in half an hour. Mao wrote to Zhai several times.

Several times a year Mao would receive visitors like Zhai. They did not stay for dinner unless they had come to say good-bye to him. When Li Liancheng and Tian Yunyu were leaving Mao, they came to see him during the Lunar New Year holiday.* Mao had dinner with them, during which he made them a toast, and even took a drink himself, which was quite unusual for Mao, since he did not usually drink. The wine made him turn red in the face immediately. Looking at them both affectionately, he said, "I want you to come and see me as often as you can. I'll miss you."

Mao never hesitated to help those who had worked for him when they were hard pressed for money. He would say, "They have helped me with my work, and I mustn't turn my back on them when they're in need."

But Mao never helped any of them get anything they did not deserve or a position in the government. His advice to those leaving him was, "Keep your mind on your work," "Be modest and prudent," and "Feel free to write to me if you're hard up."

---

*It is customary to pay visits to old friends and relatives during this festival.

Mao Bringing Up His Children

Mao, who lost six of his kinsfolk in the struggle for the liberation of China, was a loving but strict father to his children.

It is well-known in China that when Mao Anying, Mao's eldest son by Yang Kaihui, returned from studying in the Soviet Union, Mao sent him to the Shaanxi-Gansu-Ningxia border region in patched clothes to learn farming from a model peasant. Let me recount a few other incidents regarding the way in which Mao treated his children.

A girl student at Kangda (the Chinese People's Anti-Japanese Military and Political College in Yan'an) from Beiping, by the name of Fu, was very pretty. At the time few girls in Yan'an, a small town in the back country, measured up to her in looks. When Jiang Qing saw her, she hit upon an idea. One Sunday, Jiang played host to her and Mao Anying. At dinner and during the course of the conversation they had they seemed to enjoy one another's company. After the girl left, Jiang said to Anying, "You're old enough to get married. What do you think of Fu?"

After a brief silence, Mao Anying asked bashfully, "What would father say to it?"

"I'll talk to him if you like her. I don't expect any objections from him."

But Jiang's enthusiasm was dampened by Mao. Shaking his head, Mao said, "Isn't it a bit too early to be talking about marriage, after they have met only once? If the young man can't wait, you certainly can. Tell Anying I want to talk to him."

"Your father wants to see you," Jiang told Anying, adding, "now everything depends on you...."

"I think she's quite nice...." Anying told Mao bashfully.

"Or you wouldn't feel drawn to her," Mao said, smiling playfully. "I understand that. What I don't understand is why you just go for good looks."

Anying fell bashfully silent.

"Do you know anything about her," now Mao was serious, "except that she's pretty? What about her faith in the revolution, her moral character, her personality? She came from Beiping only a short time ago, and we don't know anything about her. Marriage for you is not just a personal matter; it has to do with the revolution. You're Mao Zedong's son and that's hard luck for you. What you need is discretion on this matter."

Mao was proved right. Finding the severity of life in Yan'an too much for her, the girl returned to Beiping, where she attempted to discredit the revolution in the newspapers. Mao commented upon this in his heavy, rhythmic Hunan accent: "A pretty face can be deceptive. But one can never be deceived by one's faith in the revolution."

After moving to Xibaipo, Mao Anying was sent to a nearby village, together with a girl by the name of Liu Siqi, as member of a land-reform team. Soon they fell in love with one another. With the help of Deng Yingchao, Zhou Enlai's wife, and Kang Keqing, Zhu De's wife, Anying managed to get Mao's approval for their proposed marriage.

One day, at the same time that Mao was helping me to win the hand of Han Guixin, Mao Anying went to see his father.

"Aunt Kang has told you about Siqi and I, hasn't she?"

"Yes," Mao answered, without looking up from the document which he was reading.

"Shall we go and register for marriage now?"

"How old is Siqi?"

"Eighteen."

"Is that her nominal or full age? Be honest."

(A person's nominal age is generally one or two years older than his or her full age.)

"That's her nominal age, but there's only a few months difference...."

"Not even a day's difference. No! I'm busy."

Mao Anying, who had come with high hopes, left in dejection. By contrast, Mao was much more enthusiastic about my marriage, which I found both heart-warming and a little disturbing.

Mao Anying was on C mess like us bodyguards. The administrative office had tried to put him on B mess, but the chairman said no. He said

169

to Anying, "Your sister (Li Ne) has been on C mess ever since she was a child. You're old enough to know which grade of mess is for you without my telling you."

That day we were squatting in the courtyard eating—we always ate like that—when a rooster chasing a hen kicked up a lot of dust. I rose quickly to keep out of its way. Mao Anying didn't. Looking at the chickens, he grumbled: "Even a rooster needs a hen. I'm a human being and still waiting at the age of twenty-seven."

I was gripped by a sense of guilt: here I was getting married at the age of twenty-one, whilst Mao Anying still had to wait at the age of twenty-seven. I offered him my advice: "Be patient and talk to the chairman when he's in the right mood."

One day, when the news of the annihilation of seven enemy brigades by our forces in East China reached us, I said to Mao Anying, "The chairman's singing Beijing opera now. Go and see him." Mao was often heard singing arias when he was in high spirits.

Mao Anying left for his father's office immediately.

"I'm getting married tomorrow, Dad." Mao Anying tried to give the chairman the impression that nothing could stop him now.

"Haven't I told you to wait?"

"This is something I can decide for myself, I guess."

"You can decide who you want to marry, but not at what age you can marry.* The regulations decide that."

"Lots of people get married in spite of them...."

"But you are Mao Zedong's son!" Mao slapped the writing brush on the ink stone. "Who will stick to the regulations if you don't?"

Mao Anying left feeling bitter. Mao, panting in anger, mumbled to himself, "A happy day spoiled!"

After returning to his room, in frustration and anger, Mao Anying threw himself on the bed, crying so bitterly and making such a scene that no one could stop him.

Mao flew into a rage when Yan Changlin, platoon leader of the

---

*The legal age for marriage in New China, used to be 18 years old for women, and 20 for men. Now young people are encouraged to marry late, so it is 20 years old for women, and 22 for men, in rural and remote (less densely populated) areas, and 23 years old for women, and 25 for men in the cities, due to housing shortages for married couples and couples with families.

bodyguard, told him what was happening. He threw the writing brush down on the desk and walked out of the room furiously. I immediately followed him out: I didn't want him to hit his son. But he stopped in front of Mao Anying's room, and, standing there, thundered—Mao was frightful when he shouted—"What do you mean, Mao Anying?"

That was enough. Immediately Mao Anying was stilled and the room fell silent.

Mao turned around and left; he didn't need to say any more.

A few weeks later, on one of his constitutionals on the edge of the village, Mao saw Mao Anying returning from the nearby village. After greeting his father, the young man tried to get away from him with an excuse. Mao stopped him. "Don't you try to evade me. Tell me: do you still want to marry without waiting?"

"Not any longer," Anying said with down-cast eyes. "I was wrong."

"What about Siqi?"

"She has no objection. We've decided to wait until next year."

"Now you're talking like my son." Mao was pleased, and with a wave of his hand he added, "Go on home."

Mao continued with his walk. Stopping in the middle of it, and looking at me, he asked, "Whom do you think I am closer to, my son or you?"

I thought for a while before replying, "You feel closer to us."

Mao made no comment; he said thoughtfully: "My son and I see each other only once every few years. Even when we're not separated, we don't see each other more than a handful of times a year. But you're with me every hour of the day and have become my shadow. If what occurs in my family is a secret to others, it is not a secret to you. But don't write about me when I'm still alive; wait until I die, and write truthfully when you do."

In 1958, when Mao learned that I was thinking of writing about him in response to a call for "worker-peasant-soldier" involvement in literary creation,* Mao reminded me, "Don't write about me when I'm still alive. Wait until I die."

When Jiang Qing and some others learned that Mao had decided to send Mao Anying to Korea to join the war there, they tried to talk

---

*Another movement launched in 1958, the year of great leap forward.

him out of it, saying that the work which Mao Anying was then doing was important. Mao explained his decision to them; one of the reasons that he gave, which I can not forget, was: "He's Mao Zedong's son. Who would go if he didn't?"

Mao was not told of the telegram from Peng Dehuai informing him of the death of Mao Anying in Korea.* Jiang Qing, Zhou Enlai and Ye Zilong had decided to keep the sad news a secret from Mao. It was only some time later that Jiang and Ye broke it to him.

Mao had finished the day's work and was resting in an easy chair. When he heard the news, his initial reaction was one of shock. He didn't say anything; he just looked at Jiang and Ye. The two hung their heads in silence; they knew better than to repeat the news to him or offer him their sympathy.

Mao then blinked, slowly turning his eyes away from them towards a pack of cigarettes on the tea-table. He picked up the pack and tried to take out a cigarette, but he couldn't do it; he tried again, and again he failed. I hurried over, took one out and lighted it for him.

The room was silent, except for the hissing sound which Mao made as he inhaled the cigarette smoke between his teeth. Then I noticed that his eyes had suddenly turned red and moist around the rims, caused perhaps by some stray cigarette smoke, or by past memories flooding his mind.

Ye Zilong quietly left the room.

Mao finished another cigarette. He ground the stub in the ashtray, breaking the long silence with a sigh charged with such emotion that would move anyone to tears: "He was Mao Zedong's son and that was hard luck for him...."

I looked away and cried.

Mao did not cry. He lighted yet another cigarette, and listened to Jiang Qing's detailed account of the tragedy. What I heard was only fragmentary: It happened during an air-raid, when enemy airplanes were dropping incendiary bombs. Mao Anying left the air-raid shelter never to return; he was burned to death. I did not hear any more. My mind was filled with echoes of what Mao had just said: "He was Mao Zedong's son and that was hard luck for him."

---

*November 25, 1950.

Mao Anqing was Mao's younger son by Yang Kaihui, and bore a strong resemblance to his father. During early childhood, with his father away and his mother murdered by the reactionaries,* Mao Anqing was left with no one to take care of him, and all the misfortune that life could bring to a child, which reduced him to wandering and begging, and inflicted great damage to his health. In his case, being concerned about his impaired health, Mao was more of a loving than a stern father, as he was with Mao Anying.

Early in August of 1957, Mao was in Qingdao, where Mao Anqing was then recuperating in a sanatorium. One day I brought Mao Anqing to him as instructed. They had a nice talk together in one of the rooms of the city government's liaison office where Mao was staying. Work, study and politics were the subjects which Mao discussed with Anying; with Anqing, he showed more interest in his study, daily life and health.

The nurse who was taking care of Mao Anqing was very nice to him, and something more than mere friendship had by then developed between them. When Mao learned of this, he asked the guard-office to send someone to the sanatorium to enquire about the girl and at the same time to find out about the medical treatment which Mao Anqing was receiving there. The guard who the office sent was Xu Yongfu. Xu was quite thoroughgoing with his enquiry. When he returned from the sanatorium, he sent a report to Mao. Mao read it carefully and was so well-pleased that he told Tian Yunyu to thank Xu. He said to Tian, "Go and tell Xu it's a good report. Say thanks to him for me and tell him I appreciate it very much."

With his daughters, Li Min and Li Ne, Mao never allowed his love for them to interfere with what he demanded of them, which was no less strict than what he demanded of his sons.

Li Min's pet name was Lovely Lovely (Jiao Jiao). She had got it from Deng Yingchao, who, once holding her in her arms soon after she was born, had looked at her fondly, and proclaimed, "What a lovely, lovely baby!" When she began to attend school in China, after returning from the Soviet Union in 1947, Mao had given her the name Li Min.

Mao was then known as Li Desheng. "Ne" and "Min" have their

---

*The Kuomintang.

origin in a line from *The Analects of Confucius*, that says: "The gentleman is slow in speech (ne) but quick in action (min)." Mao wanted his daughters to be like that.

The two girls never enjoyed the privilege of sharing A mess with their father; for them it was always C mess like the rest of us. When they were college students, they lived on the campus, sleeping on bunk-beds in a dormitory shared by six or eight roommates, and eating simple food like the rest of the students. They were always dressed in old blue cotton jackets and pants, attended the same classes as their fellow students, did manual labour along with them, and went about on foot, bicycles or in crowded buses, like all the other students. There was nothing about them that showed they were Mao's daughters.

One day, around 1956, during a walk, Mao asked me, "Which one of them do you like better, Li Min or Li Ne?"

"They're both fine girls," I said. "They're respectful, both of them. Some of the children of high-ranking officials turn their noses up at people like us, but they don't. They're very strict with themselves and always strive to do better."

"Not as hard as you do, I'm afraid," said Mao, shaking his head, "nor are they as promising as you are. Life has never meant as much hardship to them as it has to you. The world belongs to those who are not daunted by the severity of life."

"You don't mean they haven't suffered enough hardship, do you?" I said. "Life's been a great deal harsher to them than to the children of ordinary families."

"I don't agree with you," Mao shook his head. "You're using the wrong yardstick for comparison. You mean as my daughters they shouldn't have been exposed to so much hardship, and should live better than the children of ordinary families. True, they eat the same kind of food as you do, but isn't the food you get on C mess better than the food eaten by the majority of Chinese peasants?"

"But it's not fair," I argued, "to cite the lowest standard of living for comparison in their case, Comrade Chairman. I don't think the food most of the city people eat is any worse than the food the students get from their school canteens. I, for one, get better food at home than from the C mess canteen."

"And the people don't see anything wrong in that," Mao said with a smile, "because you've made a contribution to the revolution. But the two kids haven't contributed anything yet. It pays to think of people worse off than yourself when it comes to standards of living. A man who vies with others for material comfort and not for service to the revolution is contemptible."

It's true that life wasn't as harsh to Li Ne as it was to her sister and brothers. But I still believe that she would have been spared much of the harhship she was made to endure if she had been the child of an ordinary family. She was only seven years old in 1947 when I became Mao's bodyguard. From that year on, life for her meant, as it did for us, constant marches, exposure to the elements, enemy air-raids, the shrill of bullets cutting through the air and the pungent smell of gun smoke.

I remember what Li Ne was like when she was seven: a little girl, clutching a small enamel-coated bowl, waiting in line with the men in front of a big pot to be served her ration of black soya beans, and then retreating quietly to a wall when her bowl was full, and squatting there, dipping her tiny fingers into the bowl and putting the salty boiled beans into her mouth, and chewing slowly, slowly, ending up with a gas-filled stomach like the rest of us; or the same girl entertaining the men with selections from Beijing opera, which she sang in her lovely child's voice during the lulls of a battle.

Of all his children Mao loved Li Ne best. I don't remember how many times I saw him holding her in his arms after a hectic day, patting her gently on the back, saying, "Baby, my darling baby ..." and Li Ne, wrapping her arms around his neck, responding with, "Daddy, my darling Daddy...."

For all the tender love he possessed for Li Ne, Mao wouldn't allow her to be put on A mess like himself. After the founding of New China, Li Ne's nurse, finding justification in Mao's now being the chairman of the government, once said to him, "It's time Li Ne ate with you, Comrade Chairman." Mao, indicating his flat refusal with a wave of his hand, responded: "No. She's to continue to eat with you. She's to stay on C mess like you."

After entering college, Li Ne only returned home on Saturday evenings. The university was far out in the suburbs; sometimes, on account of campus activities, she was not able to leave for home until it was dark. Since I thought it was unsafe for a girl to make the trip at night alone, I decided, without Mao's knowledge, to take her home in a car. The car would be parked in an inconspicuous place away from the campus, and I would enter the university, and quietly leave with her in the car. To avoid any bad impression, I made sure that we left without drawing the attention of her fellow students.

But Mao found out. He gave me a good dressing down for doing that, and I protested: "But it isn't safe for a girl to walk home alone at night...."

"What about the other girls?" Mao stared hard at me. "If it's safe for them, why isn't it safe for my daughter?"

"She's different, she's Mao Zedong's child," I said in a loud voice.

Mao was taken aback by what I said, but before he had time to lose his temper, I added: "The enemy's not interested in other people's children, but they're certainly interested in yours."

Mao's rising anger gave way to a sense of satisfaction: he was apparently pleased with my alertness at a time when the Kuomintang was clamouring for a military counter-offensive on the mainland. But he stood his ground: "No more car for her. Do what I say. She can use a bicycle."

Jiang Qing, who was present, chimed in, "I was used to walking at night, when I was barely ten years old. She's old enought to take care of herself. You may go now, and do as the chairman says."

The winter of 1960 was a severe one: the country was in serious economic trouble. The days were short, and with no car to take her home, Li Ne was able to return only once every two or three weeks. Her sister, Li Min, was resting at home on account of poor health, but Li Ne had to remain on the campus. One day I sent one of the bodyguards, Yin Jingshan, to see her. The girl looked pale. When Yin asked her if she was ill, she hesitated for a long time before confiding to him, "To tell you the truth, Uncle Yin, I'm hungry."

When Yin told me about that, I decided to do something for her. The bond of affection which had formed between the two of us in northern Shaanxi, and the memory of her eating nothing better than black soya beans, but still managing to entertain us with Beijing opera, made me feel very close to her at such a time. On the quiet, I brought her a parcel of crackers.

She opened the parcel and looked furtively around. Whe she was sure that no one was watching, she shoved two crackers into her mouth and swallowed them almost immediately. Watching her, I was saddened: they were just a few crackers but she had to eat them on the sly. She put the crackers away in a secure place: they were so precious to her that she didn't want to eat them all at once, but wanted to make them last as long as possible. I said, "Go on, eat them all. I'll bring you more."

When Jiang Qing discovered this, she took me to task, but not without my answering her back. Afraid that I might pick a row with her like the last time, she wasn't as harsh with me as she would have been with the other bodyguards, but she told Mao of what I had done. Mao called me in.

"How many times do I have to tell you no one is allowed any special priviledges?" Mao was angry.

"But the other students get extra food from home...." I stammered. If Jiang Qing could not frighten me with all her fury, Mao could.

"They can, but not my daughter! No extra food for her, not even one single cracker!" Slapping the desk, he added, "She's Mao Zedong's daughter!"

I did not dare say anything more. From then on, Li Ne never got anything more from me.

That day when I returned home, I complained to my wife about what had happened, blaming Jiang Qing for the criticism which I had received from Mao. But secretly I knew that Jiang was right; anyway, Li Ne was her daughter.

One Saturday, not long after that, Li Ne returned home. Yin Jingshan, as he was pouring tea for Mao, said to him, "Li Ne's returned, Comrade Chairman. Will you have dinner with her? It's been several weeks since she was last home."

Mao gently and appreciatively looked up at him, saying, "That's a good idea. Yes."

Yin immediately went to tell Jiang Qing, who after some hesitation said in a low voice, "Make it a nice meal with extra rice and extra vegetable oil."

Mao's house did not have a dining-room. Mao ate his meals, which were brought to him by the bodyguards in a food-basket, in his bedroom or office. That day the dinner consisted of four dishes and soup, with hot pepper and preserved toufu served on saucers on the side. The cook was proud of what he had prepared: "I put in twice as much rice for this meal."

Li Ne was in Mao's bedroom telling her father about her studies at college. She wound up by complaining mildly about the food she got at the university. "I'm always runnig short of rations," she said. "The side-dishes are very small portions, cooked with nothing but salt and plain water. The vegetable oil we're allowed isn't even enough for the cooks to help themselves to. I never go to a class with a full stomach."

"These difficulties won't last long," Mao said kindly. "Stick them out like everyone else in the country. Set an example for the others, explain to them and don't lose confidence in the Communist Party." He added humorously, "I can't tell the cooks what to do."

Yin Jingshan returned. "Dinner's ready, Comrade Chairman."

"Come and eat with me." Mao took his daughter by the hand and led her to the dinner table.

Li Ne picked up the chopsticks and smelled long and hard at the steaming hot rice. It was brown rice mixed with taro roots. "How nice it smells!" she exclaimed, and smiled a lovely smile at her parents.

Jiang Qing looked at her and then at Mao. She wanted to say something but checked herself; she didn't want the bodyguard who was waiting on table to hear her. With a half-hearted smile, she picked some food from one of the dishes and put it into Li Ne's bowl.

"Come on, let's eat," Mao said, pointing at the dishes with his chopsticks.

Li Ne began to shovel the rice into her mouth, but stopped midway; it was so hot it brought tears to her eyes. She opened her mouth and blew out steam before gobbling up the rest of her rice.

"Slow down. No need to hurry," Mao said as calmly as he could manage, smiling faintly but unnaturally.

Li Ne stole a glance at the bodyguard and said apologetically, "We all eat fast at the school. Grown used to it."

"But you're eating at home now." Mao was barely audible; there was sadness in his smile.

"Eat as much as you can." Jiang Qing kept picking the food from the dishes and shoving it into Li Ne's bowl. She looked a bit off colour. That smile was still on her lips, but it threatened to disappear. The way she looked at Li Ne was characteristic of a mother.

Li Ne wasn't much inhibited in the presence of her parents. Soon she began to eat like a hungry wolf, downing the food without even bothering to chew it. She would steal a quick look now and then at the dishes to see how much was left.

In the beginning, Mao kept his daughter company by chatting in a leisurely manner with her. But it wasn't long before he fell silent and ate more slowly, taking a long time over each mouthful. Then he stopped altogether and looked at his daughter thoughtfully.

Jiang Qing had stopped eating much earlier. She looked at her daughter and then at Mao. She breathed audibly several times, fixing her eyes upon her husband. Sometimes she wouldn't come out with what was on her mind; she wanted Mao to read her thoughts and say it for her.

"Hey, why have you stopped eating?" Reluctantly, Li Ne took her face away from her rice bowl.

"Well," Mao said, smiling vacantly, "just too old to eat much. I wish I were as young as you are." He picked up a newspaper, turned half-around in his seat and began to read it; he seemed absorbed in what he was reading, nodding his head slightly and murmuring something.

Suddenly, Jiang Qing, her chest heaving slightly, picked up her bowl, emptied what was left in it into Li Ne's, rose and left the room. Her eyes were filled with tears.

Mao didn't seem to notice all that. But as soon as Jiang had gone, he looked up from the newspaper and said to his daughter, "Years ago, I was conducting an investigation in the countryside, in Hunan. I once begged a bowl of leftover rice after I had gone hungry for a whole day...."

Li Ne wasn't listening. Before Mao could finish, she said, "I'll finish what's left if you don't mind."

"Go ahead!" Mao looked at his daughter for just a fleeting second and then took his eyes away from her, as if he might have seen something he didn't want to see if he had looked any longer. He returned to his newspaper and, tapping on the table, added, "Do a thorough job of it and don't waste anything."

If Li Ne had known that her father would sometimes go with nothing more than a plate of purslane a day, she wouldn't have been so "inconsiderate." She made a clean sweep of the dishes, leaving not so much as a piece of chopped onion on them. But she still didn't want to leave the table. Looking longingly at the empty plates, she said, "I'm growing up, Dad, and have a huge appetite.... I can eat three corn buns this size," which was the size of a rice bowl, as she indicated with her hands.

Mao didn't take his eyes away from the newspaper; he responded by merely biting his lower lip.

"It's a really nice meal, but...." Li Ne stole a look at her father from the corner of her eye, and then looking at Yin Jingshan, asked slyly, "Is there any soup left, Uncle Yin? We may rinse the plates with it so nothing will be wasted."

Yin looked away; he couldn't hold back his tears. He made straight for the kitchen.

"Poor child!" said the cook. He found two buns made of mixed wheat and corn flour, and before he could roast them Yin had grabbed them and left.

Looking guiltily at her father, Li Ne broke off a piece from one of the buns, and wiped it round one of the plates, whilst Yin made "soup" for her by rinsing the plates with hot water. Mao swallowed noisily, rose from his seat and left the room in silence. He was walking towards the courtyard when he suddenly turned back for his bedroom; he took only a few steps in that direction before turning around again for the courtyard. It seemed he didn't know what he wanted to do.

That night Jiang Qing went to Mao's room and dismissed the bodyguard there. When she re-emerged half an hour later, her eyes were red around the rims; apparently she had been crying. We knew what had happened, so we all went to see Mao.

"It's too much for Li Ne, Comrade Chairman. Would it be possilbe for her...."

"No. She's not any worse off than the people in the countryside." Mao knew what the food situation was like in the countryside.*

"But...."

"Say no more. I don't feel happy about it as you may be thinking, nor does her mother. But I'm a member of the government; I get what I'm entitled to, according to the regulations. Li Ne's a student, and there

---

*There was near starvation in rural areas in China at this time.

is no regulation which allows her more than she is getting now." Then, sighing deeply, he continued in a slightly sad tone, "As I said about my other children, she's Mao Zedong's daughter and that's tough luck for her. Let's all keep things in perspective; this is especially important at a time like this."

Mao might have been summing up the love he felt for his children, and the strict demands which he placed upon them when he said, "She's Mao Zedong's daughter and that's tough luck for her." It was so eloquently said that I shall never forget it.

By 1980, my wife and I were no longer restricted in our contact with Li Ne. Jiang Qing had been convicted of her crimes as a member of the Gang of Four; Li Ne was living alone with her son and was not doing very well. When I advised her to marry again, she said, "Who'd marry a woman whose mother's a member of the Gang of Four?" This brought back to me the memory of what Mao had said about his children. So my wife and I reminded her that her father was the great leader and that she was also Mao Zedong's daughter.

Later, my wife and I found a suitable man for Li Ne. He was one of Mao's former guards, by the name of Wang Jingqing. When they married, Comrade Yang Shangkun made them wedding gifts of a large quilt cover* and a box of chocolates—chocolates were Li Ne's great favourite when she was a little girl. The congratulatory message Yang set them was co-signed by all the members of his family.

The help which my wife and I gave to Li Ne won the commendation of Comrade Wang Guangmei, who said, "You've done a good thing. She deserves your help, being the chairman's daughter."

Not long ago, Li Ne treated my wife and I to a dinner when we visited her. She told us, "I'm going to give you something Jingqing has made: bean jelly** and steamed buckwheat cakes."

We were surprised. "Jingqing can make bean jelly and steamed cakes?"

"Life with him is all sunshine. He's a very capable man, a lot more capable than I am."

---

*Traditionally, it is the custom to give a quilt as a wedding-gift—"to put one's quilts together" is a euphemism for getting married in China.

*A clear, transparent jelly made from bean curd, sweetened and served as a sweet.

I am very gratified to know that Li Ne and her husband are living happily together.

Mao's Sense of Humour

Of all the leading figures with whom I had contact, Mao was the most humorous, a quality which the screen image of Mao does not do full justice to. The Mao Zedong seen on the screen, does crack a joke or two, but there is always something about his mien that is missing, as compared with the Mao Zedong in real life. When he walked, for example, he would rock, sway and gyrate his hips, like those old people doing fitness exercises in the park. He needed this exercise to loosen his joints after a long day at the desk; he would do it even when it was only a short walk. The meeting hall at Zhongnanhai was within a stone's throw of his office, but still, he would rock and swing on his way to attend a meeting there, and in the process he could be heard breathing rhythmically and would cast a glance at his bodyguards now and then, as if to say, "Why are you looking at me like that? I'm as much a human being as you are." But the Mao on camera is always to be seen walking with firm steps or in a stately manner. He did carry himself like that, but not when he was alone.

The sense of humour Mao displayed in the face of danger, was evidence of his enormous courage as a leader and a source of strength to the men around him.

One day, when Hu Zongnan's troops were attacking Yan'an, the air-raids by waves of enemy aircraft left Wangjiaping enveloped in thick smoke. The incendiary bombs which they dropped, landed right in front of Mao's cave-room and the ground was strewn with their fragments. When the bodyguards ran into his room after the bombing, they heard Mao asking, without taking his eyes off from the map he was studying:

"Have the visitors left?"

"Visitors? You had visitors?"

"The airplanes," Mao pointed to the sky with his pencil. "Very noisy visitors and nasty."

The bodyguards laughed and felt relaxed.

One needed to have heard Mao say that, to really feel the impact of his sense of humour, which was highlighted by the lively rhythm of the Hunan accent with which he spoke. When the rest of us heard of his remark, we, too, had a good laugh, oblivious of the danger confronting us.

One day during the war in northern Shaanxi, our guide lost his way after reaching a barren hill having just left a village. There was a downpour, down in the gully there was movement of fifty to sixty thousand enemy troops, and sporadic gun-shots could be heard. The men, cold, hungry and nervous, huddled around Mao. Looking at them, Mao laughed and said, "What a strong line of defence! It beats the rain and the wind."

That set the men's minds at ease.

Mao liked to imagine himself talking to someone. That day, after leaving behind the hill with the dragon-king temple on it, we were halted by a swollen river. As the men who could swim were in the process of throwing a bridge over it, heavy firing was suddenly heard in the direction of the temple; the enemy troops were closing in on us, and with shells exploding over our heads, it looked like there would be a pitched battle right where we were, any minute. The men grew restless, darting about on the river bank. But Mao remained calm. He sat on a huge rock, studying a military map, marking it with a pencil. He looked as if he were engaging Chiang Kai-shek in a game of chess with the map as a chess-board, and with each mark he made he seemed to be saying to his opponent, "I'm sorry, my friend, if you find this move a bit too hard on you...."

Watching him playing the imaginary chess game and muttering to himself, those of us bodyguards who were holding an oil cloth over him to shelter him from the rain couldn't help chuckling.

In times of trial, Mao's witticisms were testimony to his indomitable optimism.

One night during the war in northern Shaanxi, Mao had to share a cave-room with more than a dozen of the men in a village called Tianciwan. The hostess apologized, saying, "It's a shame I don't have any place bigger. I'm sorry for that, sir." Mao replied in the same tone, "There're far too many of us. I should say sorry to you." His reply brought hearty laughs from the hostess and all of us.

Hu Zongnan's attack created a food shortage for us. Beginning with the days when we were in Liangjiacha, the only thing we could get to eat were black soya beans. One day, in the middle of drafting "The Manifesto of the Chinese People's Liberation Army," Mao rose to take a walk to relieve him of the indigestion caused by those beans.

At the entrance to the courtyard Mao saw Zhu Laosi, who was standing guard there. Perhaps because Zhu was a heavy smoker, his teeth were badly stained. This was more noticeable than it might otherwise have been, since he seemed to have some difficulty keeping his mouth closed. Taking note of them, Mao looked at them with mock seriousness, asking, "How come your teeth are so black, Comrade Laosi? The beans did it?"

Before he could close his mouth and say anything, Zhu broke wind.

As though he had heard Zhu's reply, Mao nodded in satisfaction. "No? I'm glad to hear that."

Zhu couldn't restrain himself any longer. Scratching the back of his neck and blushing, he laughed with the innocence of a child. We, too, rocked with laughter. Mao, when he stopped laughing, changed the subject and said to us:

"We won't be eating black soya beans for long. Northern Shaanxi isn't a very big place and what the peasants grow each year is barely enough to feed themselves. Now, with several hundred thousand enemy troops here eating out of their bowls and destroying their crops, the food situation is even worse. But no matter. All we have to do now is stick it out, and in a few months' time, we won't be looking for food here but will be living off the enemy." Turning to Zhu Laosi, Mao asked resentfully, "If the enemies can help themselves to our food as they're doing now, why can't we get our food from them?"

Nodding in agreement, Zhu managed to find his voice: "Why not? Those s.o.b.s!"

And that gave us another hearty laugh.

During the three bad years in the early 1960s when the country was in serious economic trouble, Mao refused to eat any meat for seven months, and in the pre-harvest season when the food shortage was even more acute, he ate nothing but spinach and purslane; no one could talk him into eating anything better than that.

One day when I was massaging him to put him to sleep, I noticed that the pressure of my hands caused the flesh around his ankles to indent. Mao was suffering from edema. I was worried. "You're terribly under-nourished, Comrade Chairman. Look...."

"What do you mean?" he cut me short. "I'm gaining weight around the ankles and you're telling me I'm under nourished."

Mao would often mark a happy occasion with his witticisms.

The victory at Shajiadian did not send Mao jumping for joy; he seemed sorry for Hu Zongnan, his adversary, commenting with sympathetic sighs: "We were unable to prevent him from doing what we wanted him to do."

We laughed, and that was how he shared his joy with us. Then, bending his fingers as he counted the number of enemy troops we had wiped out, he continued: "At Qinghuabian, Yangmahe, Panlong, Shajiadian ... we put a total of six to seven enemy brigades out of existence. Hu boasted the four generals he had; he said they're his trumps. But," Mao paused, and then shaking his head, went on, "I don't think they're any better than four lumps of mud, and they belong on the garbage-heaps in the peasants' backyards."

We roared with laughter.

"Three of the four trumps, He Qi, Liu Ziqi, and Li Kun'gang, are history now. There's only one left. He's...."

Amid the general animation someone in the audience was heard shouting, "Li Riji!"

"Yes, Li Riji," Mao bit his lower lip, "or Li Erji (twice-lucky). He's lucky this time; we didn't get him. He may be lucky again next time, but we'll certainly get him the third time."

At this, we again burst out laughing loudly. But Mao kept a dead-pan expression, like a good humorist, and that made us laugh even more heartily.

Many people in China have seen the picture of Mao sitting in a pavilion, reading a newspaper, which carried the news of the liberation of Nanjing. Those of us who worked for Mao were there when the photograph was taken. We all wanted to have our picture taken together with Mao at that happy moment, but we were too shy to suggest it.

However, Mao read our thoughts. He said to the photographer, "What did you take that picture of me for?"

"It's a great day; Nanjing's been liberated!"

"So a great day calls for a picture." Turning to us, Mao enquired, "Don't you think it's a great day?"

"We sure do!" "Let's have a picture taken with the chairman!"

So Mao walked out of the pavilion amidst our joyous shouts, and had a picture taken with us.

On another occasion during the 1950s, Mao was inspecting the navy. The officers and men, standing in ranks, greeted Mao on the deck of a ship in top military form. The men were nervous and excited, their bodies straight as ramrods, saluting Mao with their eyes, as the chairman of the Communist Party, the People's Republic and the Military Com- misssion of the Party's Central Committee, walked past them in his broad-toed, brown leather shoes.

Suddenly Mao halted. He looked affectionately at one of the men, a skinny young seaman. Immediately the reporters and officers were on alert, assuming that Mao was about to deliver an important speech or had something important to say to the men. The men felt proud that Mao was going to speak to one of them. That skinny young seaman, his chest heaving slightly, was ready to shout out his answers to whatever the chairman might ask him.

But Mao didn't do any of these things. Instead, in a soft voice, he asked the skinny young man, "Have you ever had enough to eat?"

Mao smiled, but the young seaman was stunned. Then, no longer stiff, and conscious of his slight build, he smiled too, and the men who had heard Mao also laughed gently. Immediately the air of solemnity gave way to an atmosphere of informality.

With his bodyguards and guards Mao wisecracked even more freely.

I remember one occasion just before a swim in the Yangtse River. I was changing into my swimming trunks after helping Mao into his, when I noticed he was looking at me.

"You're getting to be a great man, Yinqiao," Mao said in all seriousness, "and you'll outshine me if you go on like this."

I was perplexed by what he had said and a bit disturbed.

"It's getting bigger," Mao continued, patting me on the belly, "and is competing with mine."

I smiled and pulled in my stomach.

He then patted me on the shoulder. "Throw out your chest. You're getting to look like me."

Like Mao, I had become a bit stooped. I did what he told me, saying, "Age is creeping up on me unawares. But I don't think I shall ever accomplish as much as you have."

"How come you talk like a defeated man when you've just turned thirty? I'm an old man, but the future holds high hopes for you." And with that, Mao walked out.

When work kept Mao at his desk for long hours, it would take a lot of reminding to get him to stop and take a walk, and when he did stop he would say, "Keep the time. Ten minutes."

So as to give him longer than ten minutes, I would lie about the time. But Mao, as if he possessed an inbuilt clock, would ask at the end of the ten minutes, "Is the time up?"

"Two minutes to go," I would say.

"That watch of yours is always erring on matters of principle, and is unlikely to improve," Mao would complain, and, ignoring me, would take the one hundred steps back to his office.

Once, when Mao was out for a walk, I got some other bodyguards to help me move a large easy chair from his study to another room. We tried several times to get it out of the room, but we couldn't do it, so we gave up.

When Mao returned and found that the chair was still in the study, he asked, "Why didn't you take it to the other room?"

"The door's too narrow," said Feng Yaosong, "and we couldn't get it through. Shall we leave it where it is?"

Mao looked at us, and then at the chair, remarking with the air of a man pondering over something, "There's one thing I don't understand."

Mao had the habit of interrupting a discussion on important issues with experts, or ranking members of the Party, and asking the bodyguards who were with him what they thought about those matters under discussion; and when he did that, the bodyguards would be more than glad to let him know their opinions. So we asked him what it was that he wanted to hear from us.

"Tell me," said Mao, looking perplexed, "was the chair here before or after the house was built?"

We all flushed. Mao didn't need to say any more. We finally managed to manoeuvre the chair through the door.

These are only a few of Mao's wisecracks. When Mao got humorous, what he said was not to be taken as mere jest, or simply as a joke intended to liven up the atmosphere, for one could always draw something from his witticisms: confidence, joy, enlightenment, knowledge or strength.

Mao: a Book Enthusiast

During the first few years I was Mao's bodyguard, Mao would assign me classes to attend in elementary education and books to read. The many stories which appeared in the newspapers and magazines about Mao's helping to arrange elementary education classes for those working under him were all truthful accounts. Here I should like to add a few of my own recollections about Mao's attitude towards books and education.

Although Mao rarely asked others for favours, during the war in northern Shaanxi, he did do so, and what he asked for was books.

The Central Committee office did not evacuate Zaolin'gou until we were within ear-shot of the enemy's gun-fire. Mao had just mounted his horse when he got off it again. He went over to Ma Hanrong, one of the guards, and asked, "You're from Suide, aren't you, Comrade Hanrong?"

"Yes, Comrade Chairman," Ma, a new recruit, answered at attention.

"How many *li* is Suide from here?"

"I'm not sure, but it's within a half day's walking distance."

Mao thought for a while, and then, looking at the cases in which he kept his books, said, "I'd like to ask a favour of you. Could you...."

"Just say the word, Comrade Chairman."

"I have a few cases of books. Can I leave them in your home?"

"Certainly. No problem."

"But.... Would they cause any inconvenience to your family? For example, might they get them into trouble?"

"No. My folks live in a deep gully east of Suide. It's far from the highway, and the enemy troops won't set foot there. And even if my folks did get into trouble, they'd know what to do."

"Thank you, thank you very much. You'll have to make the trip then."

190

Mao, his brows knitted, was worried about his books at a time when we were concerned about his safety. After Ma left with the books, his knitted brows relaxed a bit. Two days later, Ma caught up with us, and told Mao that his books had been put in a secret cave-room inside the house, a place not even the bandits, still less the Kuomintang troops, could find. It was only then that Mao's face brightened up, as he thanked Ma, saying, "Thank you, thank you, thank you ever so much for your great help."

During those war years we kept on reducing our baggage. There was nothing Mao would not part with, except books; he would not even throw away sheets of paper with something written on them. Dong Biwu once remarked, "Mao Zedong is a book enthusiast, and as such he has done a great thing for the Party. He has managed to ensure the safety of volumes of documents and printed materials of historical value which the Central Committee office was unable to keep. These things are important assets to the Party."

Contrary to the conventional wisdom of sending food and fodder ahead before an army starts on a march, Mao sent his books ahead before setting out on a journey. He was never seen travelling without those two wooden crates each one square metre in size, in which he kept reference books, works of literature and political science, other documents and printed materials. Even if he was returning within just a few days, he would take them with him. If he was going on an inspection tour, we would carry the books to his special train one hour before the train was due to start, and arrange them in the order in which they were kept at home, putting those he was in the process of reading or was intending to read on his bed and desk. After aboarding the train, the first thing he would do, having wiped his face, would be to pick up a book and begin reading. Mao was quite literally an avid reader.

When Li Ne was brought back from east of the Yellow River, by Jiang Qing, in late October 1947, she then had Han Guixin as her new nurse. Mao commented, "Li Ne's seven years old now, but she can't go to school under the present circumstances. What shall we do?" Han had finished elementary school and could teach Li Ne to read and write.

The day upon which Li Ne was introduced to Han, she assured her father: "I will study hard and stay out of mischief...."

"I'm glad to hear you say you're going to study hard," Mao said, smiling, "but 'staying out of mischief' needs to be qualified. Mischief, within limits, should be tolerated. It's a sign that the child is intelligent and healthy."

In my opinion, such words should be regarded as more than merely conventional wisdom.

Once Mao criticized me, saying: "It's stupid of you to refuse to get an education as I advised."

Zhang Baojin, one of those on the list of Mao's former staff, was the only person whom Mao would see when he called, even if he was busy. Mao enjoyed conversing with him because Zhang was an intellectual, with a college education.

Zhang had been Mao's bodyguard before he went to college. Mao had once punished him by making him stand for hours, because he made too much noise with fire-wood when Mao had just gone to sleep, and woke him up. Compared with the other bodyguards, Zhang was not well-liked by Mao. But Mao became very proud of him after he made the college entrance examinations and won top scores in course tests. When Mao talked to us about him, he was full of praise. He would say, "Comrade Zhang Baojin always tries to do better. He was my bodyguard, like you, and was eager to learn. In college, he once scored the best marks in the tests. He's risen in my estimation now that he's better educated and more experienced in dealing with things."

Amongst those working for Mao, Dr. Xu Tao was undoubtedly an intellectual, and, a graduate from a prestigeous university, he was held in high regard by Mao. Mao enjoyed talkig with him and arguing with him about scholarly matters; but he was never to be heard raising his voice in conversation with the doctor.

Mao once told Xu, "In school, I liked social sciences better than natural sciences. So what I learned was lop-sided. It's time that I made up what I missed."

"It's the other way round for me," Mao's physician responded. "I have a few things to make up, too."

Their conversations covered a wide range of subjects, as diverse as philosophy, politics, history, literature, mining, metallurgy, machining, chemistry: "high-class stuff," to borrow a voguish Chinese expression.

However, when an intellectual turned up his nose at cadres of peasant or working-class origin, Mao, citing great historical figures of humble origin, would tell him that he was wrong, and would warn the latter against succumbing to an inferiority complex. When these latter displayed no interest in study and no confidence in their ability to learn anything, he would tell them not to lose heart, but to persevere, following the example set by some of China's great historical figures. Amongst the bodyguards to whom Mao recounted the success stories of such men, were Tian Yunyu, Feng Yaosong, Zhang Xianpeng and myself. As a result of Mao's persistent encouragement and patient persuasion, Tian Yunyu and Li Liancheng finally qualified for college preparatory school. Throughout the years they were in college, they received books and food from Mao, and Mao would sometimes take time off to listen to their telling about their life and studies at college. When they graduated, Mao invited them to dinner and made them a toast.

Mao set up a spare-time school at Zhongnanhai and personally selected the teachers. The students comprised members of his First Bodyguard Company and all those guards at Zhongnanhai who had never received any formal education. The curriculum consisted of six courses: Chinese, mathematics, political science, history, geography and physics. The classrooms were situated either in the buildings in the west courtyard of Mao's residence, or in the compound of the First Bodyguard Company. Mao paid for all the necessary items which he told me to purchase for each of the students: satchels, textbooks, exercise-books, stationery, and keep-fit equipment, such as horizontal parallel bars, dumb-bells, chest-expanders and spring-grip dumb bells, out of the remuneration which he received for his publications. When Mao was out of town on business, the bodyguards accompanying him would bring their textbooks along and have their teachers travel with them. From time to time Mao would ask them about their study to keep track of their progress; once in a while he would teach them himself.

Those of us who were with him every day received even more help. By the 1960s, we had basically been brought up to the level of senior high school graduates, thanks to Mao's efforts. He was the only person at Zhongnanhai ever to have set up that type of school. When Feng Yaosong recalled what he had learned at the school, he was speaking for us all: "Mao taught me seven courses, one more course than any of the teachers did. In addition to the above-mentioned six, he taught me how to undertake social investigation and how to present the findings."

The homework papers written by the guards and bodyguards which Mao had corrected, and the social investigation reports which they wrote during their home furloughs, and which Mao revised, are now in the collection of the Military Museum.

For a time, during the "cultural revolution," it was forbidden to read books other than those written by Mao Zedong. In the army, where the books we read had to be exclusive those written by Chairman Mao, even the works of Marx and Lenin were banned. It was never Mao's wish to see that happen.

One time at Beidaihe, in the 1950s, when he was taking a walk during a work break, Mao saw a bodyguard poring over a book. He went over and found that the book he was reading was *Mao Zedong In His Youth* by Xiao San. Mao took the book and thumbed through it, commenting: "What the book says is largely true, but only largely." Then, changing the subject, he continued, "I wouldn't recommend books of this kind to you. People of your generation should do better than those of my generation. How can this be achieved? Reading other kinds of books will help you to accomplish more. Don't spend much time reading books about me, but about other people. You ought to read more extensively on society and nature."

One day during the 1960s, Mao was leaving the meeting hall at Zhongnanhai, when he saw a man who worked there walking hurriedly by with a book rolled in a cylinder* in his hand. Mao asked him casually, "What's the book in your hand, Hu?"

"*On Contradiction*." Hu stopped.

Flipping through the book, Mao said, "I'm not satisfied with this book of mine, and want to re-write it. Do you think it's worth reading?" Then, turning to those of us who were with him, he remarked, "I like philosophy and have written a few monographs, but only two of these (*On Practice* and *On Contradiction*) have been published, and even these two are not well written as far as I'm concerned. Don't spend much time reading books by me or about me, but read books by and about other

---

*A "book," hand-written in ink-brush, on a scroll, which was the traditional style of Chinese manuscript. These were rolled up in cardboard cylinders, for safe-keeping and storage.

people. There should be books by Marx and Lenin on your reading-list."

Those who have come into contact with Mao all agree that he read avidly. Indeed, how could a man such as Mao, whom even his enemies acknowledge and respect as a staunch defender of China's national dignity and interest, be disdainful of knowledge? Many of his oldest followers of peasant and working class origins did look down upon intellectuals. Whilst Mao trusted them and would speak up in their defence, he would never forget to remind them that "an uncultured army is a dull-witted army." He created opportunities for them to received an education, which constituted part of his goal to make good education in science and other fields of knowledge accessible to everyone in China.

Mao Seeks Ways to Open Up China

On May 2, 1949, Mao left his residence at Fragrant Hills to meet Liu Yazi in the Summer Palace. When his car pulled up at the east gate of the palace, Mao saw Liu waiting there for him.

As he shook Mao's hand, Liu, like many other prominent democratic personages, raised his arm, proclaiming, "The Communist Party is great, so is Chairman Mao, and the People's Liberation Army."

Feeling ill at ease at such extolment, Mao said to Liu, "Such glorification is unnecessary between old friends; it can only creat a barrier between us," adding, "If anyone is great, it's the people, including you and me."

They strolled in the covered walkway in the former imperial garden, looking at the illustrations on its beams and chatting. The man whom Mao frequently discussed at this time with people like Liu, was Chiang Kai-shek, whom they referred to as "treacherous," "a dirty politician" and "the scourge of the nation." Now, as Liu looked around in the garden, his thoughts turned to the Empress Dowager of the Qing Dynasty. "We had the misfortune to be born amidst calamities," commented Liu. "That corrupt imbecile of a woman, the Empress Dowager —she thought she could go on ruling the country as its virtual sovereign by closing China's door to the outside world, but the imperialists said no. When they sent their gunboats here, she was so scared she signed all those unequal treaties* with them, subjecting our people to humilia-

---

*Following its defeat in the Opium War launched by Britain against China, the Qing government was forced to sign the Sino-British Treaty of Nanjing in 1842. In 1844, the United States and France forced the Qing government to sign the Sino-American Treaty of Wangxia and the Sino-French Treaty of Huangpu, respectively. These were followed by many other unequal treaties signed later by the Qing government, such as the Treaties of Tianjin it signed in 1858 with Russia, the United States, Britain and France, the Sino-Russian Treaty of Beijing in 1860, the Treaty of Shimonoseki in 1895, etc.

tion and untold of sufferings. She built this garden with naval funds,* and gave all the money she squeezed out of the people to the imperialists. What a traitor, a traitor to be condemned down the ages!"

"That corrupt feudal government was responsible for all that," Mao picked up the discussion. "With her heading the government she would have surrendered the navy to the imperialists even if she had had one." Then, after looking at some more illustrations on the beams, he added humorously, "Anyhow, she built this palace and that's something the imperialists could not take away. Now the people have this beautiful place for their leisure; it's better than having had the money squandered by people like her on other things."

Then their discussion shifted back to the Opium War,** and to the revolutionary pioneers since then, who fought persistently and died heroically for the cause of national independence and prosperity. Liu, sticking up his thumb, said in all sincerity, "History has proved that only the Communist Party and you can lead us to victory."

"We followed the path blazed by our forefathers. Our wisdom and experience come from the blood they shed." Mao stopped, and, taking a deep breath as he looked at the ceiling of the covered walkway, continued, "Our comrades went to France, Germany, Japan, the Soviet Union.... But we realized that we could count on no one but ourselves, upon our unflagging determination to win the struggle. We will make an effort to win outside support, but we won't stake everything on it, nor shall we do what Chiang Kai-shek did. Those warlords all had the support of imperialist countries; they got it by selling China out to them. Both they and the Empress Dowager were birds of a feather. They were not interested in the welfare of the nation; all they were interested in was creating a paradise for themselves and relegating the ordinary people to hell. It's no wonder they all ended up being toppled by the people."

When they reached the steamboat that the Empress Dowager had bought from a foreign country, Liu remarked that even such a common thing as a steamboat must have been a marvel to her.

"She paid much more than she got," Mao commented, "when she bought those few things from abroad. There can be no equality or mutual benefit for a country that does not strive to become self-reliant.

*Thus the marble boat, in Kunming Lake, in the Summer Palace.
**The Opium War (1840–42)

Remember that old saying: food begged is poison."

. Mao was extremely busy in the days following that visit to the Summer Palace. Besides meeting with representatives of mass organizations, he continued consultation with prominent public figures and leaders of the democratic parties on the convocation of the new political consultative conference, regularly working through the night until the following morning. In a speech delivered on June 15 to the preparatory committee for the convocation of the new political consultative conference, Mao declared solemnly:

"We are willing to negotiate with any foreign government for the establishment of diplomatic relations on the basis of equality, mutual benefit and mutual respect for each other's territorial integrity and sovereignty, provided that such a government severs all its relations with the Chinese reactionaries,* stops colluding with or aiding them, and shows genuine, not feigned, friendliness towards people's China. The Chinese people are willing to cooperate with peoples of all countries in the world for the restoration and development of international trade so as to promote production and economic growth."

On the day the People's Republic was founded, Mao, with his faith in the enormous strength of the Chinese people, declared to the world in Proclamation One of the Central People's Government, that the Central People's Government was the sole legitimate government representing the people of China and that it was willing to establish diplomatic relations with the government of any foreign country which respected the principles of equality, mutual benefit and mutual respect for each other's territorial integrity and sovereignty.

But what happened? The imperialist countries loathed to see our people live under socialism; they scoffed at the principles of equality and mutual benefit, they showed no respect for the territorial integrity and sovereignty of our country, they refused to recognize our government, they openly threatened to strangle us with an economic blockade. Even the Soviet Union doubted our ability to survive. It had tried to prevent our army from crossing the Yangtse River. Just before Nanjing was liberated, its embassy moved to Guangzhou,** along with the fleeing Kuomintang government.

*The Kuomintang in Taiwan.
**In the south, Guangdong Province, formerly also known as Canton.

That's what happened.

Mao was extremely busy in the first few years after the founding of New China, but he managed to take time off to go to the Soviet Union. What for? To seek loans and aid. He anticipated difficulties. When I was packing his things for the journey, he said to me, bending his thumb, index and middle finger to indicate the duration of his stay in the Soviet Union, "Maybe longer than that. It maybe several weeks, even a month." As it turned out, he stayed in the Soviet Union for nearly ten weeks. In the interests of the Chinese people and for the revival of the country's economy, Mao made concessions against his will; in return the Soviet Union promised to provide China with an annual loan of U.S.$60 million for five years.

A mere $60 million! Much less than any of the Eastern European countries was getting from the Soviet Union, and none of these countries was as big as a Chinese province in size or population.

Still, in the spirit of "returning favours done you with favours ten thousand times greater," Mao referred to the loans as "long-term, comprehensive, noble, selfless assistance." When the news of Stalin's death reached him, he had insomnia; even the sleeping pills couldn't put him to sleep. In his article, "The Greatest Friendship," he expressed his heart-felt thanks for the support and assistance which Stalin had given to the revolution and socialist construction in China.

The term, "any foreign government," which Mao declared China was willing to establish diplomatic relations with, on the aforementioned basis of equality, mutual benefit and mutual respect, included, of course, the U.S. government.

However, two days after the outbreak of the Korean war, President Truman ordered the "neutralization" of the Taiwan Strait, in an attempt to prevent the People's Liberation Army from liberating the island. It is not hard to imagine how furious Mao was at such arrogance and hostility on the part of the U.S. government, and its interference in China's internal affairs.

For three months, from June through July until August, 1950, Mao was agitated, nervous, angry, worried, even impatient at times. As I observed, what had previously claimed his attention were the remote regions of China that were yet to be liberated, such as Tibet, along with Chiang Kai-shek, who had fled to Taiwan. In addition, there was the land reform to take care of, inflation to curb, and economic revival and development to attend to. He had not, as far as I could gather from my contact with him, thought of entering the war in Korea then: he already had too many things on his plate crying out to be dealt with at home. Only when the Americans brought the war dangerously close to the Yalu River, shortly after landing at Inchon, did Mao turn his attention to Korea. What followed then were many sleepless nights, during which the cigarette ashtray had to be emptied almost every two hours.

On the day when the final decision was due to be made about sending our men to Korea, Mao could not sleep in the morning, not even after three doses of sleeping pills. As he rose from his bed, he remarked to himself in a heavy voice, "There doesn't seem to be any choice. We've got to do it whatever happens, and everything else will have to wait until we are through with this war."

The meeting continued all through the night in the east room of Mao's residence; the room was filled with so much cigarette smoke that it looked as though it were on fire. For the first few days after our men were sent to Korea, Mao again suffered from insomnia. Between 1949 and early 1950, those Mao saw had been primarily officials in charge of political and economic affairs; but beginning in late 1950, they were mostly military leaders. Amongst them were General Nie Rongzhen, then chief of the general staff. Nie remained Mao's most frequent visitor until the end of the Korean war.

On the day in 1953, when the Korean armistice was signed, Mao walked out of his room and sang a Beijing opera aria loudly. It seemed to us that Mao wanted us all to share in his joy.

Beginning that same year, Mao would go to the seaside once a year. We knew what he went there for: to watch the tide. When he looked far into the distance over the vast expanse of water, his chest would heave with the rhythm of the surging sea and his eyes would shine with emotion. What was on his mind at such moments? This is what happened one day.

After gazing for a long time at the horizon, where the sea merged with the sky, Mao asked a bodyguard, "What do you think causes high and low tides, Zhang Muqi?"

"The attraction of the moon," answered Zhang.

"Say gravitational attraction. The gravitational pull of the moon. More questions: What is a warm current? What is a cold current?"

"I'm not sure about a warm current. As for a cold current, it must be that cold thing from Siberia."

Mao smiled. "That's the cold wave that moves south. I'm asking you about the ocean current. Do you know anything about it?"

"No, I don't," Zhang shook his head.

"There are two major warm ocean currents. One flows from the Gulf of Mexico and is called the Gulf Stream; the other is the warm current from Taiwan."

Mao's gaze returned to the sea, and as he looked at it, he pointed at the horizon. "Taiwan," he said. "We are yet to liberate the island."

The treaty which China concluded with India, in 1954, was based on the five principles of peaceful coexistence. It was largely, in my opinion, Mao's brain-child; two of the principles which were included in the treaty were exact replicas of what Mao had said at the new political consultative conference, back in 1949, when he expounded the principles which would guide China's relations with foreign countries.

That day in 1955, after patronizing the mutton-and-bun restaurant on his way back from the airport, where he had seen off Sukarno, the Indonesian president, Mao told his driver to stop at the Soviet Exhibition Centre, where there was a Japanese industrial exhibition on display. Mao toured the exhibition with interest, and the Japanese made him a gift of a transistor radio—something that China was not then able to produce domestically. During this visit, Mao repeatedly called for friendly relations in the course of his conversation with the Japanese hosting the exhibition, saying that in the absence of diplomatic relations between the two governments, people-to-people contact should increase. He spoke highly of the exhibition, and declared that he hoped to see more trade between the two countries and more efforts made by both China and Japan to expand economic relations. Mao's conversation with the Japanese left me with the impression that he was looking for every possible means to defeat the economic blockade imposed on China, and, if possible, increase economic contact with the outside world—through people-to-people channels, if a hostile foreign government made diplomatic relations impossible.

By the 1970s, things had taken a dramatic turn. Previously, Mao had insisted that all matters of principle be settled before China could improve relations with any foreign country. But now, with the situation changed, he initiated what is today known as "the ping-pong diplomacy." Mao, it may be claimed, was the first to foresee the end of one era and the beginning of another; he knew that confrontation must give way to dialogue.

In 1972, Mao Zedong and Richard M. Nixon, with admirable courage and foresight, crashed open the door of ice which had separated China and the United States for more than twenty years, and met with each other. The two men, one, a great Marxist and teacher and leader of the proletarian revolution, the other, the president of the largest capitalist country in the world, and top representative of the bourgeoisie, shook hands with one another, beginning the dialogue after more than two decades of confrontation.

This meeting heralded the re-opening of China's door to the outside world.

What Mao Never Managed to Accomplish

The first time I saw Mao frustrated in an attempt to do anything was when he tried to swim the Yellow River.

Two days after the victory at Yichuan, Zhou Enlai announced a decision to all the officers. "Comrades," he said, "the Central Committee and Chairman Mao have decided to move to northern China on the other side of the Yellow River."

We cheered and jumped for joy at the decision because it meant that we had defeated Hu Zongnan and that the War of Liberation had reached a turning point.

We arrived at Chuankou on March 23, 1948, where we were to cross the Yellow River. The river bank and the hillside were crowded with people who had come to see us off. Waiting in the river were more than a dozen large canoes, all manned by strong, tough young men. Mao got into the first canoe, Zhou Enlai and Ren Bishi into the second one, and Lu Dingyi and Hu Qiaomu took the third canoe.

As our boat pulled slowly away from the bank, several bodyguards stood around Mao, who, waving good-bye to the crowd on the bank, refused to sit down.

Soon the boat began to rock, and as it moved further out into the river, we could hear the dull noise of the waves as they lashed against the sides of the boat. With my hands on Mao, I said, "Sit down please, Comrade Chairman."

Mao brushed my hands away. He looked at the murky torrents, and then at the receding shoreline of the river and the crowd. As he did so, he breathed audibly and his eyes shone brightly, signs that he had worked himself into an emotional state. Suddenly he turned to Ye Zilong, chief staff-officer of the detachment. "We now stand on the Yellow River with northern Shaanxi as a backdrop. What do you think of it? Take a picture of me."

"Sure. It's worth a picture." Ye took out his camera immediately.

Mao, no longer smiling, steadied himself in the boat and held with dignity. Just as he was ready, Ye clicked the camera.

"Good," smiling, Mao nodded in satisfaction. "The people of the northern Shaanxi plateau, and the Yellow River, all in one picture—that's something to remember."

The river became turbulent when our boat reached the middle. It was the ice-floe season. Floes the size of a millstone, riding the huge waves, were thundering their way down the river at lightning speed. Our tiny boat, caught in the swells, would one moment rise with them, as if it were flying, and the next, as they crashed down, would plummet into what seemed like a bottomless well, with nothing but a patch of blue sky above. All the while our boat, jostled by the floating ice, rocked violently. But the boatmen, rowing and pushing with their puntpoles to the soul-stirring rhythm of their work-song: "yo-ho, yo-ho," kept the boat darting forward.

Mao was visibly excited. It seemed an idea was shaping in his mind and he couldn't wait to get it out. His chest heaved, and then as he inhaled deeply, he suddenly turned around to face the bodyguards. "Which of you dares to swim this river?" he asked.

There were good swimmers amongst the bodyguards. Someone shouted his recommendation: "Ma Hanrong can do it. He swam across the Yellow River Fork when it was in flood to take a message to General Peng."

"I once swam the Yanhe River when it was in flood," said Shi Guorui.

"I swam it once in the dry season," said the usually reticent Sun Yong, in a low voice. "I may do it again."

"Good idea," said Mao, seizing upon Sun's offer in excitement. "Let's leave the boat and swim to the shore. Come on!"

I was shocked to hear what Mao had said and almost shouted my objections. Luckily, I didn't say anything of that kind: any objections at such a time would only have made him even more determined, in which case, the consequences could have been disastrous.

An uneasy silence fell on everyone in the boat. Then someone was heard saying in a low voice, "Not today. It's the ice-floe season."

"No, not today," Sun Yong followed up immediately, "not when there's this ice floating in it."

"Can't do it? Ha, ha!" Mao laughed. "You're scared, that's all." He turned his eyes to the opague and murky waters of the Yellow River, looking at the raging, foaming waves and whirl-pools. He seemed to be turning something over in his mind, sizing and weighing it up. Finally, he let out a long sigh and, as if speaking to himself, or to those of us in the boat, said, "If there's anything not to be slighted, it is the Yellow River. Slighting the Yellow River is tantamount to slighting our nation."

When we were more than halfway across, Mao looked upstream into the distance. The river was shimmering in the golden rays of the sun. "Behold! The mighty Yellow River tumbles down from the sky...." Mao was reciting Li Bai, the great Tang Dynasty poet. Then he murmured: "Just where does it rise, I wonder?"

Our boat was approaching the bank, on the east side of the river, after going round a sand islet. Mao, not watch the welcoming crowd on the bank as we were doing, looked over his shoulder at the Yellow River, and said with a sigh, "What a pity!"

The pity was, as I understand it, that he was unable to swim the river.

Mao never left a river or lake without swimming in it, during the years after the founding of New China. He would jump into the water with the air of a man taking on a challenge, and leave it with the satisfaction of having overwhelmed his opponent. But he never treated the Yellow River in this way. During his many inspection tours along the river, he would look at it with respect, thinking, sizing and weighing it up carefully, and then leave it in disappointment.

Mao was never able to swim the Yellow River.

With the advance of old age, Mao dropped the idea of going swimming in that mighty river, but he gave it up only grudgingly; he was like that old horse in a poem by Cao Cao (A.D. 155-220), a horse that remained as ambitious as it had been when it was young.

On April 19, 1962, Gao Zhi, Mao's confidential secretary, was leaving Mao for his new job in Xi'an in Shaanxi Province. Gao had been with Mao during the war in northern Shaanxi and had crossed the Yellow River with him.

"You've been working for me for a long time," Mao said to Gao, with feeling, "and we've become very close friends. Now that you're leaving me, I hope that you will always remember to do a few things for me, wherever you are. I need your help."

"I will, Comrade Chairman, and I'll do whatever you say to the best of my ability," Gao replied emotionally.

Mao took a few puffs at his cigarette and said slowly, "You remember the boat trip we made across the Yellow River, don't you? My black horse was thrown overboard, but it swam ashore." After a brief pause he continued, "When we were fighting in northern Shaanxi, you often went ahead with the advance party to mark out houses as billets. Now I want you to do the advance party job for me in Shaanxi. When I get there I'm going to make a trip along the Yellow River on horseback. I'm going there...."

Gao's wife was expecting a baby at the time. But Gao didn't want to delay his departure on account of that. With the permission of He Tingyi, deputy commander of the air force, she was flown to Xi'an, aboard an air force plane which was routed there. As soon as Gao got to Xi'an, he began to explore the Yellow River, and waited for Mao's arrival, which he thought could be any day. Like all those who left Mao after working for him for a long time, Gao couldn't get accustomed to being away from Mao. He missed the chairman so much that he would cry out in his dreams, "Comrade Chairman, Comrade Chairman!" And when he awoke to nothing but the stillness of the night, tears would slowly trickle down his face.

So Gao waited and waited, counting the days, until 1965. But Mao never came.

However, Gao did not forget Mao's request. In 1965, on his way from Xi'an to Beijing, before departing for Indonesia, he made a detailed record of what he passed by on the trip, a record that included names of mountains, gullies, the number of culverts and the length of the longest of these, roads difficult to travel, places where Mao could take a rest....

When Gao met Mao in Beijing he told the chairman about his family, his work and study.

"I never managed to do what I proposed in that study plan I gave you. It was too ambitious. Just couldn't follow it through with so much work to do," Gao told Mao.

After asking Gao in detail what he had seen on the way from Xi'an to Beijing, Mao said, "I was too ambitious, too, when I planned to make a horseback trip along the Yellow River. I couldn't take the time off for that trip after all.... I love northern Shaanxi. I lived in Jiangxi for only a short time, but I spent much longer in Yan'an. I still want to go back there for a visit, eat the millet grown there, and make a trip along the Yellow River."

That dream never came true.

He did eat the millet: Gao had it sent to him from northern Shaanxi, and he thanked Gao for that. But he never made the trip, which was something Mao always regretted.

But the thing which Mao regretted the most was that he did not see the reunification of Taiwan with the mainland.

Mao summed up what he had accomplished in his life when he said that he had founded the People's Republic of China with the support of the people and launched the "cultural revolution" in his later years. But with Taiwan still to be liberated, Mao was left with a loose end which he was unable to tie up in his lifetime, and it is not hard to imagine how disappointed this left him.

As I said earlier, every year, beginning in 1953, Mao would go to the seaside. He would gaze into the distance over the sea, saying, "We must liberate Taiwan." I don't remember precisely what else he said, but I have the impression that the "independent Taiwan separatists" incurred his wrath even more than Chiang Kai-shek did, because Chiang insisted that Taiwan is an inalienable part of China. The thing which most readily won Mao the praise of every Chinese, was his unswerving determination to defend the dignity of China and the interests of the Chinese nation. As I learned from a record of Nixon's visit to China in 1972, just when the joint Sino-American communiqué was finalized, officials of the U.S. State Department raised a lost of objections, saying that they didn't like this, they didn't like that about the document. When Zhou Enlai raised the matter with Mao, Mao said categorically, "Tell Nixon we may keep the communiqué open for further negotiation, but not the section about Taiwan; we won't agree to any changes in that section." After a brief pause, he added most emphatically, "Any attempt to make changes in the section about Taiwan will be counterproductive to the possibility of the communiqué's being made public tomorrow."

That record rang true to me: that's how Mao felt and would react. The Taiwan question had claimed a lot of Mao's attention since 1949, and had been the main obstacle to the normalization of Sino-American relations.

Wu Xujun became Mao's head nurse soon after the founding of New China. She also worked for Mao for a long time, like me, staying on after I left Mao. On Lunar New Year's Day, in 1976, she was Mao's guest for dinner. Before the dinner they watched a movie. The film was "A Struggle to Remember." Mao didn't care much for movies, but he made an exception that day. In his later years, Mao grew increasingly nostalgic for the years before the founding of the People's Republic, when a struggle of epic scope within China was shaking the world. As he watched the movie, Mao wept quietly. When the film reached the part about the People's Liberation Army marching into a city to the rousing welcome of the people, Mao asked Wu, "Were you among the students in that crowd?"

Mao knew that Wu had gone to school in Shanghai, and it happened that Wu had joined in the welcoming crowd. But she only nodded her answer, for she, too, was weeping.

Wu's response brought a cascade of tears from Mao's eyes, and everyone in the audience wept. Mao was immediately carried away by the nurses.

Could the painful realization that he would not live to see the liberation of Taiwan, be one of the many causes which made Mao cry that day?

Mao never let his time pass without reading or writing something. As far as I know he had plans for further publications, some of which never materialized, which must have been another source of disappointment to him.

I was with him at Beidaihe in 1954. When he strolled on the beach or stood there scanning the sea, he could be heard reciting poems. One day, Dr. Xu, his physician, became curious, and asked him, "Whose poem are you reciting, Comrade Chairman?"

"How does it sound to you?" Mao asked him.

"It's a great poem. Very beautiful."

"It's by Cao Cao called 'Looking at the Sea.' It's the first section of a long poem entitled, 'A Journey On Foot Out Of the Summer Gate.'"

"Cao Cao, a poet?"

"You find it surprising? He was a great statesman, great soldier and great poet."

We were all stunned. Mao said that long before Guo Moruo wrote to change men's image of Cao Cao. For ages, the man had been despised for his treachery and perfidy, and now Mao was calling him a great man! Perhaps Mao was talking about another man by the same name.

"Cao Cao?" Dr. Xu couldn't understand. "You don't mean that bad man with the hideous face, do you?"

"Nonsense!" Mao snapped. "Cao Cao unified the northern part of China and founded the Kingdom of Wei in the Yellow River Valley, which was then the most important region in China. He reformed many bad policies of the Eastern Han Dynasty (A.D. 25-220), clipped the wings of powerful families, boosted production and was the first man to put garrison troops on farming duty. He told the peasants to open up wasteland, strengthened the rule of law and encouraged frugality. And with all that, he succeeded in bringing about stability in the country, which was, at that time, badly ravaged by war, and put it back on its feet and on the road to prosperity. Wouldn't you call that great? All those books and plays claim that he was a treacherous man with a hideous face, and the people believe them. But that's a lie, told by men of letters with feudal, orthodox views. The pen can be lethal, and such people monopolized the influence of the pen and fed the people many lies. We must tell the people the truth about Cao Cao."

I had never seen Mao so agitated, so concerned about "men of past ages" as he was that day. It seemed that his comments about Cao Cao were not limited to a particular historical figure; they represented an attempt to rid people of deep-seated and long-standing prejudices.

Mao, however, never managed to write anything to rehabilitate Cao Cao. Guo Moruo did it. His article touched off intense debate nationwide, which resulted in the acceptance of Guo's views by the majority of people in China.

That night, following this conversation about Cao Cao, Mao said to us, thoughtfully, before going to bed, "I'm very much interested to know what's on the minds of young people these days. Nowadays writers seem interested in the attitude of youth towards work and marriage. But what about their understanding of history and the world?"

One day soon after saying that, Mao asked Tian Yunyu, "What have you been reading recently?"

"I'm interested in history and philosophy," said Tian.

"I'd like you to read a book. It's called *Get to Know the World*, by Feng Qi. It's a good book."

A few days later, Mao encouraged Tian to study the basic principles of Marxism, and lectured him on historical materialism. Then he repeated what he had said previously, "I'm going to write a book for young people about themselves. The world belongs to the young, and that's not going to change."

Back in 1935, Mao had written the famous line, "If we fail to reach the Great Wall, we're not men." Although he never swam the Yellow River, he paid many visits to the wall. Each time he was there, he would talk about Shihuangdi (First Emperor) of the Qin Dynasty, who ruled China from 246 to 209 B.C. As in the case of Cao Cao, his views about the first emperor of feudal China, which gave the emperor the credit due to him for his contributions to the Chinese nation, are diametrically opposed to the traditional views. True, the emperor did many things that spelt suffering for the people, but his achievements were monumental; they benefited the Chinese nation and led to the unification of the country. For over two thousand years, feudal China saw many changes of dynasty, but the system of government which Shihuangdi created, remained in operation. He unified the Chinese script, standardized the width of vehicles, and devised administrative codes of conduct for the whole nation to follow, measures which bound the country and nation into a unified whole.

Mao was the first man in China to challenge traditional views of Shihuangdi and Cao Cao. To those who made comparisons between the leaders of New China and the emperor, he would say, "You're wrong. We're one hundred times more thorough than Shihuangdi." He was not referring to the emperor as a tyrant; he was comparing the contributions which we had made to China and its people, with those of Shihuangdi.

On one occasion he said to me, "The chairman isn't an emperor; he's a servant of the people."

One day in the early 1960s, Mao was chatting with those of us working for him on his special train going to Hunan. At one point, Li Min mentioned the many fortune-tellers she had seen in the course of a visit she had paid on Mao's behalf to the family graveyard. With a smile Mao asked her, "Why didn't you have your fortune told by one of them? You could have told if the fellow was right."

Then, Li Min said that she had heard some people abusing Mao during that visit. When Yao Shuxian, the train attendant, heard what Li Min was saying, as she entered the carriage, she was shocked and almost instinctively shouted: "They must be class-enemies."

Mao, still smiling, shook his head in disagreement. "Not necessarily," he said. "It's not unusual for people to attack you with foul language; it's unusual if they don't. Not everyone who abuses me is a bad man. I'm not infallible." After a brief pause, he continued slowly and thoughtfully: "Chiang Kai-shek destroyed my family graves, and the Communist Party pushed me to the sidelines and wouldn't let me work for it. Revolution is no easy thing; it means making sacrifices. They destroyed my family graveyard to lay a curse on me, but nothing has happened to me; it's all mere superstition. Now the people have restored the graveyard, and nothing has happened to me, either. I'm just another human being like you; Mao Zedong is a human being. Like all human beings, I will die some day. They call me far-sighted, but that's boloney. I expect to be attacked for what I've done after I die; some of the things which I've done may turn out to be wrong. I'm a human being, and to err is only human. But I have my convictions; I will always remain truthful to the revolution, no matter what names they may call me."

Mao's greatest worry after the victory of the revolution, was the possibility of the waning of the revolutionary drive amongst the rank and file of the masses. In a sense, Mao was more interested in changing men's thinking than in changing the material world. Rather in the vein of a poet who sings, "One thousand years are too long/Grasp the hour, seize the day," he attempted to do a number of things which were unrealistic and for which China was not ready, amongst which were the great leap forward and the movement for rural people's communes.*

I would like to take this opportunity to make one point which, in my opinion, in conjunction with many other factors, culminated in Mao's wrong decision to launch the "cultural revolution." What happened during the "cultural revolution" has demonstrated its destructive impact upon the nation, and that it was the worst mistake Mao committed during the course of his career. However, Mao merely made a mistake, whereas the Gang of Four committed crimes, which are entirely different in nature from misjudgement. Mao's intentions regarding the "cultural revolution" were honourable; he wanted to rid the Communist Party, amongst other things, of bureaucratic practices and corruption.

Mao was a dead enemy of bureaucracy and corruption. As I mentioned earlier, during the campaign against bureaucracy, waste and corruption in the early 1950s, he asked me on several occasions, in a very severe tone, "Have you pocketed government money?" and, "If you haven't in the past, what about in the future?" He kept on reminding me: "Don't get hit by the sugar-coated bullet. You work for me, and that makes it all the more important for you to resist temptations. Never fall a prey to them"; "We're very intimate friends, but you'll be my enemy if you engage in corruption"; "You're my bodyguard, low in rank but high in position. This position may make it dangerously easy for you to seek personal priviledges. So be careful and be modest"; "Have you wasted anything even if you haven't engaged in any corrution? Waste is harmful, too; it's the first step towards corruption"; "Be economical, and make that your habit."

Mao had a confidential secretary who left after working for him for over a dozen years. The day he moved out, the only transportation he required to carry his belongings was a jeep. He was, indeed, as clean as clean could be. Mao had a picture taken with him and his family. When they were shaking hands, Mao said, "You're an honest man. I'll miss you."

A new bodyguard, who joined us not long after the three years of economic trouble, one day told the others what he had expected to obtain as Mao's bodyguard: "I thought that once I became the chairman's bodyguard I would be able to eat whatever I wanted."

---

*In 1958.

Mao would say to us, "Don't expect to become big government officials and make big money by working for me. What your work demands of you is yet more sacrifices." Mao would always ask anyone who joined his personal staff, "Are you willing to work for me?"

Mao set a fine example of what he expected of others. Those who left Mao, after serving him for a long time, would almost invariably find themselves so socially naive, like kids who have just left school, that they were unable to cope with the complexities of society, and would thus end up very frustrated or even social casualties.

Mao was not unaware of these complexities. Whenever one of his bodyguards left him, he would remind him of two things: "Be modest and remain true to the revolution, without losing your drive or becoming decadent."

Mao did not find everything about the Communist Party or the nation which he had founded to his satisfaction, and he always tried to "do something to rectify it." In my opinion, this is one of the reasons why he initiated the "cultural revolution." Unfortunately for the Chinese nation, this "something" which he did, turned out to be a mistake which triggered ten years of catastrophe.

This was Mao's ultimate regret, and the regret of history as well.

图书在版编目(CIP)数据

走下神坛的毛泽东:英文/权延赤著.—北京:
外文出版社,1996
ISBN 7 - 119 - 01445 - 5

Ⅰ.走… Ⅱ.权… Ⅲ.毛泽东—生平事迹—英文
Ⅳ.A752

中国版本图书馆 CIP 数据核字 (96) 第 03740 号

走下神坛的毛泽东

权延赤

＊

ⓒ外文出版社

外文出版社出版

(中国北京百万庄路 24 号)

邮政编码 100037

北京外文印刷厂印刷

中国国际图书贸易总公司发行

(中国北京车公庄西路 35 号)

北京邮政信箱第 399 号　邮政编码 100044

1992 年(大 32 开)第一版

1996 年第二次印刷

(英)

ISBN 7 - 119 - 01445 - 5 /K·95(外)

01580

11 - E - 2603P